Studies in International Relations

George Clarke

(Principal Teacher of Modern Studies)

Frank Cooney

(Head of Social Studies, Northern College)

Irene Morrison

(Principal Teacher of Modern Studies)

Pulse Publications

Contents

Published and Typeset by
Pulse Publications
45 Raith Road, Fenwick,
Ayrshire, KA3 6DB

Printed by
Thomson Colour Printers

British Library Cataloguing-in-Publication Data
A Catalogue record for this
book is available from the
British Library

ISBN 0 948766 47 6

© Clarke, Cooney& Morrison 1998

Acknowledgements

The authors and publishers would like to thank the following for permission to reproduce copyright material:
Illustrated London News (13), Mirror Syndication (15, 59, 85), Press Association (45, 57, 62, 83, 87, 97, 105), Associated Press (55), Gerry McCann (133, 134, 135, 138, 139, 140, 142, 146, 149, 153, 155), Photodisc, Digital Stock, David Welch (Concern Worldwide – Scotland), Graham 'Ping' Smith for his contributions to the China section.

Every attempt has been made to contact copyright holders, but we apologise if any have been overlooked.

We, the People...

DISTRIBUTION OF THE US POPULATION BY RACE AND ETHNICITY

The census figures collected by the US Bureau of Census identify the population of the USA by race or by ethnicity. Race attempts to categorise people by physical characteristics, while ethnicity categories distinguish people by culture and language.

The Bureau's race categories are American Native or Alaska Native (Aleut or Eskimo), Asian and Pacific Islander, Black and White. The only ethnic category is Hispanic. The Bureau of Census does not define the physical or biological features which create these categories but it allows people to identify their own race. Statistics are therefore given for 'no race'.

The population of the USA is made up of diverse racial and ethnic groups. Currently the dominant group is white English speakers for whom the melting pot view of society has become a reality. Whether Britain, Ireland, Northern, Southern or Eastern Europe was the origin of their family, through the generations they have become American in outlook and culture. White Americans were 73.6% of the population in 1995.

In 1991 the white population was predominantly suburban whereas the black population was overwhelmingly located in the inner cities. This reflects the post-war migration patterns with white residents leaving the inner cities to live middle-class lives in the suburbs and Blacks migrating to the inner cities and becoming trapped there.

Race & Ethnic Distribution of the Population, 1995

Race or Ethnic Group	Number	%
White	193,523,000	73.6
Black	31,591,000	12.0
Asian American	8,715,000	3.3
American Indian	1,931,000	0.9
Hispanic	26,994,000	10.2
Total	262,754,000	100.0

Table 1.1

RACE AND ETHNIC CATEGORIES

The race and Hispanic origin categories as defined by the US Census Bureau are as follows:

American Indian, Eskimo & Aleut
A person having origins in any of the original peoples of North America, who maintains cultural identifications through tribal affiliation or community recognition. The term 'American Indian' refers to the race group American Indian, Eskimo, and Aleut.

Asian and Pacific Islander
A person having origins in any of the original peoples of the Far East, Southeast Asia, the Indian subcontinent, or the Pacific Islands. This area includes, for example, China, India, Japan, Korea, the Philippine Islands, and Samoa. The term 'Asian' or abbreviation 'API' refers to the race group Asian and Pacific Islander.

Black
A person having origins in any of the black racial groups of Africa.

White
A person having origins in any of the original peoples of Europe, North Africa, or the Middle East.

Hispanic
A person of Mexican, Puerto Rican, Cuban, Central or South American other Spanish culture or origin, regardless of race.

Urban - Rural Distribution of the Black and White Population, 1991(%)

	WHITE	BLACK
Central city	28	59
Suburban	49	27
Rural	23	14

Table 1.2

DISTRIBUTION OF AMERICAN INDIANS

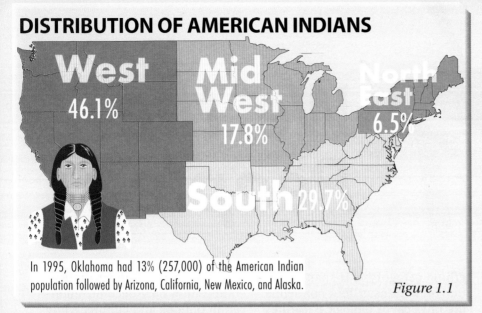

West 46.1%

Mid West 17.8%

North East 6.5%

South 29.7%

In 1995, Oklahoma had 13% (257,000) of the American Indian population followed by Arizona, California, New Mexico, and Alaska.

Figure 1.1

AMERICAN INDIANS

American Indian is the smallest of the ethnic groups counted in the Census with just under 1% of the population. It consists of the American Indian, the Aleut and the Eskimo. In 1990 there were 24,000 Aleut and 57,000 Eskimo in the US, most of whom lived in Alaska. The 1.9 million American Indians were scattered across the US with most living in or near reservations in the western or southern states.

American Indians are descended from the original settlers on the continent of America who arrived from Asia over 20,000 years ago and populated the entire length of the Americas. In North America they formed tribal groups with different lifestyles and cultures. The tribes were massacred by the white settlers and the army and were decimated by diseases such as measles which were intentionally introduced. They were herded onto reservations where their traditional ways of life were destroyed. By the 20th century they were dependent on the Bureau of Indian Affairs and its officials. They were not made citizens of the USA until the 1920s.

In the 1960s and 1970s the average income on the reservations was 25% of the US average and the residents suffered from overpopulation, poverty, unemployment, malnutrition, ill health and low educational achievement.

The American Indian Movement was set up in 1968 to reassert pride in traditional Indian cultures while demanding equality of opportunity. It did not, however, seek integration. A shift in attitude towards the Indian appeared in US literature and culture. Books reassessed Indian culture and its contribution to American history. The American Western, a cornerstone of American culture, portrayed Indians with greater sympathy and appreciation of their culture.

In 1980 the Indian Gaming Regulation Act allowed tribes to run gaming operations on their reservations while excluding them from paying federal or state taxes on the income. This made a significant difference to tribal income. The takings from gambling rose to $1 billion in 1988 and by 1992 they were almost $6 billion per annum. There was a sudden increase in the number of US citizens claiming membership of a tribe and the right to own tribal land. The population of American Indians rose from 1,420,000 in 1980 to 2,242,000 in 1995. This represented an increase of 58% in fifteen years.

A survey of reservations in Minnesota found that gambling directly accounted for 4,700 jobs with a $32 million payroll, and indirectly for around 6,000 jobs in construction and new tourism. The number of families receiving welfare in these reservations has dropped by 17% since the casinos opened while, in the rest of the state over the same period, the number of people on welfare has risen by 15%.

This money spinner has enabled rapid improvements to be made in education, health and welfare facilities on the reservations as well as providing employment.

DISTRIBUTION OF ASIAN & PACIFIC ISLANDERS

West 55.7%

Mid West 10.6%

North East 18.4%

South 15.4%

Composition of Asian & Pacific Islanders, 1990	
Chinese	23%
Filipino	19%
Japanese	12%
Asian Indian	11%
Korean	11%
Vietnamese	8%
Laotian	2%
Cambodian	2%
Thai	1%
Hmong	1%
Others	10%

40% of Asian and Pacific Islanders live in California and 10% live in New York.

Figure 1.2

In 1995 there were 8,715,000 APIs legally living in the USA. They accounted for 3.3% of the population. Over 14 different categories make up this group with the Chinese being the largest. (See Figure 1.2.) Some groups concentrate in 'little Chinas' or 'little Koreas' in the major cities where they add to the rich diversity of life providing ethnic shopping or restaurants. They also become involved in small-scale manufacturing and the provision of services. Other groups such as the Japanese have integrated into the education and business worlds and are spread more evenly across the USA. They tend to live middle-class lives integrated into white society.

HISPANICS

Hispanic Americans or Latinos are the fastest growing ethnic group in the USA and are pressing the Blacks for the position of most numerous minority group. In 1990 there were 22 million US citizens who described themselves as Hispanic. They are not a homogeneous group but consist of several sub-groups, each with its own varied history. The 3 largest groups are:

- Chicano or Mexican American
- Puerto Rican
- Cuban

Mexican Americans are by far the largest group within the Hispanic community in the USA comprising 60% of the total, followed by Puerto Ricans at 12% and Cubans at 5%. Other Hispanic Americans have migrated to the USA from countries in the Caribbean and Central and Southern America such as El Salvador, Nicaragua, and Panama but make up only a small fraction of the total.

The overall figures for Hispanics show that they were largely concentrated in the South and West regions of the USA, but this statistic obscures the significant differences in distribution between the 3 largest Hispanic sub-groups.

Chicano or Mexican American

In 1990 over 90% of this group was concentrated in the South and West of the USA where they made up significant proportions of the population. Mexican Americans were 27% of the population of Texas, 20% in Arizona, 13% in Colorado, 39% in New Mexico and 27% in California. California is the home state to over one-third of all Hispanics in the USA.

Although there is a significant number in the agricultural labour force, the population is mainly urban. Mexican Americans make up over 50% of the population in 5 major cities in Texas and 5 in California where they were also the single largest ethnic group in Los Angeles. The Mexican population of Los Angeles is second in size only to that of Mexico City .

The Mexican American population is growing rapidly in several Mid-West states and especially in Chicago where 20% of the population is Mexican American.

Puerto Ricans

There are over two million Puerto Ricans resident in the USA. More than one-third of them live in New York while the rest mostly live in other eastern seaboard cities. Figure 1.3 shows that 68.8% of Puerto Ricans live in the North East.

They are viewed as a separate group from Hispanics generally. They are US citizens as Puerto Rico is a Free Associated State of the USA. They generally suffer all the effects of inner city deprivation to an even greater extent than the Blacks. They form the lowest income group in the US.

Cubans

There were 1,044,000 Cubans living in the USA in 1990. 70.5% live in the South, mainly in Miami and other parts of Florida, but there are sizable communities in New York and New Jersey accounting for 17.6% of the population. Only 3.5% of this group live in the Mid West and 8.5% in the West (Figure 1.3).

Reasons for the geographical distribution of Hispanics

Mexican Americans

Mexicans are attracted to the United States because of the relatively high living standards which can be obtained doing even the lowest paid of jobs in comparison to the poverty experienced on the Mexican side of the border. Each year thousands of Mexicans cross the border in search of work. They may become farm labourers following the planting and harvesting work through the Western, Southern and Mid Western States up to the Canadian border. They help to maintain their families by sending home the money they earn. Many of these migrant labourers return to their land in Mexico.

In California and Texas the farmers depend on this labour force and pay for gangs of illegal immigrants to be smuggled into the country. Border patrols are not above accepting favours from farmers or

DISTRIBUTION OF HISPANICS

West 45.2%

Mid West 7.7%

East 16.8%

South 30.3%

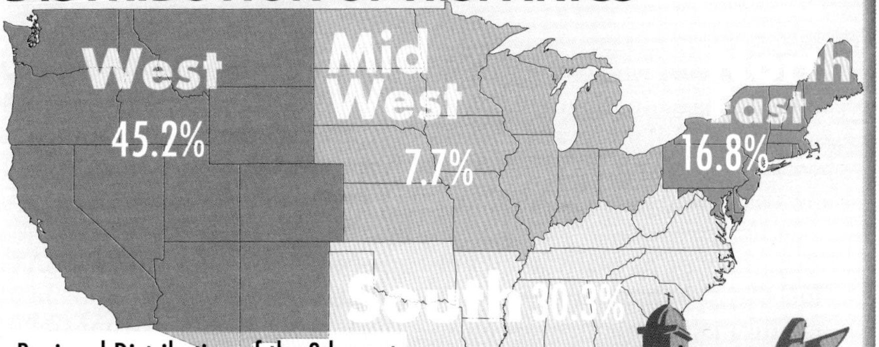

Regional Distribution of the 3 largest Hispanic American Groups in 1990 (%)

	Mexican American	Puerto Rican	Cuban
North East	1.3	68.8	17.6
Mid West	8.5	9.4	3.5
South	32.2	14.9	70.5
West	58.0	7.0	8.5

In 1995, 74% of the USA's Hispanics lived in five States. California with 9 million had the largest share followed by Texas, New York, Florida, and Illinois.

Figure 1.3

HISPANIC AMERICAN GROUPS in 1990

Total Hispanic Population	22,354,000	100%
– Mexican	13,496,000	60%
– Puerto Rican	2,728,000	12%
– Cuban	1,044,000	5%
– Others	5,086,000	23%

Table 1.3

restauranteurs who employ illegal immigrants to do the menial tasks despised by Americans. These workers are exploited, receiving low wages and harsh conditions.

There may be as many as 10 million illegal immigrants in the US and the majority of them are Mexican 'Wetbacks'. Wetback is a derogatory term for Hispanic Americans from Central and South America who enter the USA illegally. These immigrants are mostly young men who enter the USA to amass enough capital to set themselves up when they return to their homes. There are also a number who live near the border and cross to work in the USA on a daily basis. In the USA they can earn $5 to $6 per hour whereas in Mexico the minimum wage is around 22 pesos or $3 a day.

Illegal immigrants run the risk of ill-treatment at the hands of employers, police and other groups. In Rio Grande, Texas, a local lawyer obtained video recordings taken by police of officers abusing young Mexicans. The police kept the film to weed out those officers not participating. In 1996 another video recording of sheriff's deputies beating 3 Mexican immigrants in Riverside, California had the same effect on the Mexican American community as the Rodney King beatings had had on the black community in 1991. In one year fifty bodies were found having been shot by the border patrol, the Ku Klux Klan vigilantes or by Mexican gangs who prey on the wetbacks.

The Border Patrol has about 4,500 patrolmen for a border that is 2,000 miles long and largely unfenced. The service is underfunded, there are only 30 checkpoints and patrols are regularly stoned and shot at.

Many of those who started out as illegal immigrants have settled down in the states of the South and West and have become US citizens.

Central American Refugees
During the 1980s refugees from Guatemala, El Salvador, Ecuador and Colombia arrived in the USA. In one three month period 20,000 refugees arrived in New York to escape the killing and torture in El Salvador.

Becoming a refugee in the USA (as in many other countries) depends on from what or from whom refuge is sought. Those fleeing from Cuba or Nicaragua (both had socialist governments) were welcomed with open arms. Those fleeing the atrocities of the terror squads and army in El Salvador or Chile were quietly and quickly returned to death or imprisonment with little or no investigation into the merits of their case.

Puerto Ricans
The poverty in several of the Caribbean Islands has led many to seek the American Dream in the eastern seaboard cities of New York and New Jersey. Because of their special status, Puerto Ricans are free to enter the US. They were attracted to areas where traditionally their relatives had settled and form a significantly large minority in New York City.

In the 1990s, 20% of all the immigrants to New York came from the Dominican Republic, a neighbouring island to Puerto Rico, in the Caribbean. A majority of these settled in Washington Heights, a particularly run-down and violent area of the city. They came to New York to escape the absolute poverty of their home and worked in the low paid service industries such as cab driving.

Cubans
Florida is 90 miles from the coast of Cuba. Cubans were political refugees from the Communist government of their country. When Fidel Castro and his followers overthrew the dictatorship of General Batista in 1959, 200,000 rich and middle-class Cubans fled to Florida. The USA, as part of its anti-communist stance, always encouraged refugees from Cuba and criticised Cuba for preventing people from leaving. In 1965, Castro allowed another wave of Cubans to leave and in the next 8 years a further 300,000 Cubans arrived in Miami. Most Cubans who have settled in the USA since 1960 have done so reluctantly. The Cubans call themselves exiles, not immigrants, and claim they would like to return to their country of origin.

In 1980 Cuba exiled 126,000 to Florida, 5% of whom were convicts and patients from mental hospitals, and, in 1994, Castro allowed tens of thousands to flee the country for the USA. This was an economic exodus resulting from recession, poverty and unemployment mainly created by the US trade embargo which has been in place since 1959. These refugees became known as 'the boat people' because many attempted the 90 mile crossing in unseaworthy and overcrowded boats.

The people of Miami (including the Cuban residents) became alarmed during the 1980s over the constant influx of refugees from Cuba. In the 1990s the US government reversed its open door policy towards Cuban refugees and began to return 'the boat people' to tented camps at Guantanamo Bay—a part of Cuba still controlled by the US military.

DISTRIBUTION OF BLACKS
In some counties within the states listed in Figure 1.4 the black population accounts for 80% to 90% of the total. There is also a significant rural population of Blacks in these states.

While 78% of Blacks live in metropolitan areas in the South, 22% still live in rural counties and make their living as farm labourers or truck farmers. In the cities of the South there is a far more even spread between those living in the inner city areas and those who live outwith the central city areas in the suburbs. There is far greater integration between Blacks and Whites as far as housing is concerned than there is in the cities of the North and West.

Blacks form the majority population in many of the cities in the

BLACKS in the South		
TOTAL	18,531,000	100%
Non-metropolitan Areas	4,086,000	22%
Metropolitan Areas	14,445,000	78%
Inside central city	8,102,000	44%
Outside central city	6,343,000	34%

Table 1.4

DISTRIBUTION OF BLACKS

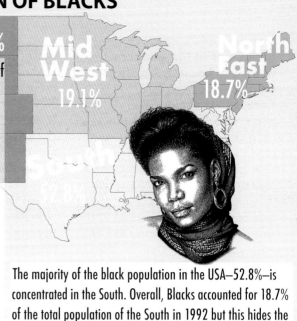

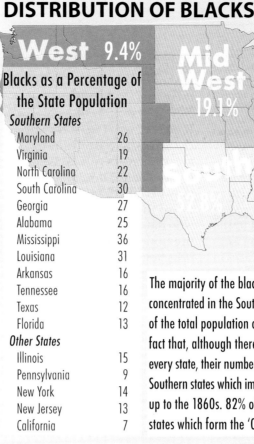

West 9.4%

Mid West 19.1%

North East 18.7%

Blacks as a Percentage of the State Population

Southern States	
Maryland	26
Virginia	19
North Carolina	22
South Carolina	30
Georgia	27
Alabama	25
Mississippi	36
Louisiana	31
Arkansas	16
Tennessee	16
Texas	12
Florida	13
Other States	
Illinois	15
Pennsylvania	9
New York	14
New Jersey	13
California	7

The majority of the black population in the USA–52.8%–is concentrated in the South. Overall, Blacks accounted for 18.7% of the total population of the South in 1992 but this hides the fact that, although there is a significant black population in every state, their numbers are particularly concentrated in those Southern states which imported slaves to work in the plantations up to the 1860s. 82% of Blacks living in the South live in the states which form the 'Old South'.

Figure 1.4

southern states. Outside the South the geographical distribution of Blacks is concentrated in the industrial cities of the North and West. 18.7% of Blacks live in the North East, concentrated in the larger cities of New York, Newark and other cities in New Jersey which were heavily industrialised.

In 1990, 19.1% of the Blacks in the USA lived in the Mid West, but again this disguises the fact that they had a limited presence outwith the major industrial cities like Detroit, Toledo or Gary. Blacks made up 9.6% of the population of the Mid West in 1992 but 89% of them were concentrated in just five of the twelve states which make up this region—Ohio, Illinois, Indiana, Michigan and Missouri. The industrial centres dominating these states are Toledo in Ohio, Chicago in Illinois, Gary in Indiana, Detroit in Michigan and St Louis in Missouri.

Over 9% of the black population of the USA lives in the West. Blacks make up just 5% of the total population of these states but are concentrated in just two of the thirteen states which make up this region—California and Washington. 83% of Blacks living in the West live in these two states. Indeed California is home to 77% of all Blacks in the West and they are concentrated in cities such as Los Angeles and San Francisco.

Reasons for the geographical distribution of Blacks

The majority of Blacks live in the 'Old South' for *historical reasons*. They are the descendants of the original black slaves who were imported to work on the cotton and tobacco plantations. Although they were emancipated after the Civil

War (1861–65), most remained to become truck farmers and seasonal labourers.

The political system and the Ku Klux Klan kept them segregated and isolated within their own communities. High levels of illiteracy, caused by lack of education, and little or no access to radio reinforced their ignorance of the world outside their county.

There was *movement out of the rural South* to southern towns where new industries required labour or jobs could be found in the service industries, for example, domestic servants or entertainers. In the twentieth century increasing numbers made the move to the cities of the North and West to escape the segregation and hostility they faced in the South. In 1900, 90% of Blacks in the US lived in the South, but by 1940 this figure had fallen to 77%.

World War II had a dramatic impact as Blacks were drafted into the forces to fight or were attracted to the cities of the North and West to work in the industries which were supplying the war effort. After the war this movement north and west continued as post-war reconstruc-

tion meant that there were jobs in the industries of the North and West. Soldiers returning from the war did not want to return to the grinding poverty and injustice of the South and they moved to these cities as well.

By 1970 a little more than 50% of the black population of the USA lived in the South. However, elsewhere Blacks either found themselves trapped in the inner city ghettos of northern towns facing deteriorating social and economic conditions or living in segregated middle-class suburbs.

In the 1970s and 1980s the traditional industries which had provided employment either closed down because of foreign competition or moved out of the suburbs to the Sunbelt South—Arizona, New Mexico and Texas—where wage levels were lower and workers were non-unionised. Thus in the 1980s and 1990s the trend for the migration of Blacks from South to North and West went into reverse and the black population in the South stopped falling and began to rise marginally.

Conditions in the southern states were more favourable to the Blacks than they had been up to the 1960s. Racial discrimination and violence which were used to keep Blacks in an inferior position were largely eradicated by both the civil rights movement and the affirmative action programmes that followed.

The South was not affected to the same extent by the economic segregation which affected the races in the northern cities. Black and white people lived in the same areas and sent their children to the same public schools—unless they were rich and sent their children to private segregated schools. With industry moving to the South and social conditions at least as good if not better than they were in the North, many Blacks decided to remain in the South and many from the North were encouraged to make a move down South.

The Black population in northern metropolitan areas

The traditional pattern of settlement for each new wave of immigration to the USA is for the new immigrants to move into the central city areas where there is cheap accommodation and jobs in the manufacturing industries or in the service sector. They work hard and they or their children become upwardly mobile. They get better paid work and move out to the suburbs to live in better surroundings.

As Table 1.5 shows, only 2.5% of Blacks live outwith the major metropolitan areas of the North and West. They are also more concentrated in the city centre areas. 69% live in the ghettos of the inner cities while less than half that number have managed to find housing in the suburbs. There is less integra-

BLACKS in the North & West		
TOTAL	14,821,000	100%
Non-metropolitan Areas	374,000	2.5%
Metropolitan Areas	14,447,000	97.5%
Inside central city	10,220,000	69%
Outside central city	4,227,000	28.5%

Table 1.5

tion of housing between Blacks and Whites in the northern cities than there is in the South.

In the cities of the North and West the Blacks moved into the inner city areas where there was cheap housing available. They found work but they became trapped in the ghettos of the northern towns. Those who did find better paid work and promotion moved out to the suburbs but rapidly found that as they moved in Whites moved out. Recent studies have shown that as the number of Blacks moving into a suburb rose beyond 8% of the residents, house prices began to fall and Whites moved away to other white only suburbs.

Some white residents' committees would buy a house from owners who were moving out and control its sale to new owners, thereby ensuring that only Whites could buy a house in their neighbourhood. Thus these cities had a black underclass trapped in the decaying inner city core, living in dilapidated houses or in the vast soulless 'projects' which were built to replace them. Meanwhile middle-class Blacks found themselves living on segregated suburban housing estates.

THE IMPACT OF POPULATION GROWTH

The population of the US is growing as a consequence of both childbirth and immigration. The growth rates are different for each of the race and ethnic groups. This fact is having a profound effect on the economic and social cohesion in certain areas of the US and is making an increasing impact on the politics of the country. Tension is growing between the ethnic groups. When the dominant cultural group in an area is challenged numerically by a minority group, it can have several effects. The dominant group might simply move elsewhere. This happened when Whites fled from the city centres to the suburbs to get away from the increasing number of Blacks. The groups may come into conflict over

US Birth Rates (per 1000 people)

	1980	1990	1993
Average	15.9	16.7	15.5
White	15.1	15.8	14.7
Black	21.3	22.4	20.5
American Indian	20.7	18.9	17.8
API	19.9	19.0	17.7
Hispanic	NA	NA	NA

Table 1.6

One reason for the different levels of population increase between the ethnic groups is the birth rate. In the black community it is about one-third higher than the national average while that for Whites is below the national average.

US Fertility Rates, 1995

	Number of children per woman
Average	2.055
White	1.826
Black	2.398
American Indian	2.114
Asians	1.919
Hispanic	2.977

Table 1.7

gang territory or job allocations. In Washington, for example, Hispanics have demonstrated against what they see as discrimination in favour of Blacks by City Hall when allocating jobs. They feel that this is being done to the detriment of Hispanic applicants. In such cases prejudice begins to develop and can be used and fostered by some politicians for their own ends. For instance, Blacks and Hispanics in some areas are prejudiced against Asian entrepreneurs and accuse them of taking their jobs and businesses; Louis Farrakhan has used the tension between Jews and Blacks in New York for his own political gain within his own community. (See page 45)

Whites feel their political control slipping as concentrations of Blacks and Hispanics become the majority populations in certain urban areas. Forward projections into the next century see Whites becoming another ethnic minority group in several states and this

8

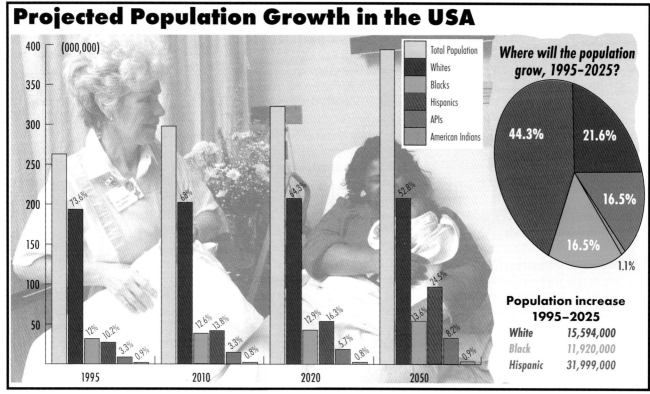

Projected Population Growth in the USA

400 (000,000)
350
300
250
200
150
100
50

1995   2010   2020   2050

Total Population
Whites
Blacks
Hispanics
APIs
American Indians

1995: 73.6%, 12%, 10.2%, 3.3%, 0.9%
2010: 68%, 12.6%, 13.8%, 3.3%, 0.8%
2020: 64.3%, 12.9%, 16.3%, 5.7%, 0.8%
2050: 52.8%, 13.6%, 24.5%, 8.2%, 0.9%

Where will the population grow, 1995-2025?

44.3%   21.6%   16.5%   16.5%   1.1%

Population increase 1995-2025

White	15,594,000
Black	11,920,000
Hispanic	31,999,000

Figure 1.5   Source : US Bureau of the Census

makes many right-wing Whites very nervous. Similarly, Blacks who have recently become the dominant force in certain areas see their political power slipping as the Hispanic community grows and becomes the majority population. When the Hispanics become more politicised they will use their majorities to ensure their own political ascendancy.

Population projections predict that the size of all ethnic groups will increase into the next century, but proportionately the rate of increase for Hispanic people will rapidly outstrip that of all other groups. On 1 July 1996, the Census Bureau announced that officially Hispanic children formed the second largest group of children in the USA. There were 12 million Hispanic children and 11.4 million black children while white children still formed the largest group with 50.8 million. By 2050 the white group will only just be in the majority in the USA and on some predictions by that date the US will be a nation of minority groups with the Whites simply being the largest.

This will have profound conse-

quences for the political, economic and social life of the USA over the next half century. It has already created tensions in both the white and black communities who see their culture and way of life being radically altered by the rapid growth in the Hispanic population.

Many people realise that they cannot directly influence the growth in the Hispanic population by controlling the birth rate. However, they can reduce the rate of migration into the US and try to remove illegal immigrants who are already in the country.

IMMIGRATION TO THE USA

The population of the USA has been regularly increased by successive waves of immigration from various parts of the world. It has given the US a vitality for growth which is part of the American Dream and it is the American Dream which has been the magnet for countless generations who migrate to improve their lives.

Immigration to the USA passed through distinct phases. Between 1820 and 1970 the dominant source of immigrants to the USA was Eu-

rope. In the period 1971 to the 1990s, the source of migrants to the USA swung away from Europe with Asian and Hispanic immigrants becoming the main groups to seek the American Dream.

Between 1965 and 1990, five immigration measures altered the numbers allowed into the USA and the basis on which they were admitted. Less emphasis was placed on nationality, which favoured European immigration, and more on admitting relatives of US residents or those who had skills that were in demand, which favoured Hispanics and Asians.

By the end of the 1980s, none of the European countries was a leading source of immigrants. Almost half of all immigrants to the United States were coming from Asian countries, with at least 25% of the remainder coming from Spanish-speaking nations. Throughout the 1990s legal immigration to the USA was running at between 700,000 and 800,000 people per year. Family reunification accounts for over half of all legal immigration each year and it includes brothers and sisters as well as adult children.

The 1986 Immigration Reform and Control Act (IRCA) offered legal status and possible future citizenship for illegal immigrants who were in the country before 1982. This mainly benefited Mexican Americans who, having entered and remained in the country illegally, could become US citizens. After several years they could legally apply to bring their families in. Between 1990 and 1993 the US government legalised more than two million people who were already living in the United States. Official estimates suggest there are over 4 million illegal immigrants in the US and some unofficial estimates put the figure as high as 10 million. These illegal immigrants are concentrated in 6 main states with California and New York bearing the brunt. In New York before 1986, Mexicans made up 1% of the city's immigrant population, but following the IRCA they accounted for 7% of those seeking amnesty.

In 1990, 29% of the women in New York were foreign born, but they had 43% of the children born in the city. A 1993 survey of households found that a third of the city's residents were immigrants, but on top of that a further 20% were their children. Thus in 1993, 53% of New York's population were foreign-born immigrants and their children.

The combination of this level of immigration and the fact of there being so many illegal immigrants has led to pressure to take action to stop or reduce immigration and to take harsher steps against those living in the country illegally. Arguments centre around cost to the taxpayer, job competition and conflict between different cultures.

Job Competition
During the late 1980s and early 1990s when thousands of jobs were disappearing, particularly in manufacturing, blue-collar workers and their trade unions found themselves in a shrinking labour market where they increasingly came into competition for employment with newly arrived workers. This was also true of the middle classes who saw competition for skilled jobs and professional jobs developing, particularly from the Asian community. When other areas of the US began to pull out of the slump, California continued to have economic problems. Angry white males increasingly blamed immigration policy as a major cause of their economic problems.

"Joe Six-pack has found a scapegoat for the cushy job he lost during the state's 4 year recession and for the fading of the California dream." (*Economist* 3 September 1994)

The need to find scapegoats also existed in poor black communities. In California, for example, Korean immigrants were becoming successful shopkeepers in the black ghettos of Los Angeles. Yet their hard work and success were resented by sections of the black community. One black politician was quoted as saying, "I am continually served food and drink by someone who not only isn't black but can't even speak English. It's a wonder how they were even able to get these jobs." The Koreans were accused of making money and then taking it out of black areas.

Almost every sector of California's economy depends on illegal immigrant workers for cheap labour—from the construction industry to nannies and housekeepers. This competition has driven down wage rates and annoyed poor Blacks and Whites who were in competition for these jobs.

Culture shock
Many poor Whites felt that not only their livelihoods but also their neighbourhoods were under threat as migrants concentrated in the poorer areas of the cities. Demands grew for an end to immigration and for the deportation of illegal immigrants. Daniel Stein, the executive director of the Federation for American Immigration Reform which has 70,000 members, claims that concentrations of immigrants who do not try to assimilate create a culture shock for the existing residents. *"Suddenly, in what used to be their own neighbourhood shops, there's not a sign in English."*

What unsettles white and African Americans is that increasingly large numbers of Hispanics do not appear to be assimilating into the US population and culture. Hispanics have already altered the language used in schools in certain districts. Their growing influence can also be felt in food, music and architecture.

In southern California, chains of Hispanic supermarkets have opened to cater for the tastes and shopping experiences of Hispanics. One chain, 'Tianguis', plays mariachi music to create an atmosphere for its customers.

Though individually poor, the combined spending power of Hispanics in California is $140 billion and growing. This makes them increasingly attractive to producers and advertisers. It has enabled the creation of Univision, a TV station transmitting solely in Spanish to Los Angeles and Miami.

Developments like this provide fuel for the argument of other organisations such as

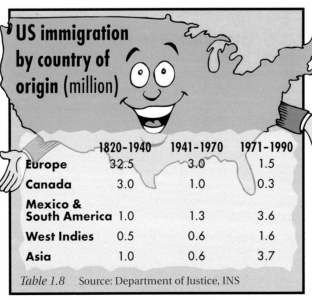

US immigration by country of origin (million)

	1820-1940	1941-1970	1971-1990
Europe	32.5	3.0	1.5
Canada	3.0	1.0	0.3
Mexico & South America	1.0	1.3	3.6
West Indies	0.5	0.6	1.6
Asia	1.0	0.6	3.7

Table 1.8 Source: Department of Justice, INS

US English which was formed in 1983 to pressure for an 'English only' amendment to the Constitution. It has 350,000 members and has managed to get 16 states to become 'Official English' states through the use of referendums including Proposition 63 in California. Its members believe that English is one of the 'glues' which binds Americans together even though they come from different cultural backgrounds. They claim that teaching children in a language other than English will divide America. Their critics claim that they are racist since they are trying to eliminate cultural differences and to protect their privileged position in the USA.

Other groups argue that immigrants inject a much needed vitality into what were run-down areas. If the Koreans had not made successful small businesses, many black neighbourhoods would be without the basic amenities their shops provide. In response to criticisms, Mayor Rudolph Guiliani said in 1997, "*For those people in New York who are concerned—'Oh there are too many foreigners coming here and there are too many people who look different and act different'—please remember, that has been the key to our success.*"

OPPOSITION TO IMMIGRATION

Immigration levels, both legal and illegal, mixed with the downturn in the US economy in the early 1990s, led to political pressure to end or reduce immigration and to curtail welfare and education programmes for illegal immigrants.

Demands have been made to tighten security along the Mexican – US border which, for much of its length, is open and only lightly patrolled. Between 1 million and 3 million illegal immigrants enter the USA over this border each year and while most return to Mexico when they have earned enough money, about 100,000 remain permanently in the USA. The Border Patrol employed about 4,500 staff in 1996 and the intention was to double that number to about 10,000 and to increase the budget for equipment from $400 million in 1994 to $716 million in 1997.

Some more extreme politicians have called for electrified fences and the laying of land mines along the border, but even with the more reasonable suggestions serious questions have been raised about potential human rights abuses by the border patrols. Many illegal immigrants die as the result of accidents. Between 190 and 330 die each year as they try to cross the Rio Grande river into Texas.

The government also has to avoid the accusation of racism against Hispanics being made by the Mexican government and Hispanic politicians.

Visa regulations

Officials estimate that about half the illegal immigrant population entered the country legally but then stayed on after their visas had lapsed. Having tighter visa controls would reduce the number of visas issued and measures are being investigated to tighten up on policing the visas in the US to catch those outstaying their welcome.

Hiring illegal aliens

The 1986 Immigration Reform and Control Act made it illegal for the first time to hire illegal aliens. Employers could be fined and imprisoned. However, in ten years the federal government has devoted few resources to enforce the provisions of the Act. The law, therefore, has very little effect in deterring illegal immigration. Some people have called for the provisions to be tightened up and enforced more vigorously. Nevertheless, there is strong opposition from powerful vested interests who claim inappropriate government interference in the workplace, but who really want a constant supply of compliant cheap labour. There are problems in applying such legislation. It would essentially be discriminatory since only those with Hispanic appearance or Hispanic-sounding names would be scrutinised and accusations of racism and discrimination would certainly be levelled at the government.

Reduce immigration quotas

In the mid-1990s the annual level of immigration was 800,000. Many people want to see sharp reductions or a complete moratorium on immigration. In May 1995 the Clinton Administration announced that it would no longer give automatic safe haven in the US to Cuban refugees.

Restrict benefits

The Welfare Bill passed in 1996 denied most Federal benefits to non-citizens, legal or illegal, on the assumption that their sponsors had arranged work for them.

Denial of citizenship

Another proposal is to deny automatic US citizenship rights to children who have been born in the US but whose parents are illegal immi-

CASE STUDY

Dario Miranda Valenzuela

Dario Miranda Valenzuela lived at home with his wife and two children. He often crossed the border to work in construction in Phoenix or Tucson. He was saving hard to build a house in Nogales, Mexico. In 1992, when he was crossing the border illegally, he was shot in the back and killed by Border Patrol agent Michael Elmer who then hid the body under shrubs. Eventually Elmer was turned in by a colleague and he admitted what he had done. Despite this he was acquitted by two juries of all criminal charges. The US government made a cash payment in an out-of-court settlement before the trials took place. Elmer eventually resigned the Border Patrol when his ex-wife told investigators that he and another patrolman has consumed five kilograms of cocaine they had seized from drug smugglers.

(Adapted from *To Have and Have Not* by John Enders, *Scotland on Sunday* 8.10.96)

Cost to the taxpayer of immigration

A survey in 1992 estimated that it cost the US $30.59 billion to provide education, health care, welfare benefits, prison places etc. for immigrants. Other research, however, calculates that legal immigrants are net contributors to government finances if broader economic factors are taken into account such as the strong record they have for starting small businesses or their contribution to the labour market.

California claimed in 1993 that it faced a tax bill of $2.3 billion to cover aid for the immigrant population. It requested Federal help and complained that the Federal Government is in charge of immigration policy and policing but that individual states have to pay for welfare, education and prison programmes. California and five other states have tried to sue the Federal Government to reimburse them for providing services for illegal immigrants.

The Federal Government will set aside $650 million each year between 1996 and 2000 to meet the costs of keeping illegal immigrants in prison. In the 1996 budget the government set aside $250 million to help states pay for certain medical and education costs caused by immigrants.

Tax bill for immigrants ($billion)

	Legal Aliens	Illegal Aliens	Amnesty Aliens*	Total
Cost of various programmes	35.23	10.10	5.51	50.85
Taxes paid	-15.72	-2.49	-2.04	-20.25
Net public cost of direct services	19.51	7.61	3.47	30.6

Table 1.9

* Illegal immigrants who were granted amnesty and allowed to apply for legal status and citizenship in the 1980s.

grants. At present if a child is born in the US it automatically becomes a US citizen with full rights to residency, benefits, education etc. Its parents, as legal guardians, cannot be deported and effectively have the right of residency in the US until the child is grown up. If enacted it would severely restrict the number of illegal immigrants allowed to stay in the US.

PROPOSITION 187

On 8 November 1994, Californians voted 59% to 41% in favour of denying over 2 million illegal immigrants resident in California access to the state's welfare, public health and education services.

A breakdown of the vote (Table 1.10) shows the strength of feeling in the various ethnic groups towards illegal immigrants in particular, but perhaps also provides a measure of the unease felt at the growth of the Hispanic community.

The anti-immigration mood in California is linked to the state's economic troubles. Almost every sector of the Californian economy uses and often depends on illegal aliens for cheap labour. This annoys poor Blacks and Whites who are in competition for these jobs. The voting figures also suggest that nearly one-third of the Hispanic community see a problem with illegal immigration. Partly these are poor Hispanics who are in competition for low paid jobs, but mainly this vote is from those wealthy middle-class Hispanics who have made money and integrated into suburban culture.

Catching the anti-immigration mood Pete Wilson, the Republican candidate for governor who was trailing his Democrat rival by 20% in the polls, made immigration the central plank of his 1994 election campaign. After tying his campaign to that of Proposition 187, he rapidly closed the gap and won the election. On 9 November, the day after his re-election and the referendum, Governor Wilson ordered the health service to stop providing ante-natal care to illegal immigrants.

Immediately, attempts to implement the proposition were halted in the law courts while challenges to its legality were considered. Plyer v Doe (1982) was a Supreme Court decision which gave illegal immigrants the right to free public education. Opponents claimed therefore that the implementation of Proposition 187 violated people's constitutional rights and that the state could not intrude on federal jurisdiction over immigration matters. Until such legal questions are resolved Proposition 187 cannot be fully implemented, but it had immediate social and political ramifications.

Effects of Proposition 187

Immediately following the vote for Proposition 187, immigrants were afraid to go to California's health and welfare centres because forms had been issued for officers to report illegal immigrants. Also, major confusion was caused in schools and health services because they have a statutory duty to provide services under other laws. Many children were adversely affected as parents kept them away from school or clinics, fearing that through their children their illegal status would be uncovered and they might be deported.

However, the most profound effect of Proposition 187 was the politicisation of the Hispanic community. In the 1996 Presidential Election in California, the Hispanic turnout increased by 40% over 1992 and was the largest ever recorded. It voted 3 to 1 in favour of Clinton— a significant switch towards the Democrats in order to punish the Republican Party. This pattern was repeated in several other states with big Hispanic communities.

Voting by Race on Proposition 187

	Yes	No
White	64	36
Black	56	44
Hispanic	31	69
Asian	57	43

Table 1.10

Minorities and Political Progress

A HISTORY OF EXCLUSION

When the Declaration of Independence (1776) stated that "all men were created equal", it did not include the black population of the USA. Most Blacks were slaves in the southern states and were considered to be the property of their masters. The northern states refused to recognise black slaves as equal citizens because that would have given too much power to the southern slave owners. Article 1 of the Constitution (1787) identified the existence of black slaves in the US, calling them "all other persons" and reached a compromise between North and South by giving slave owners three extra votes for every five black slaves they owned. Thus the Constitution created a country based on racist principles with white supremacy as the cornerstone of its legal system.

Contrary to common belief, overtly racist laws were not confined to southern states. In the North many states passed laws that prevented 'free' Blacks from owning property, voting or doing certain jobs. From the eighteenth century until late in the twentieth century, thousands of Blacks were victims of murder, lynching and burning at the hands of white individuals and vigilante groups and had little recourse to law for the indignities and violence perpetrated on them.

The Civil War was not waged to abolish slavery, but was a clash between two diverging cultures. During the Civil War, approximately 190,000 Blacks enlisted in the Union armies and fought and died for half the pay of white troops. The Emancipation Act (1863) was an attempt to promote a slave uprising in the South to cripple its economy and divert troops from the battlefield. Essentially it was a military strategy, not a moral position.

In the immediate aftermath of the Civil War—the period of Reconstruction—Blacks made political

Organisations such as the Ku Klux Klan used terror to intimidate Blacks and murdered those who tried to vote or stand up for black rights.

and economic gains but by the 1880s the modest gains were being swept away. The Supreme Court declared many discriminatory laws to be constitutional. These were known as the 'Jim Crow' laws. For example, in 1900 in Alabama 180,000 Blacks were eligible to vote, but by 1902 the figure had fallen to a mere 3,000. Organisations such as the Ku Klux Klan used terror to intimidate local black populations and murdered people who tried to vote or stand up for black rights. Between 1882 and 1903, 2,060 Blacks were lynched in the United States. Some of the victims were children and pregnant women and many were burned at the stake.

Up to the 1950s, exclusion from the political process continued, as did organised violence against Blacks. This was not confined to the southern states. In a race riot in Chicago in 1919, 70 Blacks were lynched, 537 were injured and nearly 1,000 black families were burned out of their homes.

CIVIL RIGHTS – THE CAMPAIGN FOR INCLUSION

The Second World War left the USA with a major dilemma. It had fought against fascism so how could it continue to support racism at home? Blacks returning from the army, where they had fought in segregated units, or those working in the factories of the North and West, where they had moved as part of the war effort, were not going to resume their role as second-class citizens. Organisations such as the National Association for the Advancement of Coloured People (NAACP) and the Congress for Racial Equality (CORE) encouraged Blacks to participate in the political process, tried to educate more liberal Whites to support their cause and tested discriminatory laws through the courts. Pressure mounted to obtain civil rights and equality for the black community.

Protest

The Civil Rights Movement developed in the mid-1950s. Several non-violent protests against institutionalised racism were staged, particularly in the southern states. An example was the Montgomery Bus Boycott where the black community en masse refused to use the city buses for a whole year until the Supreme Court outlawed segregation on these buses. Bus boy-

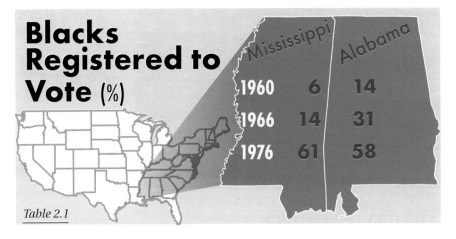

Blacks Registered to Vote (%)

	Mississippi	Alabama
1960	6	14
1966	14	31
1976	61	58

Table 2.1

cotts rapidly spread throughout southern cities.

In 1960 Blacks began to 'sit-in' in segregated restaurants, theatres, parks, beaches and churches. The spectacle of black youths being dragged and beaten from public places and imprisoned became nightly news on national TV. Within months 50,000 black and white students had joined the movement. This was followed by 'freedom rides' in which black and white people boarded buses and trains to demonstrate that interstate travel was still segregated despite this being outlawed by the Supreme Court. Parents went to court to secure places for their children in previously segregated schools and colleges. In Brown versus the Board of Education of Topeka, in 1954, the Supreme Court declared that segregation was inherently unequal and thus unconstitutional.

These activities raised the political consciousness of the black population throughout the USA. They began to demand the right to vote. Many felt that if they secured equality in the political arena, then equality of opportunity would follow in social and economic life.

The Voting Rights Act (1965)

This Act made it illegal to prevent people from voting by putting obstacles such as literacy tests or property requirements in their way. The result was a dramatic increase in the number of Blacks who registered and turned out to vote even in the most racist states (see Table 2.1) and in the number of black candidates who stood for election. In areas where there was a substantial minority of black voters their concerns had to be addressed by those seeking office.

Disillusion in the 1970s

However, the 1970s were marked by a period of disillusion in the black community. The hope that political advance would help the black underclass to break out from its poverty and enable Blacks to secure social acceptance in white communities on an equal basis did not materialise. Apathy and hopelessness replaced hope. When Martin Luther King was assassinated in 1968, Blacks lost the one national figure who was able to give voice to their hopes and fears and to provide focus and direction for their movement. The 1970s saw many Blacks lose faith in the electoral process and in many areas voter registration and turnout fell. Some

Martin Luther King

Black State Legislators, 1964–1990								
	1964	1968	1972	1976	1980	1984	1988	1990
State Legislature	94	172	238	295	318	384	416	440
State Governors	0	0	0	0	0	0	0	1

Table 2.2

Jesse Jackson emerged as the leader of the black community in the late 1970s

politicians began to write off the black vote as a waning political force.

This was to change again in the early 1980s. When Ronald Reagan became President, he introduced a series of economic and social policies which adversely affected many poor communities. Blacks realised that while they might not be able to cure all their economic ills through the political process, if they ignored it they might find their conditions deteriorating even further.

At the same time Jesse Jackson emerged onto the national politi-

cal scene and began to act as a focus for black participation. He toured the country exhorting young Blacks to reject drugs and to work hard at their education. His organisation used boycotts to force white businesses to provide more jobs for Blacks and he spearheaded several registration drives which were very successful in increasing the number of Blacks who were eligible to vote.

In 1984 Jackson entered the race to become President. With his Rainbow Coalition he tried to widen the base of his support to include all those who felt disenfranchised by the political system—including

Hispanics, women and poor Whites. These groups had not fared well under the Reagan Presidency. He did not secure the Democratic nomination. Despite winning 77% of the black vote, he won only 5% of the white vote. He was also criticised for his registration drives. In the South he increased black registration by 31%, but this prompted a white backlash which resulted in white voter registration increasing by 300% and Ronald Reagan, a Republican, won all the southern states. Jackson ran again in the 1988 Primaries and polled enough votes to come second to the eventual Democratic candidate. In spite of this, Jackson was not asked to be his running mate which angered his supporters. Jesse Jackson continued as a national political figure but his standing in the black community diminished in the 1990s.

BLACKS AND THE POLITICAL PROCESS IN THE 1990s

The first point to consider is that despite recent gains the black community has not achieved parity in representation. At 12% of the population, proportionately there should be twelve black Senators not one (see Table 2.3) and 52 members of the House of Representatives instead of 39. To that extent, Blacks are currently underrepresented in Congress. They are also under represented at the local government level. As Table 2.3 illustrates, they only account for 2.7% of locally elected officials.

However, these figures do not illustrate the extent of the influence of the black vote. Traditionally, black voters form the most solid bloc of all ethnic groups. While other ethnic groups are more fragmented in their voting patterns, Blacks, whether poor or rich, vote overwhelmingly and unvaryingly for the Democrats. Since 1964, 90% of black voters have supported Democratic Presidential candidates. For this reason, black voters have more influence within the Democratic Party than the number of black representatives in that Party would indicate.

Many Democratic representatives depend for their majorities on the black vote in their State or District. There may not be sufficient numbers to elect a black representative, but there is a sufficient bloc of votes to swing the result. Therefore many white Democratic representatives are particularly sensitive to black issues on Capitol Hill.

Increase in Minority Representation

The Voting Rights Act (1965) guaranteed one person one vote, but it did not guarantee equal representation for Blacks in the USA. In 1982 amendments to the Voting Rights Act led to the creation of 'majority-minority districts' in an attempt to boost the number of black and Latino representatives in Congress. In 1992, new gerrymandered districts returned more Blacks and Latinos to Congress than ever before. (See Table 2.3.) These districts have very strange boundaries. The 12th District in North Carolina, which unites widely dispersed pockets of Blacks, is 160 miles long and no wider than the state highway in many places. The number of Black, Hispanic and Asian members elected in 1992 increased by over 50% compared with the election two years earlier and included two black representatives elected from North Carolina for the first time since 1901.

MEASURING MINORITY POLITICAL PROGRESS

	1981	1983	1985	1987	1989	1991	1993	1995	1997
Members of the House of Representatives (out of 435)									
Black	17	21	20	23	24	25	38	40	39
API	3		3	4	5	3	4	4	5
Hispanic	6	8	10	11	10	11	17	17	21
Members of the Senate (out of 100)									
Black	0	0	0	0	0	0	1	1	1
API	3	2	2	2	2	2	2	2	2
Hispanic	0	0	0	0	0	0	0	0	0

Local Elected Officials by Race 1992

White	400,046	95.3%
Black	11,542	2.7%
Native American	1,800	0.4%
API	514	0.1%
Hispanic	5,859	1.4%

Table 2.3   Source: US Bureau of Census

Decrease in Minority Influence

Paradoxically, this "affirmative action gerrymandering" may have reduced the influence of the minority vote. In order to create a minority dominated district, several surrounding districts lost substantial numbers of their minority electorate. Grouping minority voters in districts concentrated the Democrat vote and left neighbouring districts more prone to vote Republican. This led to the loss of some traditional Democratic seats in the South in 1992 and 1994 and reduced the Democratic vote share in other districts. (See *Georgia's 8th*

District below.) In 1994 the Republican Party won a majority of Congressional seats in the South—the first time for over 100 years.

There will also be a loss of influence throughout the Democratic Party. If more seats are lost to the Republicans than are gained from the new districts, then the Democrats will find themselves with less influence in Washington. Secondly, if fewer Democratic congressmen and women depend on sizable groups of minority voters in their districts, then they will not be influenced to the same extent by those issues most important to minority groups. Where Democrats continue to be returned they owe their election to groups other than Blacks—consequently, black influence will diminish.

The new gerrymandered districts were immediately challenged in the courts. In 1993 and 1995 Supreme Court rulings cast doubt on using race as the means to determine electoral boundaries. It did not declare the use of race unconstitutional, but it did demand a very "strict scrutiny" of every individual case where race was taken into account when structuring districts. In 1995 it ordered Georgia to restructure its districts and this left the door open for other minority-

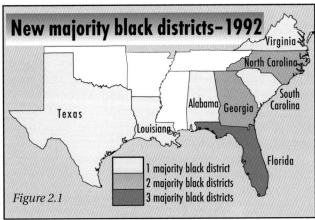

New majority black districts-1992

Virginia, North Carolina, South Carolina, Alabama, Georgia, Texas, Louisiana, Florida

- 1 majority black district
- 2 majority black districts
- 3 majority black districts

Figure 2.1

case study

Georgia's 8th District

In Georgia's 8th District the black population was reduced from 35% to 21% after redistricting. In 1992 the incumbent Democrat, J Roy Rowland, was re-elected with only 56% of the vote after winning 69% or higher in previous years. Rowland retired in 1994 and his seat was picked up by Republican Saxby Chambliss. Redrawing the boundaries to create a majority black district had lost the Democrats a seat.

majority districts to be challenged and for their boundaries to be redrawn.

It looks as if the experiment to increase the number of minority representatives in Congress by restructuring the boundaries was of short duration and it may have done more to damage minority influence in the Democratic Party than any numerical gain made in the 1990s. Redrawing black and Hispanic district boundaries may increase rather than diminish minority influence in Congress.

Motor-Voter Law

In 1995, Congress ordered states to open voter registration at sites such as drivers' licence and public assistance offices to enable the public to register to vote when they got their driving licence or welfare cheque. It was felt that this would increase registration among poor people—particularly the ethnic minorities—and benefit the Democratic Party. Because of this it was opposed by the Republican Party.

In the event the opposite was the case. Over 20 million people signed up to vote under motor-voter registration. An estimated 9 million of those were either new voters or people re-registering after having been dropped from registration rolls for not voting. (The others used the opportunity to update information on their registration, such as changing to a married name or entering a new address.) However, it was the Republican Party which gained most from this change to the system. Republicans gained in 8 of the 26 states where voters had to declare a party affiliation in order to register and lost numbers in only two states. The Democrats saw their registration numbers grow only in Maine while their numbers fell in 22 states.

"We laboured for years under the mistaken notion that more Democrats would take advantage of a new, easy registration programme," said Mike Singel, chairperson of Pennsylvania's Democratic Party. Instead "it seems to be middle- and upper-middle-class car owners who are registering."

The registration figures reflect national trends which started years ago. Democrats have seen registration drop in the South. In North Carolina, for example, more than 300,000 new voters registered. The Democrats worked hard but gained only 29% while the Republicans gained 42%. Those newcomers were crucial in the Senate battle. Jesse Helms, a very right-wing, anti-minority, anti-welfare Republican, was under threat but was returned with an increased majority over the Democrat. In the Presidential race the Republicans won the state by 49% to 44%.

HISPANICS AND THE POLITICAL PROCESS

Traditionally, most Hispanics do not become involved in the political process. There are a number of possible reasons for this.

✗ Firstly, there are language and cultural barriers. Many Hispanics have Spanish as their first or only language and until the 1980s registration, election literature and voting forms were printed only in English. Language was thus a major barrier preventing awareness of the importance of, or indeed the existence of elections. Also, politicians addressing mainstream issues have limited appeal to people whose specific problems are not being addressed. Of course this is a 'chicken and the egg' problem. If politicians feel that the Hispanic vote will not turn out in any significant numbers, then they will not address those issues which matter to the Hispanic community. If the community does not hear issues which matter to them, then they will not turn out to vote.

BLACK & WHITE VOTING IN PRESIDENTIAL ELECTIONS

(%)	1988 Democratic	1988 Republican	1992 Democratic	1992 Republican	1996 Democratic	1996 Republican
White	41	59	53	47	49	51
Black	92	8	94	6	90	10

Table 2.4 Source: US Census Bureau and ABC News exit poll

WHY DO BLACKS SUPPORT THE DEMOCRATIC PARTY?

✗ Firstly, the solid nature of the black vote stems from their recent political experience of fighting as a unified force for inclusion as equals in the mainstream of American society. The only significant variation throughout the period from the mid-1960s to the 1990s has been the turnout.

✗ Secondly, Blacks tend to favour the government using state power to rectify social ills more than Whites, Asians or Hispanics do. They also support Affirmative Action Programmes more strongly than Hispanics or Whites and they tend to support spending on social welfare programmes particularly those which redistribute wealth to the poor. This is true across the social classes.

✗ The Democratic Party fell heir to this solid voting bloc because it was the party which forced through the Voting Rights Act (1965) and which came to be identified with support for Affirmative Action Programmes. Between the 1960s and the 1990s the Democratic Party was felt to be more sympathetic towards social welfare, whereas the Republican Party was seen to favour small government and low taxation. The Democratic Party therefore won the overwhelming support of the black vote.

Voter Registration & Turnout (%)

	TOTAL		WHITE		BLACK		HISPANIC	
	Registered	Voted	Registered	Voted	Registered	Voted	Registered	Voted
1984	68.3	59.9	69.6	61.4	66.3	55.8	40.1	32.6
1988	66.6	57.4	67.9	59.1	64.5	51.5	35.5	28.8
1992	68.2	61.3	70.1	63.6	63.9	54.0	35.0	28.9
1996	65.9	54.2	67.7	56.0	63.5	50.6	35.7	26.7

Table 2.5 Source: Bureau of Census

Voter Concentration: Black voters living in an area provide overwhelming majorities for their favoured candidate. Therefore many voters do not bother to turn out to vote because their candidate will be elected anyway.

Life style: Many Blacks do not buy newspapers or watch the news. A diet of 'soap operas', 'chat shows' and MTV mean that many are ignorant or ill-informed about elections. Many Blacks do not know or are only vaguely aware that elections are taking place.

Access: making the trip to register to vote or to the polling station may be difficult or dangerous for many. Therefore many do not make the attempt.

Average black turnout at elections varies but it tends to be 6% to 9% less than that for Whites. There are a number of reasons for this.

Apathy: Limited economic and social improvement for those living in the ghetto means they see little value or point in voting.

Education: A high proportion of Blacks drop out of education at an early stage and have major problems with literacy. This makes filling out complex voter registration forms and long ballot papers extremely off-putting.

✗ Secondly, another aspect which must be taken into consideration is legality and transience. Many Mexican Americans currently living in the United States are there illegally and therefore cannot vote. Others are there only for a short time or are moving around the country following jobs during the harvesting season. They are never settled in one area long enough to register or vote. Puerto Ricans are in the US legally, but often are there only to improve the living standards for their families back home. They still feel bound to their native island and are not interested enough to vote.

✗ Thirdly, the Hispanic community has had no national *role models* with the prominence of black leaders like Martin Luther King or Jesse Jackson urging them on to vote. The Hispanic community has not had a Civil Rights Campaign to unite and encourage them to realise the importance of the political process in their lives.

✗ Finally, the process of integration may have robbed the Hispanic community of leadership. While large numbers of Hispanics do form identifiable groups in many states, many Hispanic families integrate quite successfully into mainstream American life. They do not face social and economic exclusion on the same scale as the Blacks, so their politics may well merge into the mainstream and become an indistinguishable part of it. Many Hispanics down the generations see themselves as Americans, not Hispanic Americans, and are accepted as such.

As a group, Hispanic turnouts have been traditionally low. Around one-quarter to one-third of Hispanics bother to turn out to vote (see Table 2.5), although this is not true for all Hispanics. Cubans in Florida have taken a much more active role in the politics of the state.

Since 1990 there has been an increase in the number of Hispanic

representatives in the House of Representatives. However, this was a consequence of the creation of gerrymandered majority-minority districts. (See pages 16–17.)

Hispanics and the major Political Parties

When they turn out to vote, the majority of Hispanic voters support the Democratic Party, but not in the same overwhelming numbers as the black community. In the 1996 Election the Democrats got 70% of the Hispanic vote while the other, more conservative, candidates won 30% of this group. The Hispanic community is divided in its support. Mexican Americans in the Southwest and Puerto Ricans in the East are predominantly Democrats, whereas many successful Hispanics identify with the Republican Party and its philosophy of small government, low taxation and rewarding enterprise. The Cubans in Florida in particular are very pro-Republican because of the Party philosophy and its hawkish

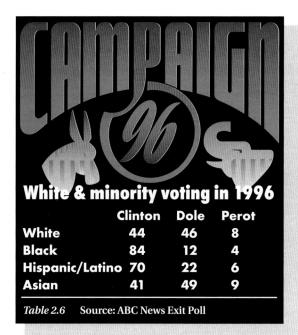

White & minority voting in 1996

	Clinton	Dole	Perot
White	44	46	8
Black	84	12	4
Hispanic/Latino	70	22	6
Asian	41	49	9

Table 2.6   Source: ABC News Exit Poll

1996 PRESIDENTIAL ELECTION RESULTS

IN **1996** only 54% of American voters bothered to vote. If Whites alone had voted then Dole would have won by 46% to 44% and if white males alone had voted the figure would have been 49% to 38% in Dole's favour. As it was, Clinton won by 49% to 40%. This demonstrates the importance of the minority vote to the Democratic Party.

The Million Man March had an effect on the Presidential Election in 1996. The march encouraged more black males to register and several advertising campaigns aimed at them increased black male voter turnout. Although black voter turnout fell from 54% in 1992 to 50.6% in 1996, turnout for black males rose by 1.7 million which was against the trend in all other categories. Most of the black vote went to the Democrats and this won them several marginal seats.

stance towards the socialist government of Cuba.

Therefore, while the majority of Hispanic voters currently register as Democrats, this cannot be assumed to be the position for the future. In 1984, 37% of the Hispanic community voted for the Republican candidate, Ronald Reagan, in his second term Election. Of the 18 Hispanic members of Congress, 15 are Democrat and 3 are Republican (two from Florida and 1 from Texas) and for the first time ever a Latino Republican was elected to the California Assembly. However, in 1996 the inroads which the Republicans had made into the Hispanic electorate were swept away because of their policies.

The Hispanic vote

The Hispanic electorate is concentrated in certain areas where it can be very influential in elections. Overall, in 1996, it accounted for 5% of the voting population of the US, but that figure increased to 10% in Arizona, 12% in Texas and 15% in California. Until 1996 the Hispanic electorate lagged well behind most of the US population in election participation. However, their registration and turnout rate rose in response to their growing concern at Republican programmes intent on cutting Hispanic immi-

gration and reducing civil rights protection and welfare benefits for immigrants already in the country. Turnout also rose because an increased number of Hispanic immigrants took out citizenship and because of registration drives and efforts by the Democrats to get the Hispanic vote out on election day.

Throughout the USA, 6.6 million Hispanics registered to vote in 1996, an increase of 30% over 1992. Of those, at least 5 million voted. In Texas the Hispanic vote increased by 60% on the turnout for 1992 and in California it was up 40%.

1996 elections

Bill Clinton got between 70% and 75% of the Hispanic vote in 1996, depending on which exit poll is used, compared with only 60% in 1992. In California, 87% of first-time Hispanic voters voted Democrat.

Of the 1.4 million Hispanics who voted in California, over 70% voted for the Democrats, marking a significant switch towards them. Where the Republicans had been making gains in the Hispanic vote throughout the 1980s and 1990s, they lost it all at the 1996 elections. Control of the California State Assembly switched from the Republicans to the Democrats who won

43 of the 80 seats and 14 Hispanic members were elected. Significantly, the Assembly elected Cruz Bustamante as the first Hispanic Speaker to the California Assembly.

The Hispanic vote proved critical in some congressional districts. In Orange County California, where the Hispanic population has been growing, the extreme right-wing Republican representative was defeated by a liberal, Loretta Sanchez, who was a Democrat. Orange County has a long tradition of electing conservative Republicans and was considered safe territory for them.

This pattern was repeated across those states with significant Hispanic populations. In Arizona, a state which had not voted Democrat since 1948, Bill Clinton claimed victory over Bob Dole by 47% to 44% because of the overwhelming support from the Hispanic community. In Texas 75% of Hispanics voted for the Democratic candidate and in New York the vote was 91% for the Democrats.

The Republican Party thought it could count on solid support from the Hispanic voters in Florida. However, Clinton's stance on Cuba and the anti-immigration stance of the Republicans led the Hispanic vote for Clinton to double from 22% in 1992 to 44% in 1996. Although the Republicans still had 46% of the Hispanic vote, the defection of so many Hispanics to the Democrats lost the the Republicans the state.

Significantly, the increased Hispanic turnout increased the number of Hispanic members of the House of Representatives in Washington. Table 2.3 shows the increase from 17 in 1995 to 21 in 1997—nearly a 25% increase.

Hispanics are the fastest growing section of the electorate and their vote is there to be won by both parties. As a consequence of Hispanic concentration in particular areas, they are influential. As the Hispanic population grows and becomes more aware of the relevance and influence of mainstream politics to its social and economic circumstances, the interests of this group will have to be accommodated by the two main parties. The Hispanic voter will become a decisive factor in future Presidential elections.

ASIANS AND THE POLITICAL PROCESS – THE 1990s

There is a growing Asian electorate in the USA but it is not a single force. There are Asians such as the Chinese who traditionally have not become involved in the political process. This is partly due to the fact that in the past they were le-

Hispanics were ultimately faced with the reality that politics does have a major effect on their lives. They realised that the Republican Party had a series of policy programmes which adversely affected them. Anti-immigration policies, opposition to affirmative action programmes and opposition to bilingual education alarmed and politicised the Hispanic community. They went to the polls to oppose the Republicans. The Spanish media called it the punishment vote – "El voto castigo".

El voto castigo

gally prevented from voting and partly because they have chosen to look inwards to their own communities and have refrained from drawing attention to themselves by becoming involved in the mainstream of US politics.

More recent immigrants from Japan and Korea have become more integrated in the mainstream either through business involvement or through the education system. They have been absorbed into the community at large and reflect their successful business or academic careers in the way they vote. Being traditionally conservative in nature and having a belief in success through individual effort and private enterprise, they have tended towards the Republican

Party as their natural home. In 1996 49% of this group voted Republican which was a greater proportion than the white population.

Although they record high percentage turnouts, the API population is not concentrated in significant numbers in any particular area except for the Pacific Islanders in Hawaii. There are a small number of Asian elected officials, but as a group they do not tend to promote themselves in the political arena. The few Asian representatives there are do not depend on gaining overwhelming majorities from their own community, but rather on winning votes from the electorate at large, which in the long run may be healthier for US politics and society.

Social and Economic Inequality

The early 1990s witnessed a growth in social and economic inequality in the USA. In this chapter we will consider the inequalities faced by the ethnic minority groups in the USA today including:

economic inequality
+ income levels – including welfare
+ unemployment rates – as a consequence of education and discrimination

social inequality
+ housing
+ family structures
+ education
+ health
+ crime and chemical abuse

All of these factors are closely interrelated.

SOCIAL AND ECONOMIC INEQUALITIES IN THE BLACK COMMUNITY

There is a tendency to consider the black community in the USA as a single entity but this would be an error. In general terms there are effectively two black communities in the USA. There are middle-class Blacks who have improved their living standards and have left the ghetto. Their lifestyle is very similar to that of the middle-class white population being centred around work, home and the traditional family. Then there is the black underclass who live in the ghetto. Their lifestyle is one of disadvantage, poverty, crime, unemployment single-parent families etc. While we will concentrate on this latter group and highlight its disadvantage we should not ignore the former.

Black Progress?

Although they remain considerably behind Whites with regard to income and levels of employment, Blacks as a group are much better off than they were before the civil rights movement of the 1960s and the adoption of various remedial programmes, including affirmative action. Writing in 1994, Henry Louis Gates Jr. noted that "never before have so many Blacks done so well." Economist Peter Drucker sums up the post-World War II changes:

> "In the 50 years since the Second World War, the economic position of African Americans in America has improved faster than that of any other group in American social history. Three-fifths of America's Blacks rose into middle-class incomes; before the Second World War the figure was one-twentieth."

Ironically, as Richard Nathan writes, the identification of the black situation with the ghetto poor stems from the fact that "members of racial minority groups who are educated, talented, and motivated can assimilate in ways that a generation ago would have been thought inconceivable." Few note the Blacks who 'make it.' As William P O'Hare and his co-au-

There are three themes to be aware of.

1 There has been an improvement in the social and economic conditions within the black community.

2 This improvement has not been equally distributed. There has been a significant divergence in the economic and social conditions between middle-class Blacks and the underclass remaining in the ghettos.

3 Despite the improvements, Blacks continue to suffer more economic and social disadvantage relative to Whites. Blacks who have the same levels of educational attainment as their white counterparts suffer from higher levels of unemployment and lower levels of income. The middle class to poor ratio for Whites is 70:30, whereas the comparable figure for the black community is 47:53. As the figures we use to compare ethnic groups are averages, they will reflect the larger numbers of Blacks in the underclass.

thors noted in a 1991 article, the record is clear:

"The black suburban population grew by 70% during the 1970s, fed primarily by an exodus from central cities. This trend has continued into the 1980s as the number of black suburbanites swelled from 5.4 million to 8.2 million. Between 1986 and 1990, 73% of black population growth occurred in the suburbs."

It is important to recognise that the situation of a major portion of black America was improving during the 1960s and '70s. Census data indicate that the percentage of Blacks living in poverty declined from 55% in 1959 to 33.5% in 1970. The rate has fluctuated somewhat since then, depending on the state of the economy.

The stability in the poverty rate figures conceals significant changes within the African American population which have produced a sizable better-educated and more affluent sector. The proportion of Blacks aged 25 and over who are high school graduates has increased from 51% in 1980 to 85% in 1993. According to the Census Bureau, "The annual dropout rate for Blacks declined from 11% in 1970 to 5% in 1993. In 1993, there was no statistical difference in the annual high school dropout rate of Blacks and Whites."

These drastic social and economic changes have led to growing differentiation within the black community. As a National Academy of Sciences panel, writing in the late 1980s, noted:

"Conditions within the black community began to diverge sharply in the 1970s. This divergence can be seen very clearly in the experience of young men. By the early 1980s, black men aged 25–34 with at least some college education earned 80–85% as much as their white counterparts. They also achieved some gains in private sector white-collar positions. In terms of education,

these black men represented the top one-third of their age group. At the other end of the group were the one-quarter of black men aged 25–34 who had not finished high school and who could not compete in the stagnant 1970s economy. An increasing number dropped out of the labour force altogether … .

The two largest groups in the black class structure are now a lower class dominated by female-headed families and a middle class largely composed of families headed by a husband and wife. The problem is that most black adults live in stable family and economic situations while most black children do not. They are the offspring of the large number of black women who are single mothers neither living with nor supported by a male head of household.

(Two Americas, Two Systems: Whites, Blacks, and Debate Over the Affirmative Action by Seymour Martin Lipset)

WHY DO MORE BLACKS THAN WHITES SUFFER FROM POVERTY ?

Relatively high levels of black poverty can be explained by several interrelated factors:

● higher than average levels of unemployment
● lower educational achievement
● discrimination in employment opportunities and in promotion

● numbers of single parent families
● welfare cutbacks
● the cyclical nature of deprivation and poverty

Unemployment

Unemployment rose in the early 1990s and then began to fall. Traditional sources of employment for young Blacks such as the armed forces no longer recruited in such large numbers because of the ending of the 'Cold War'. Also, faced with recession and stiff competition in the 1980s and 1990s, many firms resorted to downsizing.

Black unemployment rates were between two and three times higher than those faced by Whites. The disparity was even more acute for young Blacks. In 1995 more than 35% of Blacks aged 16–19 were unemployed compared with 14.5% for Whites. Although this figure was a drop from the high point of 39.8% recorded in 1992, it was still 4% higher than the figure for youth unemployment in 1990.

Such high levels of unemployment are all too visible in the inner city communities. They contribute to the incidence of crime, drug abuse and gang membership and affect the attitudes of the next generation towards education. What is the point of achieving in school if the end result is unemployment? It leads to peer group pressure to underachieve.

UNEMPLOYMENT IN THE USA (%)						
	1990	**1991**	**1992**	**1993**	**1994**	**1995**
All						
White	4.7	6.0	6.5	6.1	5.3	4.9
Black	11.3	12.4	14.1	13.0	11.5	10.4
Hispanic	8.0	9.9	11.4	10.8	9.9	9.3
16–19						
White	13.4	16.4	17.1	NA	NA	14.5
Black	31.1	36.3	39.8	NA	NA	35.7
Hispanic	19.5	22.9	27.5	24.0	NA	NA
20–24						
White	7.2	9.2	9.4	NA	NA	7.7
Black	19.9	21.6	23.9	NA	NA	17.7
Hispanic	9.1	11.6	13.2	11.8	NA	NA

Table 3.1   Source: Statistical Abstract USA 1994 & US Bureau of Labour Statistics 1996

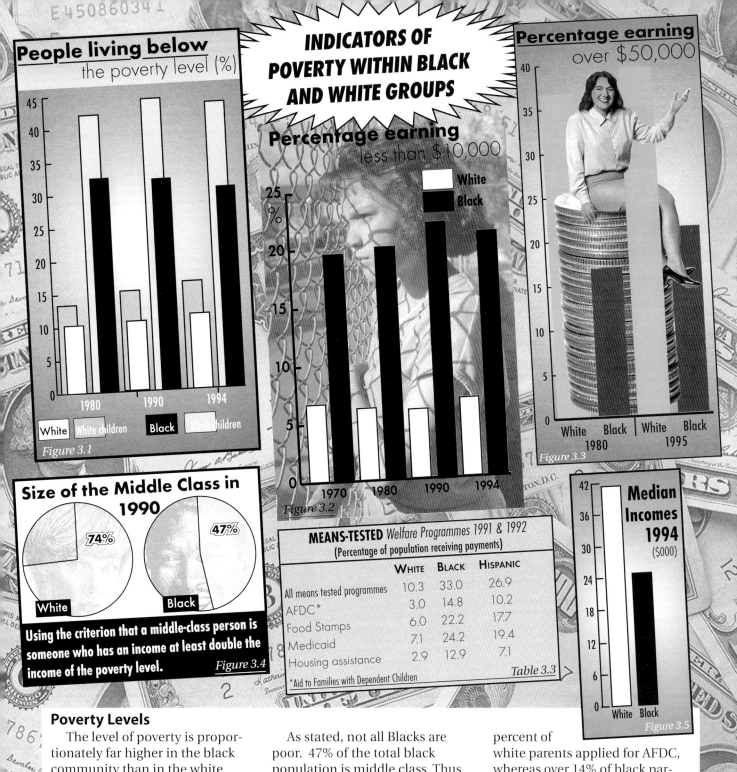

INDICATORS OF POVERTY WITHIN BLACK AND WHITE GROUPS

People living below the poverty level (%)

White | White children | Black | Black children

1980 1990 1994

Figure 3.1

Percentage earning less than $10,000

White
Black

1970 1980 1990 1994

Figure 3.2

Percentage earning over $50,000

White   Black | White   Black
1980   1995

Figure 3.3

Size of the Middle Class in 1990

74% White

47% Black

Using the criterion that a middle-class person is someone who has an income at least double the income of the poverty level.   *Figure 3.4*

MEANS-TESTED Welfare Programmes 1991 & 1992 (Percentage of population receiving payments)			
	WHITE	BLACK	HISPANIC
All means tested programmes	10.3	33.0	26.9
AFDC*	3.0	14.8	10.2
Food Stamps	6.0	22.2	17.7
Medicaid	7.1	24.2	19.4
Housing assistance	2.9	12.9	7.1

*Aid to Families with Dependent Children   *Table 3.3*

Median Incomes 1994 ($000)

White   Black

Figure 3.5

Poverty Levels

The level of poverty is proportionately far higher in the black community than in the white community. In 1994, almost 12% of whites were officially classed as poor in the USA, whereas the number of Blacks living in poverty was just over 30%—nearly three times the white rate.

The largest group to suffer poverty in the USA is black children. In 1994, more than16% of white children lived in poverty while over 43% of black children were officially recognised as poor. It is staggering to realise that in the USA, one of the richest countries in the world, nearly half of all children in the black community live in poverty.

As stated, not all Blacks are poor. 47% of the total black population is middle class. Thus almost half of the black population have an income which is double that of the official poverty level. Nevertheless, compared to Whites, where nearly 3 out of every 4 people are middle class, Blacks lag far behind. This is reflected in the comparative median incomes for Blacks and Whites. (See Figure 3.5)

More black families than white depend on welfare for their source of income. In 1991–92, just over 10% of Whites were on some form of welfare programme whereas 33% of Blacks had to apply for means-tested benefits. Three

percent of white parents applied for AFDC, whereas over 14% of black parents received payment from this source. Approximately five times as many black children as white children depended on AFDC payments.

If we consider cash income only in 1992, Blacks had a median income of 57.6% of the white median income. If we consider cash plus food stamps, free lunches, subsidised housing and medical cover, the black median income rises to 64.3% of white median income. Nonetheless, despite welfare payments, a higher percentage of Blacks live in poverty than Whites.

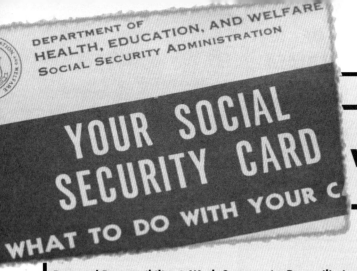

DEPARTMENT OF
HEALTH, EDUCATION, AND WELFARE
SOCIAL SECURITY ADMINISTRATION

YOUR SOCIAL
SECURITY CARD
WHAT TO DO WITH YOUR C

The Welfare Bill

Personal Responsibility & Work Opportunity Reconciliation Act 1996

When President Clinton signed the Welfare Bill in August 1996 he ended 60 years of guaranteed assistance for the poor of America and the black underclass in particular. The Bill turned over administration of the system to the individual states and reduced federal funding of these programmes by $54 billion over the subsequent six years. It is unlikely that the states will make up the shortfall.

In the short term it will seriously reduce the income of the poor underclass. In 1992, the median income for Blacks was only 64% of white median income. If welfare benefits are taken away black median income falls to only 57% of that for Whites. Therefore, because more Blacks depend on welfare for their income, more Blacks will suffer if welfare payments are cut. The biggest losers will be the children. With a higher proportion of black children dependent on welfare the adverse

effects of the Welfare Bill will fall disproportionately on the black underclass in the ghettos.

The medium- to long-term effects will either be to further impoverish the poor, increase crime statistics in the ghetto or force poor Blacks to improve their living standards by their own efforts. Whatever happens this Bill has started a far-reaching experiment in social engineering in the US which will radically alter the conditions of the poor. This may provide a lever for people like Louis Farrakhan to detach completely the black ethnic minority from mainstream American life. The 1996 Welfare Bill will be seen as a watershed in America's social commitment and may well place further strains on the fabric of US society.

PROVISIONS OF THE WELFARE BILL

The Welfare Bill ends the federal government's sixty year commitment to supporting unemployed families with children.

Its main provisions are:

☞ the states are to run the system and set many of the rules, such as ending benefits sooner than the five year lifetime set by the Federal Government.

☞ states are given a block grant by the federal government to fund the system but it will vary from state to state.

☞ a lifetime limit of five years is placed on anyone receiving Aid to Families with Dependent Children.

☞ able-bodied adults must work after receiving welfare assistance for two years.

☞ states must ensure that 90% of two-parent households receiving welfare must have jobs or be enrolled in job-readiness programmes by 1999.

☞ states can cut Medicaid cover for adults who lose welfare benefits because they do not go to work within two years.

☞ people aged 18 to 50 with no children, including the unemployed, will have to work to become eligible for food stamps.

☞ non-citizens, even those who are in the US legally, will not be entitled to most benefits because it is assumed that their sponsors have arranged work for them.

☞ reduced Supplemental Security Income assistance to handicapped children.

Education and employment

Educational attainment is an important factor in determining employment and income levels. The statistics show that unemployment levels are lower for those who have attained higher levels of qualification. Since they have higher educational attainment, more Whites will end up with better paid employment and will be less likely to suffer from unemployment.

The shortage of teachers in inner city schools is twice the national average, but this disadvantage for many ghetto children is compounded by their attitude towards education. Living in an environment which does not prize educa-

tion as a means of upward mobility, many young ghetto Blacks underachieve. Black ghetto schoolchildren "believe that studying is 'white' and that failing tests is part of being black" (John Jacobs, President of the National Urban League). This sentiment prevents many black children from taking advantage of the limited education system they find themselves in. Even where students may wish to study, uncooperative students can disrupt classroom activities sufficiently to defeat the process of education.

Dropout rates for black male students are rising. More than 13% of Blacks drop out after elementary schooling while 9% of Whites drop

out. The high school dropout rate in the first 3 years for Blacks is double that for Whites. Only 32% of Blacks make it to college and only 12% finish 4 years or more, whereas nearly twice as many Whites complete 4 years.

The subjects studied are also important. Blacks are severely under-

UNEMPLOYMENT by educational attainment 1995		
(%)	White	Black
No high school diploma	9.2	13.7
High School diploma	4.6	8.4
Bachelors degree	2.3	4.1

Table 3.3

Some facts about education

- In 1991, 40% of black adult males were functionally illiterate.
- 40% of black males in big cities do not graduate from high school. In the ghetto, black dropout rates are well above 50%.
- In 1992 there were 20,000 fewer black men in colleges than there were in 1980.
- Throughout the 1980s there was a marginal increase in the overall number of Blacks entering college but the gains were confined to black women.
- There are more young black men in prison than there are in college.

Blacks & Whites completing school in 1995 (%)

	White	Black
High school graduate or higher	83	73.7
Bachelor degree or higher	24	13.2

Table 3.4

represented in subjects such as maths, science and engineering—the subjects for which modern industry is crying out. This has a significant impact on employment opportunities and subsequent lifestyles.

In the 1950s and 1960s, high school dropouts could find work in the local mill or car factory. In the 1990s these jobs do not exist and dropouts become unemployed. For many in the ghetto, street crime is the best chance of finding wealth.

It is certainly true that for both Black and White, the higher the level of educational attainment, the less likely a person is to suffer from poverty. Those who have no high school diploma are about three to four times more likely to be unemployed than those who hold a Bachelor degree, but even those Blacks who hold a Bachelor degree are more than twice as likely to find themselves unemployed as comparable Whites. (See Table 3.3.) Where the educational skills are the same and at a high level, then the factor which determines such a large difference in unemployment rates must be race discrimination.

Discrimination and Employment

Table 3.5 indicates that discrimination continues to exist in spite of educational attainment. Blacks in comparison to Whites suffer from higher levels of unemployment, are paid lower wages and have higher levels of poverty no matter what educational level they achieve.

If we analyse the link between level of education and the monthly income of Blacks and Whites, we can see that there is a pronounced difference. From the least educated to those who have taken their learning to the highest possible levels,

MEAN MONTHLY INCOME by highest degree gained, 1993

	White ($)	Black ($)	Difference (%)
Not a high school graduate	951	713	33
High school graduate	1422	1071	33
College but no degree	1649	1222	35
Vocational	1768	1428	24
Bachelor degree	2682	2333	15
Masters degree	3478	2834	23
Professional degree	5590	3445	62
Doctorate	4449	3778	18

Table 3.5

there is a considerable difference in the earnings of Blacks compared with Whites. Indeed, the worst disparity is between those who have taken a professional degree.

People with professional degrees are doctors, dentists and lawyers and they are promoted to the highest income levels. One might assume that at this level employers would be interested in hiring the best qualified and most experienced professionals and that discrimination would not be a factor. Yet the mean monthly income of a black professional would need to increase by 62% to achieve parity with a similarly highly educated white counterpart. Obviously corporate America does not want to employ the best lawyers—it wants to employ the best white lawyers. Sick, rich America appears to want the bedside manner of the best white consultants money can buy, not the best consultants. If promotion and hiring were colour blind then there would be no disparity between the incomes of Blacks and Whites. The fact that a gap of 62% exists in this area points to discrimination at the top.

The Glass Ceiling – There are very few of the minority groups in senior positions in major US companies, thus commanding the high salaries that these positions offer. The Glass Ceiling Commission, set up by Congress in 1991, reported that the top executives in most large American Corporations continue to be white males.

The Poverty Trap

Despite being able to point to numerous examples of people from poor ethnic minority backgrounds improving their living standards and lifestyles, the cycle of poverty captures the vast majority. Most people who are poor do not attain the qualifications or have close role models to help them to improve their situations. In fact the negative effects of peer group pressure serve to pull them back into the situation into which they were born. The lack of economic opportunity makes it difficult for young people to find avenues out of their predicament.

Effectively, being born into a poor background with parents who are unemployed addicts, being taught in schools with limited resources, having restricted goals because of the limited job opportunities and suffering the negative effect of peer group pressure lead most Blacks into a life of poverty. This cycle repeats itself down the generations.

HOUSING AND POVERTY

Discrimination in housing means that Blacks also suffer from *residential segregation*. This is a major contributor to the development of the black underclass. 'White flight' occurred from some inner cities between the 1950s and 1970s causing these cities to be described as "a negro central city encircled by white suburbia." In 1968, the Kerner Commission warned the nation that it was divided "into two societies; one largely negro and poor, located in the central cities; the other predominantly white and affluent, located in the suburbs." Unlike Latinos or Asians, upward economic mobility did not lead to residential integration for Blacks.

Residential segregation was less extreme at the start of the twentieth century. However, over the course of the century, following the influx of large numbers of Blacks, Whites took action to prevent residential integration.

● Blacks found it harder to get mortgages. A Boston study found that twice as many black applicants

Households by Tenure and Race (%)

	BLACK		WHITE	
	Owner	Renter	Owner	Renter
1980	48.6	51.4	70.5	29.5
1990	42.4	57.6	67.5	32.5
1995	41.9	58.1	68.7	31.3

Table 3.6   Source: US Bureau of the Census

In 1995, far more Whites than Blacks owned the house they lived in. Many Blacks do not have a stable or large enough income to enable them to get a mortgage. Being forced to rent restricts where people can live. Most rented accommodation is in the inner city. Many urban Blacks are denied freedom of choice and are forced to live in the inner city areas and face the social deprivations associated with inner city life.

were refused mortgages as white applicants.

● Another method was outright intimidation. Black families attempting to move into a neighbourhood were visited by the local police and told to leave. Their house became the target for a hostile mob or a firebomb. More subtly, a neighbourhood association might have the right of first refusal on any property being sold. It

would then sell the house ensuring that it got the kind of neighbours whom local people wanted.

● Federal housing policies in northern cities during the 1970s exacerbated segregation. Urban renewal knocked down the old housing and concentrated the Blacks in vast housing schemes— the projects.

Housing in the South

In southern cities poor Blacks lived alongside poor Whites and more affluent Blacks lived among more prosperous Whites. When some southern cities tried to pass local ordinances to specify where Blacks and Whites could live, they were declared unconstitutional. The result was that southern Whites did not have the option of moving to white suburban communities with an exclusively white school system. Today, housing patterns are not as segregated in the South as they are in the old industrial cities of the

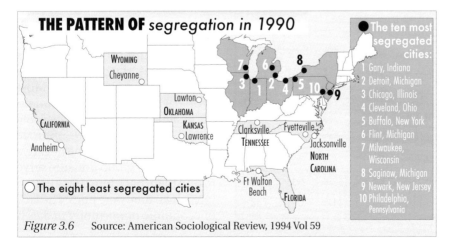

Figure 3.6   Source: American Sociological Review, 1994 Vol 59

Family Life in America

Family Households by Race

	1970	1980	1990	1995
White				
– Married couple	89	85	83	82
– Male head only	2	3	4	4
– Female head only	9	12	13	14
Black				
– Married couple	68	56	50	47
– Male head only	4	4	6	7
– Female head only	28	40	44	46
Hispanic				
– Married couple	81	75	70	68
– Male head only	4	5	7	8
– Female head only	15	20	23	24
Asian & Pacific Islander				
– Married couple	NA	84	82	81
– Male head only	NA	5	6	6
– Female head only	NA	11	12	13

Table 3.9

There has been a marked trend away from the traditional structure of the two parent nuclear family in the USA over the past quarter century. In 1970, 89% of Whites lived as married couples, but 25 years later this had fallen by 7% with most of the burden of family leadership falling to the female. This trend was more marked in the black community. In 1970, 68% of black households were led by married couples and 28% were led by women, but by 1995 married couples accounted for less than half of the black households in the US and 46% were led by females. If we consider only those households with children under 18 years of age the statistics are even more stark—53% of black households are maintained solely by women.

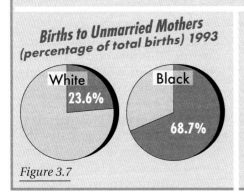

Births to Unmarried Mothers (percentage of total births) 1993

White 23.6%

Black 68.7%

Figure 3.7

Households with children under 18, 1995 (%)

	BLACK	WHITE
Two-parent family groups	41	79
One-parent family groups:		
– maintained by mother	53	17
– maintained by father	6	4

Table 3.8

Female family householders– reasons for status 1995 (%)

	BLACK	WHITE
Never married	42	19
Married, spouse absent	19	17
Widowed	14	21
Divorced	25	43

Table 3.9

Source: US Bureau of the Census

North and West. Increasingly in the 1980s and 1990s Blacks are attracted to these areas where segregation is not so entrenched.

FAMILY LIFE

For the middle class, black or white, the role of the traditional family is still strong. The breakdown is in the underclass in the ghetto. Here it has had a profound effect on family life and the roles of male and female. The increasing reality of family life is of transient relationships in which males father children and then disappear. The only permanency is the female line through the generations and illegitimacy is the norm. In 1993 just under a quarter of all white women giving birth were single but more than two-thirds of black mothers were single. Table 3.9 shows that the main reason for black women be-

ing sole heads of households is that they did not marry, but most have children. Whereas in the white community there is still a commitment to the concept of marriage, even if it ultimately fails as can be seen by the high statistics for divorce, for the black underclass the concept of marriage as an institution for bringing up children is rapidly diminishing.

One consequence is the development of a welfare dependency culture in the ghetto community. In 1992–93, 33% of the black population was dependent on some form of welfare which was three times the rate for the white population. If we consider Aid to Families with Dependent Children, 14.8% of the black population received payments—nearly 5 times the percentage of Whites. (See Table 3.2.)

Children's perceptions of 'family' and parental behaviour have been radically altered. The female is seen as the head of the family but as it is increasingly dysfunctional she earns little respect. Unmarried males are seen as transient begetters of children who need not take responsibility for the upbringing of the family. The family has lost the respect of its children and many have turned their focus on the gang which becomes the 'real' family because it is permanent, trustworthy and demands respect.

Young women are becoming more involved in gang activities. The reasons for girls joining gangs are the same as for men. They join in their early teens because their family life has been destroyed by abuse, alcohol, drugs, poverty and jail. The gang offers companionship, security and protection. As one new recruit said, "they treated me like a little sister. And if I ever had any problems, they'd help me out. I'd never had that before."

Female gangs are rapidly growing across the USA. In 1990 women made up 10% of the gang membership in the USA. By 1995 this figure was up to 15%. The girl gangs are as heavily involved in drug dealing and violence as the male gangs.

Million Woman March

Another reaction to the social and economic problems was the Million Woman March. As many as 700,000 black women filled the streets of Philadelphia in 1997, standing shoulder to shoulder for almost a mile in a show of unity and strength. Hundreds of buses brought women from dozens of states to the march which was organised by two relatively unknown Philadelphia women, Phile Chionesu and Asia Coney. They declined offers of help from established black politicians but instead publicised the gathering by word of mouth and through a Website.

The Website 'mission statement' for the event stated that as women "we no longer bond as a family unit, we no longer teach and prepare our children in the way we wish for them to go. How do girls learn to become women?" … "We will no longer tolerate disrespect, lack of communication, negative interaction, antisocial and dysfunctional behaviour…"

The Philadelphia march was organised by ordinary women fed up with crime, unemployment, teen pregnancy and other social problems. It was an attempt to address the ills of the inner city through a massive show of unity against inadequate health care, poor education, high unemployment and crime. It was intended as a catalyst for positive change in black communities and to energise black women to strengthen families and communities.

[1] prison – state or federal institution

[2] jail – city or county lockup

BLACKS AND CRIME

In June 1994 the US sent its millionth person to prison[1]. There were also 500,000 in jail[2], 600,000 on probation, 3,000,000 on parole and 100,000 in juvenile correction facilities. That year 14,000,000 people were arrested. Crime is a major part of life in the USA and is a particular problem in the ghetto.

The statistics reveal that there is a higher incidence of crime in the inner cities. They also indicate that crime is a way of life for a high proportion of black males born in the ghetto. In 1992 there were more black men in prison (583,000) than in college (537,000). One out of every four black men will go to prison in his lifetime. 42% of black men aged 18–35 in Washington, DC were under some form of criminal justice control in 1992. Black people are 8.5 times more likely to go to prison than white people. (See Table 3.11.)

Victims of crime

The ghetto is where most people are affected by crime as both perpetrators and victims. Black inner city households were most likely to identify crime as a neighbourhood problem and it increased significantly between 1985 and 1991. People with household incomes of less than $15,000 per year suffered significantly higher violent crime rates for all categories of violent crime and crimes against property were greatest for ethnic minorities,

Households identifying crime as a problem (%)	1985	1991
All households	4.7	7.4
White	4.0	6.0
Black	8.5	16.5
Hispanic	7.7	12.1
Place of residence:		
Central city	9.1	15.0
Suburban	2.9	4.6
Rural	1.4	1.9

Table 3.10   Source: American Housing Survey

city inhabitants and those who are tenants rather than owners of houses.

The reason most crime is in the inner city is because many convicted offenders committed crimes near where they lived. A 1991 survey of state prison inmates disclosed that 43% of prisoners were serving time for offences committed in their own neighbourhoods. This included 45% of violent offenders and 52% of drug offenders.

Statistics from the US Department of Justice for 1995 suggest that the most likely victim of a violent crime would be a young black male. In 1995, about one-third of all victims of violent crime were aged 12 to 19. Almost half of all victims of violence were under the age of 25. Blacks were more likely than Whites or Asians or Native Americans to be victims of robbery and

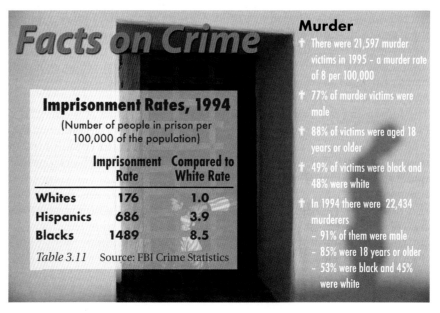

Facts on Crime

Imprisonment Rates, 1994
(Number of people in prison per 100,000 of the population)

	Imprisonment Rate	Compared to White Rate
Whites	176	1.0
Hispanics	686	3.9
Blacks	1489	8.5

Table 3.11   Source: FBI Crime Statistics

Murder

✝ There were 21,597 murder victims in 1995 – a murder rate of 8 per 100,000

✝ 77% of murder victims were male

✝ 88% of victims were aged 18 years or older

✝ 49% of victims were black and 48% were white

✝ In 1994 there were 22,434 murderers
 – 91% of them were male
 – 85% were 18 years or older
 – 53% were black and 45% were white

were also more likely than Whites to be victims of aggravated assault. One in eighteen Blacks was the victim of violent crime compared to 1 white person in 23. Apart from rape and sexual assault, 1 male in 19, compared to 1 female in 27 was a victim of violence. 80% of the 1.3 million violent crimes against Blacks that year were committed by other Blacks.

Similarly, Blacks are more likely to be victims of murder. In 1995, almost identical numbers of Blacks and Whites were murder victims—49% of all victims were black, 48% were white and 3% were Asians, Pacific Islanders, and Native Americans. Since Blacks account for only 12% of the population, it means that they are over-represented as murder victims. Most were likely to be male and relatively young.

Drugs, gangs and violence
Street violence has always been part of American culture, but during the 1980s it mushroomed in the urban areas of the US. It also developed into previously unknown random violence and drive-by shootings.

The social and economic policies of the Reagan and Bush Administrations increased poverty. As people lost their jobs these Administrations cut social welfare, thus denying many the hope of improving their lifestyle through hard work. The USA was moving from a manufacturing to a service based economy. Jobs were being relocated from the industrial cities to the suburbs and the South. Furthermore, the economy was under threat from the countries of the Pacific Rim and was feeling the effects of recession.

Simultaneously, crack cocaine hit the streets and spread like wildfire throughout the ghetto. The profits from its sale were enormous and it provided wealth for dealers. This was the incentive for gangs to grow in order to control territory—the means to make wealth and attain status. Estimates for Los Angeles County alone have traced the

growth of gang numbers and membership from 400 gangs with 30,000 members in 1983 to 800 gangs with 75,000 members in 1990. There was an explosion of urban crime as a direct consequence of the introduction of 'crack'.

The gang involvement with drugs has resulted in a level of violence which is unprecedented in US urban history. Gang members, flush with drug money, can afford to arm themselves with the latest automatic and semiautomatic weapons. Crack provides a delusion of escape and a removal from reality. A person high on crack or some other drug, having had their inhibitions reduced and being armed with automatic weapons, is a murder waiting to happen.

HEALTH
The figures on page 30 show the disparity in health between Blacks and Whites in the US. If we look at life expectancy (Figure 3.9) we can see that there has been a slight narrowing of the gap from a 7 year difference in 1960 to a 5.7 year difference in 1990. However, this hides the fact that black life expectancy has been decreasing since 1985. A black child born in 1985 expected to live longer than one born in 1995.

The life expectancy figures for males show a wider gap between the races. The seven year difference demonstrates the inequalities in health which result from lifestyles and living standards. Access to work often means access to health insurance and in the US black males have a much higher rate of unemployment than white males or if they are in employment they tend to have lower paid jobs. Blacks, therefore, are more likely to be uninsured or underinsured.

Add to that the lifestyle of many black males in the ghetto—gang membership and drug abuse—and the gap in life expectancy can be understood. An African American who lives in the inner city has less chance of reaching the age of 65 than a man in Bangladesh.

Homicide (murder) is the main cause of death for black males aged 15 to 24. The homicide rate for Blacks is 6 times the rate for Whites. The death rate from guns and violence is so high that a team of military surgeons joined the MLK Medical Center in South Central LA because black gang and drug warfare offered the best practice in treating gunshot trauma victims anywhere outside an actual battlefield.

Health Insurance
There is a large and growing number of people in the USA who are either uninsured or underinsured. This is particularly evident in the black and Hispanic communities. As Figure 3.8 shows, the number of uninsured people in the USA increased by nearly 25% between 1979 and 1990 from 29 million to 37 million.

The lack of health care insurance in the black community shows up in the statistics for childbirth. As indicated in Table 3.13, nearly 10% of black mothers get health care late on in their pregnancies if at all which means that the care which is available to help both mother and child is denied them. The consequences of this can be seen in the statistics for low birth weight and infant mortality. Due to the lack of health care during pregnancy and the poor lifestyles faced by these pregnant mothers—poor diet, bad living conditions, drug and alcohol abuse—13.3% of babies born to black mothers are underweight at birth and the infant mortality rate for black infants is more than twice that for white infants.

HISPANICS

Hispanics and Poverty
The Hispanic underclass live in the 'barrio' which is their equivalent of the ghetto. Many of the social and economic disadvantages which face the Blacks in the ghetto are present for Hispanics in the barrio. The statistics illustrate that, compared to Whites, more Hispanics are poor, are unemployed and are

Health Care

Health Cover in the USA

Inadequate insurance
Uninsured

Figure 3.7

(bar chart, y-axis: million people 0–60; x-axis years 1979, 1990, 1992–94)

Looking after the baby

(Percentages)	WHITE	BLACK
Infant mortality rate (1993)	6.8	16.5
Births with low weight* (1992)	5.8	13.3
Mothers beginning prenatal care in 3rd trimester or no care (1992)	4.2	9.9

*less than 2500 grams (5lb 8 oz) at birth

Table 3.13 Source: National Center for Health Statistics

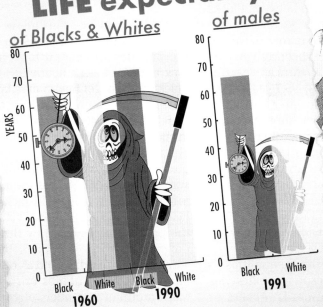

LIFE expectancy: of Blacks & Whites of males

(bar charts, YEARS on y-axis)

Black   White   Black   White
1960   **1990**

Black   White
1991

Figure 3.9

DEATH RATES (Per 100,000) by cause

	Firearms (1993)	Drug induced (1993)	Alcohol induced (1990)
White			
• male	20.7	10.0	9.9
• female	3.9	3.6	6.8
Black			
• male	68.8	13.0	26.6
• female	8.0	4.0	7.0

Table 3.12 Source: US National Center for Health Statistics

Facts About Health Care
in the USA in the 1990s

✚ 15 million people with no health insurance have incomes which are twice the poverty rate.

✚ 1 million Americans who seek health care are turned away each year.

✚ 14 million do not seek medical attention because they know they cannot afford it.

✚ two-thirds of those with serious health problems (eg. spontaneous bleeding, loss of consciousness, unexplained weight loss) do not go to see the doctor.

✚ 12 million children live in families with no health cover.

✚ 35% of poor children (more than 4 million) get no health cover because of gaps in the system of Medicaid.

✚ two-thirds of pregnant women who are uninsured do not get prenatal care which pushes up the infant mortality rate. (The US is in nineteenth position in the world league table of infant mortality rates despite being the leading country for health spending.)

✚ 40% of children do not get childhood vaccinations.

at a disadvantage in education and in health. Yet the figures also show that Hispanics are not as badly off as the black community.

Large sections of cities like Los Angeles are occupied by the Hispanic underclass which is formed by new immigrants, illegal immigrants and those of longer residence who have not yet found the American Dream. Nevertheless, they are not trapped to the same extent as the black community and can retain the hope of upward mobility. They also have far greater social cohesion through the strength of the extended family structure.

Poverty has been a growing problem in the Hispanic community throughout the 1980s and 1990s. In 1980 the poverty rate for Hispanics was twice that for Whites, but by 1994 it was approaching three times the level. By 1994 nearly one-third of Hispanics in the USA were below the poverty level. The figure for children was worse with 41.1% living in poverty. (See Table 3.15.)

Poverty is not distributed equally throughout the Hispanic community. While the Puerto Ricans are the poorest Hispanic sub-group, and indeed the poorest identifiable group in the US, the Cubans have a much smaller proportion of their community suffering from poverty. (See Table 3.15.)

Why has poverty increased?

The *economic recession* was one reason for the growth in poverty. Many well-paid blue-collar jobs, particularly in the defence industry, disappeared and others in the computer assembly industries in 'Silicon Valley' were exported to the countries of the Pacific Rim where wage costs were lower. Jobs in small-scale manufacturing enterprises, such as clothing manufacture, were also badly affected during this period.

Another major factor was the influx of *Hispanic immigrants.* Many worked for low wages which increased the numbers living in poverty. This also helped to drive down wage rates in service sector industries which adversely affected the incomes of Hispanics already well established in the US.

New immigrants start off poor, which explains the relatively high figures for Hispanic poverty, but their economic and social upward mobility is better than it is for

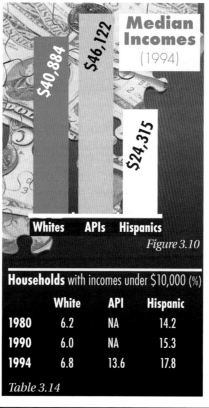

Figure 3.10

Households with incomes under $10,000 (%)			
	White	API	Hispanic
1980	6.2	NA	14.2
1990	6.0	NA	15.3
1994	6.8	13.6	17.8

Table 3.14

Living below the poverty level (%)					
	White	API	Hispanic	Children	
				White	Hispanic
1980	10.2	NA	21.8	13.4	33.0
1990	10.7	14.1	26.2	15.1	37.7
1994	11.7	14.6	30.7	16.3	41.1

Hispanics below the poverty level by sub-group (%) 1995			
Hispanic	Mexican	Puerto Rican	Cuban
30.7	32.3	36.0	17.8

Table 3.15

Hispanic Unemployment 1995				
White	Hispanic	Mexican	Puerto Rican	Cuban
4.9	9.3	9.7	11.2	7.4

Table 3.16   Source : US Bureau of Labour Statistics 1996

Blacks. They do not reach the middle class via education, but by setting up small businesses or by working hard in blue-collar jobs and pooling their resources.

Although poverty was on the increase within the Hispanic community, it was as a consequence of the influx of new immigrants who were poor. Those who were born in the US or who had been resident for many years were more likely to be moving up the economic ladder.

A recent survey analysed household incomes rather than individual incomes because the extended family tends to pool its resources and several wage earners may live under one roof. The survey demonstrated that even during a period when poverty was on the increase in the Hispanic community, increasing numbers of Hispanics were becoming 'middle class'. The results suggested that half of the households of American-born Hispanics were 'middle-class' in 1990 and that "American-born Latinos were four times more likely to belong to middle-class households than to poverty-stricken ones."

Many Hispanics have managed to become middle class without losing their cultural identities because in California and the border states cheap travel, telephones and the proximity to Mexico means that they are close to their roots. Only 21% of Hispanic men obtained citizenship or could speak proficient English after ten years residence in the USA.

Integration

Socially, Hispanics are able to integrate far more effectively with the white community than Blacks. Hispanics are more readily accepted as neighbours. They may occasionally meet with opposition which is racially motivated, but it is nowhere near the scale of that faced by Blacks

Educational Attainment 1990 (%)	White	API	Hispanic
Completed 4 years of High School or more	79.1	80.4	50.8
Completed 4 years of College or more	22.0	39.9	9.2

Table 3.17

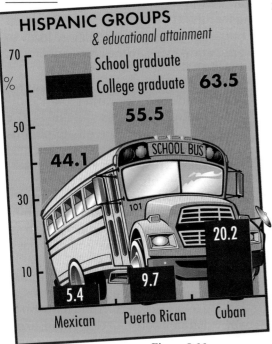

Figure 3.11

attempting to move into middle-class white areas. 40% of middle-class Hispanic householders are 35 or younger. Most live in 'white suburbs'.

Evidence for integration can also be found in the rate of intercultural marriages which take place. In 1970 just over half a million Hispanics married non-Hispanics. This had increased to 1.2 million in 1992. In 1990 the Census identified 1.5 million children born to 'mixed' parents. One-third of American-born Latinos marry non-Latinos. Education and employment lead to an increasing number of multicultural marriages.

Mixed marriages have fewer children. Whereas Mexican American couples have an average of 2.9 children and white couples have an average of 2.0, the average for mixed-marriage couples is 1.7. This is because these parents tend to be better educated and to have careers.

The rate of inter-marriage increases as we move farther away from the heavy concentrations of the Hispanic population in California, New York and Miami because of the greater chance of meeting someone from a different cultural background. Hispanic women are marginally more likely to 'marry out' than men. This indicates that the Hispanic community is more readily accepted by the dominant white community which enables a greater degree of upward mobility. It may also indicate that the predictions that the Hispanic population may rise very rapidly throughout the twenty first century and threaten the social cohesion of the USA may not prove to be correct. For Whites and Hispanics the melting pot view of society may turn out to be the reality.

Education and employment

Education makes an important contribution to poverty and unemployment. While Cuban stay on rates are closer to those for the white population than to the Hispanic average, Mexican Americans tend to leave school very early. While in some areas the temptation of the gang and drug culture is very strong, its appeal to young Hispanics is not as pronounced as it is for young Blacks. Hispanic unemployment is worse than that for Whites but it is not as bad as that for Blacks. This is because Hispanics do not depend to the same extent as Blacks on getting an education which will enable them to secure employment generated by affirmative action programmes in the public sector or in middle management with a large corporation. Instead, the Hispanic community has embraced the enterprise culture of the American

Dream. Many have become small business entrepreneurs in retailing, small-scale manufacture, construction and throughout the service sector. Consequently, young Hispanics leaving school early can find work in some local enterprise which is usually owned by a family member or a friend of the family.

Family life

Family life is still important within the Hispanic community, even in the barrio. While the figures do illustrate a movement away from traditional family patterns in the Hispanic underclass, it is not as far-reaching as in the black ghetto. Research has shown that births to unmarried mothers and traditional two-parent families are very similar to those for the white communities if we consider only those Hispanics who have managed to make their way into the middle class. In 1993 there were fewer births to unmarried mothers in the Cuban population, which is the most settled Hispanic group, than there were in the white group. However, the figures are far higher for Mexican Americans and Central and South Americans because they include large numbers of recent immigrants and for Puerto Ricans who tend to be more transient in their stay in the US.

ASIAN AND PACIFIC ISLANDERS (API)

Asians and Poverty

Asian immigrants to the USA are people of ambition and drive. Statistics show that they are more likely to get a job and less likely to be on welfare than native-born Americans. Most come to the USA seeking a better life for themselves and, more importantly, for their children. Their commitment to their new country is evident. 53% of Asian women were proficient in English and 67% of Asian men had taken out US citizenship within 10 years of arrival in the USA.

They work long hours in tough jobs to accumulate capital. They open businesses and regenerate many rundown city areas. Old properties are renovated, streets are cleaned up and the incidence of street crime—drugs, prostitution etc.—is reduced.

In New York several areas have been regenerated by recent Asian immigrants—Flushing in Queens and Sunset Park and Red Hook in Brooklyn. In Los Angeles, Monterey Park now calls itself the Chinese Beverley Hills. 120,000 Vietnamese have transformed Westminster and Garden Grove from being scruffy rundown areas into hives of economic activity called 'Little Saigon'. Another lively and even more prosperous part of downtown LA is 'Koreatown' with its restaurants, shops, factories, offices and homes.

On average, the statistics show that economic and social conditions for Asian Americans are equal to or better than those for the majority white population. While there are more APIs living in poverty, there are fewer APIs than Whites living in the harshest of poverty with incomes below $10,000 and a higher proportion have incomes above $50,000. Between 1980 and 1990 the average income of Asian men doubled from $19,800 to $39,000 making them the most rapid upwardly mobile group in the USA.

Asians have overtaken Whites in educational attainment and far more stay on to complete college degrees. Their belief in marriage matches that for Whites exactly. The rates of births to unmarried mothers is far lower than for Whites which illustrates the importance placed on the role of the family in Asian culture. The health statistics also show that Asians are just as mindful of their health as the white community and also have jobs and incomes which enable them to have access to adequate levels of health insurance.

Yet these averages disguise some significant differences that separate the subdivisions within the Asian group. The Japanese have successfully integrated into the US business community, especially in the export-import business with the East. An increasing number are becoming prominent in the education world. Significant numbers live in the USA but they usually remain aloof from US politics and lifestyle, preferring to focus on their own culture and way of life. They either form part of a silent sub-culture or are totally integrated with few socioeconomic problems.

The Koreans have an entrepreneurial reputation. They run businesses such as greengrocers' shops, sandwich shops and service stations and have become very visible especially in Los Angeles. Many recent Asian immigrants to the USA are highly trained graduates who can command high salaries. Also, many Asian parents and children place a high value on education and so do better than other groups including white Americans.

Not all Asians are doing well. Most of the refugees from Indo China (Cambodia, Vietnam and Laos) have not achieved the American Dream.

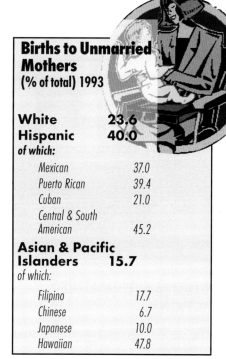

Births to Unmarried Mothers (% of total) 1993	
White	**23.6**
Hispanic	**40.0**
of which:	
Mexican	37.0
Puerto Rican	39.4
Cuban	21.0
Central & South American	45.2
Asian & Pacific Islanders	**15.7**
of which:	
Filipino	17.7
Chinese	6.7
Japanese	10.0
Hawaiian	47.8

Table 3.18   Source: US National Center for Health Statistics

Many of the original Vietnamese refugees started off well, finding assembly jobs in Silicon Valley. Then, when the electronic companies found that they could buy parts much cheaper from Hong Kong and Taiwan, the Vietnamese workers became unemployed. Untrained and with little English, they turned to social welfare or any low paid job they could find. Some of their children dropped out of school and joined street gangs. They made a living by demanding protection money and defending their turf for the profits from drugs.

Filipinos do the mundane jobs and are falling behind the rest. There are more Filipino women than Filipino men in the US. Many are the wives of white Americans who 'ordered' their wives from mail-order firms which advertise 'submissive' brides from the Philippines. There is also a huge demand for nursing staff in the USA. Many female nurses arrive to work in the US from the Philippines and later send for their families, thus reversing the usual pattern.

Figure 3.12

Affirmative Action

WHAT IS AFFIRMATIVE ACTION?

The term 'affirmative action' first appeared in Executive Order 10925 issued by President JF Kennedy in 1961. It referred to measures designed to eliminate discrimination in employment. Affirmative action became the umbrella term used to describe a variety of programmes designed to remedy contemporary discrimination and eliminate the current effects of past discriminatory practices. It covered ethnic and racial minority groups (as well as women and the disabled) and referred to procedures which enable minority groups to compete equally for jobs, education and promotion opportunities with the dominant white male population.

The programmes, collectively known as affirmative action programmes (AAPs), developed in two areas—education and employment. Education was seen as a means to give all Americans, regardless of race or ethnicity, the same opportunities to progress towards the American Dream. Equality of opportunity in employment was going to enable the minorities to have an equal chance to live the American Dream.

A BRIEF HISTORY OF AFFIRMATIVE ACTION

For much of the twentieth century, racial and ethnic minorities and women were either discriminated against in economic life or were excluded from it. Blacks and Hispanics were segregated into low skilled and low paid employment. Asian Americans were forbidden by law from owning land.

Labour shortages during and following World War Two brought ethnic minority workers into many industries which previously had predominantly employed white workers. Even so, into the 1960s Blacks continued to be segregated into low paid jobs and into the 1970s employment opportunities for Hispanics remained highly restricted. In department stores, the clerks were white while the lift operators were black. In factories, floor sweepers were black while the skilled and more highly paid machine operators were white. Asian Americans were not only excluded from becoming managers, they were housed in physically separate living quarters.

It was common for Blacks who were college trained to find jobs only as bellboys, porters or domestics. Their main avenue into the professions was either to become a preacher or to find a teaching post in an all-black school.

Presidential support

While affirmative action programmes had their roots in the 1950s and 1960s, it was the Nixon Administration of the 1970s which enabled them to flourish. They did not develop until it was realised that anti-discrimination laws alone would not be enough to remove the discrimination which was deeply embedded in US society.

Examples of Affirmative Action

IN EMPLOYMENT
- placing job advertisements in locations which are likely to be seen by a wide range of people.
- eliminating discriminatory practices in hiring and promotion.
- setting flexible goals which increase opportunities for those who were previously discriminated against. These would include training and promotion.
- setting target dates to achieve the goals and holding employers accountable. Firms with more than 50 employees or who won contracts of more than $50,000 had to develop a written affirmative action programme (AAP). The firm had to change its worker profile to be more like the population profile in the district.

IN CONTRACTS
Affirmative action programmes require
- federal, state and city government to set aside a small percentage of the contracts they issue for firms which are minority owned or which show some form of disadvantage
- the bidding process for all government contracts to be open to firms which are traditionally excluded.

IN EDUCATION
- busing
- outreach programmes
- recruitment and retention programmes
- diversification of admission procedures

IMPORTANT LANDMARKS

IN AFFIRMATIVE ACTION

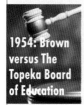

1954—The Supreme Court ruled that 'separate but equal' facilities were inherently discriminatory and therefore unconstitutional.

1964—Civil Rights Act prohibited discrimination based on race, gender, national origin and religion in employment and education.

1965—President Johnson signed Executive Order 11246 requiring federal contractors to institute affirmative action measures to increase their number of employees from minority groups.

1969—President Nixon required construction companies seeking contracts from federal and state agencies to introduce 'goals and timetables' to measure progress towards increasing the number of employees from minority groups. In **1970** he extended this to all federal contractors.

1978—Allen Bakke was refused entry to the University of California despite having better grades than applicants from the ethnic minorities who were admitted. The Supreme Court ruled that universities could take race into consideration as a factor in admissions when trying to create diversity on the campus, but the use of quotas was unconstitutional as it represented reverse discrimination. In 1995 the University voted to drop race as a factor in admissions.

1978—President Carter set up the Office of Federal Contract Compliance Programme (OFCCP). Initially, all federal agencies monitored their own programmes and some were more rigorous than others at implementing affirmative action. OFCCP monitored all programmes with the same rigour.

The Supreme Court ruled that AAPs based on racial preferences will receive "the strictest judicial scrutiny" and will "seldom provide a relevant basis for disparate treatment". Effectively, AAPs designed to benefit minorities are unconstitutional. Each contract must be reviewed individually to ensure it passes a 'strict scrutiny' test which means that it has to serve a compelling government interest and is narrowly tailored to address past bias.

1995—Cheryl Hopwood was denied a place in a Texas university "solely because she was the wrong skin colour." The US Circuit Court ruled that the Texas policy of "giving preference to minority applicants violated the Constitution's equal protection guarantee." The Supreme Court allowed the ruling to stand.

1996—Under Proposition 209, 54% of the voters of California voted to end affirmative action programmes in California.

1997—The US Circuit Court of Appeals turned down a request from civil rights groups to block Proposition 209 pending a decision by the US Supreme Court on whether or not it is constitutional.

The Kerner Report (1968) analysed the conditions faced by ethnic minority groups in the USA and shamed the nation with its findings. Blacks were "living in a state of crisis". It also warned of potential dangers to a society which tolerated such disadvantage.

The Nixon Administration pushed affirmative action forward. Over the next few years, succeeding Presidents, Ford and Carter, backed by strong supportive majorities in Congress, passed legislation which extended the process. Simultaneously, a series of decisions by the Supreme Court on suits filed under the Civil Rights Act extended the scope of affirmative action programmes.

The first major reverse to affirmative action came in 1978 with Bakke versus the Regents of the University of California. Allen Bakke was denied a place in the University because less qualified ethnic minority applicants were offered admission on a quota system. He successfully claimed that quotas were a form of reverse discrimination. If less qualified ethnic minority students were allowed places in medical school while better qualified white males were denied entry, then white males were victims of a discriminatory procedure. Therefore programmes which relied solely on a quota system to encourage minority access to higher education were no longer constitutional.

AFFIRMATIVE ACTION IN EDUCATION

There are many affirmative action programmes designed to increase the number of minority students in college and university.

- Outreach Programmes
- Recruitment and retention programmes
- Busing
- Magnet Schools

Outreach programmes

These are designed to help students from minority backgrounds,

CASE STUDIES OF DISCRIMINATION

In July 1970, a federal court ordered the State of Alabama to stop discriminating against Blacks when hiring state troopers. The court found that "in the thirty seven year history of the patrol there has never been a black trooper." Eighteen months later, not a single Black had been hired either as a state trooper or in a civilian position connected with the troopers. The court then ordered Alabama to hire one qualified black trooper or support person for each White hired until 25% of the force was composed of Blacks. By the time the case reached the Court of Appeals in 1974, 25 black troopers and 80 black support personnel had been hired. The US Supreme Court ultimately ruled that the court order was constitutional.

Similarly, seventeen years later in 1987, the San Francisco Fire Department was ordered by a federal court to increase the number of Blacks in officer positions from 7 to 31, Hispanics from 12 to 55, and Asians from 0 to 10.

Federal courts also had to order trade unions to stop discriminating against non-white workers in recruitment, training and admission to the union. Union membership is essential in some jobs before workers can find employment. In 1975 a court found that the Sheet Metal Workers' International Association had "adopted discriminatory admission criteria, restricted the size of its membership to deny access to minorities, selectively organised shops with few minority workers and discriminated in favour of white applicants seeking to transfer from sister locals". The court found that the union's record was full of instances of "bad faith efforts to prevent or delay the admission of minorities". The court ordered the union to set a 29% membership goal for minorities. The Supreme Court ruled the decision constitutional.

who may not be achieving the grades necessary to gain admission to higher education, to get extra tuition to improve their grades. An example is part of *The Programme to Encourage Minority Students to Become Teachers.* This programme prepares and places minority students as teachers in elementary or secondary schools which have at least 50% minority enrolment. Part of the programme identifies and encourages minority students in the 7th to 12th grades to aspire to and prepare for careers as teachers.

Recruitment and retention programmes

These are designed to encourage students from minority backgrounds to consider a career in a particular discipline or profession and to encourage institutions to make greater provision to enable them to take up and retain places. The National Science Foundation Programme encourages students from the ethnic minorities to take up a science, engineering or mathematics course. They provide funding for students and support for institutions trying to increase numbers. The National Centre for Research Resources provides similar support in certain natural sciences to help those from particular racial or ethnic backgrounds to undertake biomedical or behavioural research.

Busing

Initially two ideas lay behind busing. Firstly, it was an attempt to create *equality of opportunity* in school facilities. After Brown versus the Topeka Board of Education in 1954 it was recognised that segregated schools could not be equal and therefore all schools had to be desegregated. However, in many northern cities the demographic patterns meant that most inner city schools were almost exclusively attended by ethnic minorities whereas the suburbs were almost exclusively white. Thus busing was introduced to move black and white schoolchildren across town and city boundaries to achieve a more integrated school community providing equal opportunity for all.

Secondly, busing was an attempt at *social engineering.* Advocates of the system argued that if schools were integrated then integrated communities would follow. Whites and Blacks would develop communities around their local schools. Students who attended integrated schools would be more tolerant of each other and in the medium term this acceptance of each other would develop into mutual respect and equality.

Unfortunately, busing will be remembered because it created resentment rather than integration. It is doubtful if any neighbourhood has integrated as a direct result of busing in the USA. Busing transported thousands of children long distances at great expense using finance which could have been spent on upgrading school provision. The expense of busing caused many school districts to question its usefulness. In Cleveland, Ohio, the local Representative claimed that between 1978 and 1996, over $500 million dollars was spent on busing black children to predominantly white schools on the other side of town.

Role of the Supreme Court

The Supreme Court and the US legal system have played a major role in both the imposition and the impotence of busing as a means of

Last week the Seattle School Board voted unanimously to abolish forced busing, finally owning up to the flaws of this decade-old attempt at promoting desegregation. This 'Band-Aid' approach, consisting mostly of transplanting minority youth to suburban schools, has done more harm than good, and I'm glad to see it go.

I spent 17 years growing up in Ballard, but I never went to school there. Throughout my elementary and middle school years I was bused to the Central District to participate in a programme for gifted students. Although my displacement wasn't a result of forced integration, I know what it feels like to be carted off to a school in a distant neighbourhood. And although my experience was a positive one overall, I know that many students have not benefited from attending school across town.

To catch the bus to Madrona Elementary School I had to wake up a whole hour earlier than the boys who lived across the street. Their house was still dark as I trudged to my bus stop every morning – they were all still asleep. I would often fall asleep too, during the 45-minute bus ride, but the unyielding green vinyl seats never quite compared to my Star Wars comforter.

Extra sleep is one of the many luxuries of attending a school in your own neighbourhood. Not only do you have an extra couple of hours to do homework and play outside, you get to hang out with your school friends outside of school. You are not precluded from participating in after-school sports

A STUDENT'S VIEW
GETTING RID OF BUSING IS A BLESSING

by Alison Dahmen

and activities. You might even be able to run home to get that assignment you left on the kitchen table.

Parents of children who attend neighbourhood schools find it much easier to get involved in their children's education, since they don't need to travel out of their way to attend PTA meetings and the like. According to Superintendent John Stanford and many others, parent involvement is the key to student success.

The forced busing policy never had an equal impact on Seattle's public school students. The majority of students bused to non-neighbourhood schools

over the past decade have been children of colour. For example, during the 1994–1995 school year only 12% of those bused for racial integration purposes were white. School Board members admit that busing has not helped children academically, and that it has placed an unfair burden on minority youth.

Although I am a firm supporter of integration and equity in education, I can't help but see the forced busing fiasco as a misguided attempt at achieving this goal. Instead of just sticking as many kids of colour as possible into the schools that happen to be doing well, public money should

be spent on improving the quality of education at the schools that already exist in urban and/or less affluent areas.

Before the arrival of forced busing, neighbourhood schools helped bind communities together. Even if they had nothing else in common, parents at least shared the experience of having their kids educated in the same place. How dare anyone criticise Seattle's inner-city communities for perceived dysfunction? Seattle has spent the last ten years intentionally dispersing its children of colour all across the city. I can think of few better ways than that of discouraging community.

I'm glad the School Board finally figured out that surface changes in enrolment percentages do not represent a 'cure' for school segregation. The challenge lies in changing the underlying reasons why our schools tend toward segregation in the first place. We cannot ignore the fact that Seattle is sectioned off into neighbourhoods based on race and class divisions.

One of the most reasonable concerns about ending busing is that the disparity between schools will get even worse. Without forced integration, many fear that ethnic minorities will be concentrated in failing schools. Civil rights groups threaten to sue if we slide further backwards in this respect. From now on, I would advise the Board to focus its energies on making every school academically successful.

Adapted from *The Daily of the University of Washington, 1996*

achieving integration. In 1954 the Supreme Court decided that separate facilities could not be equal and therefore it was unconstitutional to segregate schools, colleges and other facilities. However, by 1964 only 2% of black children attended school with white children.

In 1968, the Supreme Court declared that discrimination should be "eliminated root and branch." In 1971 the Supreme Court decided in Swann versus Charlotte–Mecklenburg Board of Education that the federal courts could order busing to desegregate schools. One federal court then ordered the City

of Detroit school district to integrate its schools with the 53 surrounding school districts outside its city limits because there were not enough Whites within the city. This was immediately challenged all the way to the Supreme Court.

In 1974, in Milliken versus Bradley, the court struck down the order because it said that suburban areas could not be ordered to help desegregate a city's schools unless the suburbs had been involved in segregating them in the first place. On the one hand, therefore, the legal system used its authority to order school districts to desegregate their

schools, but almost immediately prevented them from taking steps to overcome the major obstacle to integration—the distribution of Whites and ethnic minorities in the northern cities.

The Milliken ruling eliminated any hope of school desegregation in most of the country's urban areas. By 1990, 94% of Detroit's public school system was attended by minority students. In the eighteen largest metropolitan areas in the USA, 78% of the black community would have had to move to achieve an evenly distributed residential pattern.

Magnet Schools were neighbourhood schools provided with extra funding to enable them to develop as centres of excellence in particular fields. This was to lure white parents to send their children to these schools rather than to their local, suburban schools or to private schools, thus encouraging a better racial mix. Many school districts turned to magnet schools after the Milliken ruling said that forced busing between city and suburbs should not occur. (See page 37.)

Ligon Middle School in downtown Raleigh, North Carolina is an example of a magnet school. Left as a neighbourhood school it would be 90% black, but its population profile is 50% white, 40% black and 10% other minorities. Fewer than 10% of students live close enough to walk so most are brought by 70 buses to and from the school. Ligon is attractive because it has a strong performing arts programme and separate classes for the academically gifted. However, the attempts at integration appear to be flawed. In the lunch rooms, hallways and in games the student body is a swirling mixture of white, black and other minorities. Yet when the period bell goes the many Whites go to the classes designed for the educationally gifted and classes seem less racially diverse than the school as a whole.

Ironically it was in the South, where the struggle for civil rights was fought so bitterly, that busing had the most effect. This was because in the South, school districts extended beyond the city limits so that both black and white students could be transported between schools in different neighbourhoods. In 1964 only 2% of black children attended school with Whites, but by 1972 over 36% of black children attended majority white schools.

Opposition to Busing

White Racists—Busing was vehemently opposed by white racists. Their attitude was candidly voiced by one white mother in Richmond Virginia in 1972 when she said, "It's not the distance, it's the niggers." There are, however, more thoughtful arguments put forward in opposition to busing as a process.

Parental Involvement Lost—From its introduction, busing met deep opposition from both sides of the racial divide. Parents wanted to be involved in the education of their children. Busing children to another area gave parents no control over those who administered the schools which their children attended. It often made it difficult, if not impossible, for parents to visit the school to be given reports on their children's progress by the staff.

Black Students—The burden of desegregation usually fell on ethnic minority students because it was they who were forced to take long bus journeys into often hostile environments where they did not have role models on the teaching staff. Busing did not lead to an appreciable improvement in the academic success of students from an ethnic minority background.

Middle-Class Flight—Busing encouraged middle-class flight. Initially it was white flight, but busing encouraged the growing black middle class to move to the suburbs where they could enrol their children in a neighbourhood school free from busing.

Community Spirit—Busing was blamed for the breakup of communities. The concept of community is very important in the USA and the school is often the focal point for creating community spirit and binding the community together. For example, it is part of the school curriculum in many schools that on Friday afternoons the whole student body gathers together to practise their chanting and cheering for the football or basketball game that evening. Parents and the community fill the stands and cheer on their teams. Busing weakened or destroyed these activities and alienated local people who believed in community spirit.

Black Leaders and Busing

Currently, an increasing body of opinion in the black community is of the view that white Americans have believed incorrectly that the problem of race is a black problem instead of an American problem. The whole approach to desegregation, therefore, is flawed. The 1954 Brown ruling, it is suggested, was based on a false and insulting premise that black schools were inherently inferior and that black children could not learn adequately unless they were sitting next to white children. Although this interpretation of the Brown ruling is arguable, it leads an increasing number of Blacks to welcome the end of attempts to desegregate education.

Representative Polly Williams of Wisconsin, who tried and failed to create an all-black school district in Milwaukee, said, "I fought against segregation that was ordered by the courts...I did not fight for integration, ...which implies that anything that is all black is all bad. I have always chosen to put my children in schools that are close to me, and the fact they are black to me is an asset. That's the best for my children, to be taught by people who understand them, who want to teach them and who expect that they will achieve. It is the opposite when you send your children into the white community. There's a low expectation. They're not challenged. And they don't care."

There is a growing body of opinion among city officials, both black and white, across the USA, that busing has outlived any usefulness it had. Sharon Sayles Belton is black, a life-long campaigner for civil rights and the Mayor of Minneapolis. She wants to end the court-ordered busing in her city. It would, she argues, be better for Blacks if the millions of dollars currently spent on transporting children across the city were spent on improving the quality and quantity of school places. In Massachusetts the Governor wants to end a state law which mandates racial balance in the classroom.

Busing is criticised for encouraging the parents of both black and white students to pull their children out of the public school system and place them in private schools. Many black officials and educators now oppose busing because it has failed to show any significant gains for minority schoolchildren and has cost a great deal in stress and loss of community.

Support for the Continuation of Busing

Research has shown that desegregation appears to have "a modest positive impact" on the achievement of black youngsters and has "no negative effects on white students."

College Students—In 1989 a survey of first year college students found that a majority of both white and black students supported busing if it helped to achieve racial balance.

A Wrong Signal—Intolerance is growing on college campuses and is trickling down into the schools. If attempts to integrate society are abandoned, a signal will be sent that segregation and intolerance are now acceptable.

The End of Busing

In 1995, the Supreme Court ruled in *Missouri versus Jenkins* that the courts had no authority to order states or districts to pay for plans aimed at attracting suburban students. Once the effects of legally enforced segregation were eliminated, it would be perfectly legal for districts to run schools that happened to be all black or all white.

> "The Constitution does not prevent individuals from choosing to live together, work together, or to send their children to school together, so long as the state does not interfere with their choices on the basis of race."
> (Justice Clarence Thomas)

The court's direction is clear. Education is ultimately a local issue. Desegregation orders cannot eliminate differences in student performance caused by poverty, poor family structure and other socio-economic factors.

This ruling effectively ended such affirmative action programmes as busing and magnet schools. In the first nine months following Missouri versus Jenkins, increasing numbers of school districts applied to end court ordered integration schemes including Minneapolis, Indianapolis, Cleveland, Pittsburgh, Denver, St. Louis, Florida, Louisville and Wilmington. Many of the school leaders in the 800 school districts under federal desegregation orders are tired of busing because it has failed to end segregation or improve the academic performance of minority students and, at the same time, has swallowed up large sums of money which could have gone to improve the academic standards in the school districts. Furthermore, significant numbers of the ethnic minorities no longer see school integration as the way forward for education in the USA.

Busing—success or failure?

While public opinion favoured integration, busing was not a popular method of achieving it. Some critics argue that busing was partially responsible for the geographic segregation of the races as Whites rushed to leave the inner city areas and move to all-white suburbs to escape having to submit their children to long journeys into hostile environments. Black public opinion was resentful because busing usually meant that their sons and daughters were the ones transported miles across cities, away from their own neighbourhoods each morning, only to do the reverse journey in the evening.

Latterly, many within the black community have turned their backs on busing because they question one of its basic tenets, namely that it is bad for Blacks to be segregated into black-only schools and better to be integrated into the dominant white society. In the 1990s, black educators no longer argue that black children will benefit from integrating with Whites. Indeed the current thinking is that black children learn better in predominantly black schools.

HOW SUCCESSFUL WAS AFFIRMATIVE ACTION?

Figures from the US Equal Employment Opportunity Commission show that affirmative action has led to some real progress. In California the number of Blacks and Hispanics finding employment as officials and managers in major companies has shown a significant increase. Between 1975 and 1993 the number of Blacks in this category rose from 2.6% to 4.5% and Hispanics went from 4.8% to 8.3%. Nevertheless, these groups are still not represented in the higher levels of companies in proportion to their numbers in the population. In 1990 Blacks were 7.4% of the population of California and Hispanics were 25.8%. While the two decades show a measure of success for affirmative action programmes in the economy of California, it is apparent that equal opportunities for minority groups is still a goal and not a reality.

There has been an increase in the size of the black middle class from 1% in 1940 to 39% in 1970 and to 47% in 1990, but there are analysts

ARGUMENTS FOR CONTINUING AAPs

AAPs benefit employers

In March 1992 a survey of top executives from corporations such as AT&T and IBM found that 68% of them rated affirmative action programmes as "good, very good or outstanding". Only 2% described them as "poor". The reason most gave was that these programmes extended the pool of qualified labour and expertise which strengthened their companies.

AAPs benefit community relations

In public services such as the fire service or the police, studies have shown that a force which more closely mirrors the ethnic and racial composition of the community it serves, develops a greater degree of respect from that community and is able to lower tension in moments of hostility.

Discrimination continues to exist

In 1992, the black unemployment rate remained at more than twice that of the white unemployment rate. In the same year, a survey of the top 1,000 corporations in the USA found that 97% of senior managers were white males. A 1993 survey found that Hispanic men were half as likely as white men to be managers or professionals and only 0.4% of senior managers in the top 1,000 corporations were Hispanic.

In a series of studies between 1990 and 1992, the Fair Employment Council of Greater Washington showed that 24% of the time Blacks were treated significantly worse than equally qualified Whites, and that Hispanics were treated worse than Whites 22% of the time. In one test of a national employment agency, black testers were given no job referrals whereas the white testers who appeared minutes later were interviewed by the agency, coached on interviewing techniques, and referred to and offered jobs as switchboard operators. On another occasion, a black female tester applied for employment at a major hotel chain in Virginia and was told she would be called if they wished to pursue her application. She never received a call. Her equally qualified white counterpart appeared a few minutes later, was told about a vacancy for a front desk clerk, interviewed, and offered the job.

In 1996, 154,000 complaints about employment discrimination were lodged with the federal, state and local authorities and thousands of other complaints alleged discrimination in housing, voting, and public housing.

who claim that the increase over the period 1970 to 1990 would have happened without affirmative action programmes. If anything AAPs (see page 34) held back the development of the black middle class because they encouraged Blacks to become public employees or find jobs with big corporations instead of becoming entrepreneurs. Asian Americans and Hispanics increased the size of their middle class at a faster rate during the same period because more became involved in starting their own businesses, the area where most new jobs and wealth has been created.

Compared to the size of the white middle class, Blacks still lag behind. The white middle class rose from 70% of the white population in 1970 to 74% of the white population in 1990. This means that three out of every four white people were considered to be middle class in the USA in 1990 compared to only one black person in two. Black income gains relative to white income gains halted in 1974 just as affirmative action was developing.

For poorer Blacks, affirmative action programmes have been worse than useless. In helping middle-class Blacks to improve their standards of living and upward mobility, AAPs also enabled them to detach themselves from the black underclass which developed. Deprived of middle-class role models, interest, and investment in the poorer communities, the underclass grew. Since 1970 the proportion of black families living in poverty has increased from 20% to 25%.

Education is regarded as the gateway to opportunity and has been a central focus for affirmative action. In 1955, only 4.9% of college students aged 18–24 were black. This figure rose to 6.5% during the next five years, but by 1965 it had fallen back to 4.9%. When affirmative action programmes began to be introduced in the late 1960s and early 1970s the percentage of black college students began to increase steadily. In 1970, 7.8% of college students were black, a decade later the number had risen to 9.1%, and in 1990 it was 11.3%.

The decision to end affirmative action programmes for admission to university by the Regents of the University of California and the court ruling in the Hopwood case in Texas have led to a dramatic fall in the number of ethnic minority students in these states and on some campuses threatens to all but wipe out minority enrolments. At UCLA's law school, black admissions fell by 81% in 1997, this being the lowest number of Blacks admitted since 1970. At Berkeley law school there were only 14

ARGUMENTS AGAINST CONTINUING AAPs

AAPs disadvantage small companies

AAPs are a major paper-work burden for smaller contractors. This can deter them from tendering for government contracts.

The elimination of AAPs would save money

Government agencies would not have to fund the administration of the programmes and the price on some government contracts would fall because they would be able to take the lowest bid without reference to the company's record of minority hiring or sub-contracting to minority-owned companies. The savings could run into tens of millions of dollars annually. California spent $156 million in 1993–94 on the administrative cost of affirmative action.

AAPs lead to reverse discrimination

Affirmative action promotes the hiring of the best workers from among the minorities rather than the best workers overall. By not choosing from everyone on an equal basis the programmes create reverse discrimination.

AAPs stigmatise the minorities

People who get jobs under AAPs are suspected of and are accused of being second best. Therefore although AAPs have increased the number of minority workers they are stigmatised by the process.

Affirmative action programmes have served their purpose

Blacks and Hispanics have made far more gains than their leaders will admit. Those leaders seeking even more from society justify their demands by pointing to all the problems still faced by those they seek to represent rather than pointing out the improvements.

AAPs help those who do not need it

AAPs mainly help the middle-class minority groups. Middle-class Blacks and Hispanics have access to good quality education and can afford to fund their children through college.

AAPs helped to create the conditions of social disadvantage

Poverty is concentrated in the ghetto and the underclass contains all racial and ethnic groups including Whites.

Throughout the years of affirmative action the social and economic position of the underclass has deteriorated and the main 'success' of these programmes has been to enable the middle class to more easily detach itself from the ghetto.

AAPs create tension between the minority communities

Hispanic groups in California and Washington are highly critical of the high percentage of Blacks in government jobs. Asians are in conflict with organisations such as the NAACP over programmes whose effects they feel prevent their children from gaining admission to elite colleges or public 'magnet' schools.

Blacks out of a class of 792 in 1997, down from 75 the previous year. Only 10 black students were admitted to the law school in Austin, Texas compared to 65 in 1996. In Texas there were 400 fewer black and Hispanic undergraduates in 1997 compared to 1996. In contrast, the number of white and Asian students is rising.

OPPOSITION TO AFFIRMATIVE ACTION

In the 1980s affirmative action programmes continued to assist minorities to gain ground, but Presidents Reagan and Bush were antagonistic towards them, vetoing civil rights legislation and stopping several programmes designed to fight discrimination. By 1989, these two presidents had appointed a majority of Supreme Court justices who were known to be unsympathetic towards affirmative action and the judgments they made in the 1990s reflected this. In decisions such as *Richmond versus Croson* and *Adarand versus Pena*, they severely restricted the scope of affirmative action programmes. The Supreme Court's message was that lawmakers should pursue economic and social equality through race-neutral legislation and forsake proposals based on race categories.

The Clinton Administration did not accept the thrust of this decision and used its considerable influence to preserve and retain existing race preference programmes. This led to increasing conflict and confusion in the area of affirmative action. However, the electorate was becoming more conservative.

Popular opposition

By the 1990s the popular mood in the country, particularly among white males, had swung against affirmative action. Many Whites deeply resent affirmative action programmes, not because they oppose racial equality, but because they feel that these measures violate their individual freedom. Most Whites and many Blacks feel it would be better if disadvantaged groups worked out their problems through individual improvement and self-help rather than depending on a collective approach involving mandatory government programmes. Others take the view that affirmative action programmes are racially based and lead to reverse discrimination which is equally wrong. They feel that there should be programmes to overcome eco-

---

nomic and social disadvantage based on the level of disadvantage faced by recipients and that such programmes must be race-neutral.

This antipathy to AAPs was further fuelled by fear of increased unemployment. In a period of economic growth such as the 1970s and 1980s, the added value in the economy could accommodate programmes which set aside extra help for particular groups because all groups would experience economic improvement. However, in a period of recession like the early 1990s, many white Americans were increasingly uneasy about their future. They feared the spectre of unemployment for themselves and their children. Liberal white Americans began to join their more conservative countrymen and women in questioning affirmative action programmes. Why should the sons and daughters of ethnic minorities get special treatment in access to education which might be to the detriment of middle-class white children? When jobs were becoming increasingly scarce, why should one group be given an enhanced chance to get access to qualifications, hiring and promotion? When people were being laid off, why should population profile count more than length of service, seniority or ability?

Liberal white America also felt that it was time to cast off its collective guilt about the historical treatment of the minorities. Was it not the case that after 30 years of civil rights and affirmative action the white population had done enough to atone for the years of slavery and discrimination? Was it not time for the ethnic minorities to gain the American Dream through their own hard work on an equal basis with the white majority?

Thus the mood of white middle America swung against affirmative action programmes. This was articulated by the 1996 Republican presidential contender Bob Dole when he said, "After 30 years of government sanctioned quotas, timetables, set-asides and other racial preferences, the American people sense all too clearly that the race counting game has gone too far." The Republican Party benefited from developing an anti-affirmative action stance. In 1990 Jesse Helms in North Carolina used an anti-affirmative action stance to secure victory as governor as did ex-Klansman David Duke in Louisiana. They won because their policy appealed to a majority of the white electors. In the 1996 Presidential election, 49% of white men voted for the Republican Party, while only 39% voted for the Democrats.

California kills Affirmative Action

In California, Pete Wilson won the 1994 Election for governor, following a campaign conversion to an anti-immigration, anti-affirmative action platform. In 1995 he issued an executive order banning all state affirmative action programmes which were not protected by state law. He was highly influential in the decision by the University of California to end affirmative action in admissions and hiring.

In 1996 Proposition 209, known as the California Civil Rights Initiative by its supporters, was passed by 54% of the voters in California. This law required that the state "not discriminate against, or grant preferential treatment to, any individual or group on the basis of race, sex, colour, ethnicity or national origin in the operation of public employment, public education or public contracting".

The effect of its passage, once legal objections have been tried through the courts, will be to end all affirmative action programmes in public employment, education and contracting in California. In 1997 a federal appeals court ruled that there was no doubt the measure is constitutional. The judges lifted a lower court injunction blocking the enforcement of Proposition 209.

No doubt the case will continue its way through the labyrinths of the legal system of the USA until it reaches the US Supreme Court for final adjudication. However, should the composition of the Supreme Court remain as it is at present when Proposition 209 arrives, then it is more than likely that it will be upheld and come into force in California. It may well be closely followed by Washington, Florida, Arizona, Colorado, Ohio and Michigan. These states are all in the process of initiating similar propositions.

Affirmative action programmes continue to operate in the USA, but the picture is somewhat muddied by conflicting court rulings and antagonism between the Supreme Court and the Clinton Administration. What is certain is that the mood of the majority white population has swung against the processes involved in affirmative action. If Proposition 209 and its imitators in other states are ultimately declared constitutional by the Supreme Court they will have a negative impact on affirmative action. Even if they are struck down they are indicative of the mood of the country and affirmative action programmes where they continue will be in a much restricted form. The historical imperative seems to favour a move away from race-based preference programmes which could be replaced, perhaps, by programmes based on economic and social disadvantage but which are race-neutral in construction.

The future of Society in the USA

America is a society based on relatively recent immigration. This constantly fermenting mixture can lead to tensions both within and among different ethnic groups. Although many immigrants have successfully integrated with the dominant culture, some have been unsuccessful in their attempts whilst others have not even made the attempt.

The 1990 Bureau of Census lists those groups whose first language is not English (See Table 5.1) and this gives us some measure of the complexity of US society in the 1990s.

A number of social theories have attempted to describe the relationships between the ethnic groups in the USA. The three main theories are the Melting Pot, the Salad Bowl and the Mosaic.

Languages of the USA

Spanish	17 million	French	1.7 million
German	1.5 million	Italian	1.3 million
Chinese	1.2 million	Tagalog	800,000
Polish	700,000	Korean	600,000
Vietnamese	500,000	Portuguese	400,000
Japanese	400,000	Greek	400,000
Arabic	400,000	Hindi (Urdu)	300,000
Russian	200,000	Yiddish	200,000
Thai (Laotian)	200,000	Persian	200,000
French Creole	200,000	Armenian	200,000
Navaho	100,000	Hungarian	100,000
Hebrew	100,000	Dutch	100,000
Mon-Khmer	100,000	Gujerati	100,000

Table 5.1

The Melting Pot
The idea of a Melting Pot suggests that through time all groups will fully integrate and fuse together to create an American population, each member of which is indistinguishable from his/her neighbour —racially, ethnically or culturally. Eventually all immigrants will be absorbed and come to share the same hopes, expectations and values as all other American citizens.

This theory has dominated both the official government approach to education and the media's portrayal of US society. Education has been a vehicle of social and cultural engineering to mould immigrants into Americans and through that process to encourage equality of opportunity. All children have been taught, in English, to honour an American heritage through respect for flag, nation, community and fundamental religious belief.

The Salad Bowl
Alternatively, the Salad Bowl theory views society as a blend of various cultures. Here the mainstream 'American' is enriched by the variety of cultures, languages and traditions which are nurtured by the various ethnic groups. The American 'way of life' is still developed. However, this is not done by absorbing other cultures but by co-existing with them and being enriched by them.

The Mosaic
This views the development of US society as the aggregation of a number of coexisting cultures. These remain distinct—each culture is aware of the others but remains apart and retains its own purity by developing in isolation.

An Assessment
The problem with the integrationist view of American society is that as we enter the new millennium, nearly 40 years on from the civil rights era, the distance between black and white cultures seems to be growing. Blacks have never been integrated into US society as the Melting Pot view of history would like them to be. Indeed, some sociologists argue that the 'Melting Pot' was a racist theory which only ever applied to white people. It may have been true for Germans, Italians, Greeks or Poles, but Blacks remain victims of the white supremacy which permeates US society. Even where middle-class Blacks have been able to leave the ghetto, they have been condemned to live in middle-class ghettos—forever segregated from middle-class white society.

In housing, middle-class Asians and Hispanics are far more readily accepted in white areas and do not appear to harm the property values when they move in. There is an increasing number of intermarriages between Whites and Hispanics. For Hispanics and Asians, then, the Melting Pot model might apply in time, but for Blacks there is no integration.

Whites are increasingly turning their backs on affirmative action programmes because in a period of uncertainty in the economy they do not want to see what they consider to be reverse discrimination in education and employment which might disadvantage themselves and their children. They do not want to see their tax dollars spent on expensive government programmes and they feel that after more than 30 years Blacks should stop depending on the state for help and should now make the effort to stand on their own feet. White liberals in the USA feel that they have done enough to atone for the sins of their forefathers. Proposition 209 in California (see page 42) and the Welfare Bill (see page 24) passed in 1996 are indications of this growing divide.

Division was also seen at the time of the OJ Simpson trial. White America universally decided that Simpson was guilty and that his acquittal was due to incompetence on the part of the police and the prosecution and the fact that Simpson could afford to buy himself the best justice available in America. Black America universally declared him to be innocent. He was the victim of a white conspiracy to punish a token black man who had 'got above his place'.

A growing mood for separation is slowly gaining ground in the black community. It is born out of the sheer frustration of living in the ghetto conditions endured by so many black people. Growing black pride and self-reliance seems to demand all-black schools, with black teachers acting as inspiring role models teaching about black culture. Communities with black owned banks, businesses and shops would keep the profits within the black community.

Increasingly, the black community is becoming disillusioned with its lack of social and economic equality. The burning of black churches, the demands for separate education facilities, and even for the recognition of a separate 'language' all seem to be signals that there is a growing racial tension forcing the

races apart. The views of leaders like Jesse Jackson, the inheritor of Martin Luther King's integrationist philosophy, are being eclipsed because they failed to deliver. Centre stage has been occupied by Louis Farrakhan and his Nation of Islam with its demands for a separatist solution for Blacks in the USA.

Burning Black Churches

The church traditionally plays an important role in black culture and was pivotal in the civil rights movement. The church is a potent symbol of the struggle for racial equality and an attack upon a church is seen as an attack on black culture itself. In 1995 and 1996 when arson destroyed 39 black churches throughout the southern states, the immediate assumption was that there was an organised campaign of racist attacks developing against the black community. For a period the media tried to connect the arson attempts with the Ku Klux Klan. Some commentators suggested that the burnings were an organised reaction to a growing divergence between white and black communities.

However, the facts did not support these theories. At the same time as 39 black churches were destroyed by arson, 23 white churches suffered the same fate as well as several synagogues and mosques. After an investigation of 64 cases of black church arson in 11 states, the conclusion was that the crimes stemmed from teenage vandalism, drunkenness, revenge, derangement, and insurance fraud as well as some obvious racial motives. In Tennessee and the Carolinas there was evidence to suggest that there was a pattern to church burning and that it was racially motivated. However, both clusters were unconnected. The report concluded that there was no new wave of arson.

LOUIS FARRAKHAN & THE NATION OF ISLAM

The Million Man March in October 1995 was the largest civil rights assembly in US history. Around

400,000 black men assembled in Washington DC to assert pride in themselves and to listen to speeches. The success of this demonstration was seen by the media as proof of the ascendancy of Louis Farrakhan and the growing influence of the Nation of Islam in the black community.

The Nation of Islam (NoI) was set up in the 1930s and was an organisation distinct from that of orthodox Islam. In the mid-1970s the then leader of the NoI disbanded the movement and steered its members towards orthodox Sunni Islam worship, but Louis Farrakhan broke away and recreated the NoI. There are between 20,000 and 25,000 members of the NoI compared to six million Moslems living in the USA, around 40% of whom are Blacks.

Orthodox Moslems believe that Allah (God) created all human races, that all are equal and should live in harmony. The Nation of Islam, on the other hand, preaches that Blacks were the original race on earth and that the white race was created 6,000 years ago as the result of experiments carried out by a mad scientist called Jakub and that the Whites have, in that time, enslaved the black race. The NoI believes that the races should be separated. Essentially the Nation of Islam is a social reform movement which uses religion as a vehicle to improve the social and economic position of the Blacks in the USA to the exclusion of all other people. It gives black men (and women) some positive role models and a belief in their own self-worth.

The main philosophy of the NoI was to reassert the power and strength of the family within the black community along with the demand for black economic empowerment. This would be achieved by Blacks taking control of their own lives and communities: "We cannot … keep on blaming white people for our shortcomings. We have to know our own sins … and repent of the evils that are destroying our own communities... ." Farrakhan believes in the traditional family in which women stay at home with their children.

Farrakhan also preaches that there was a major conspiracy against Blacks involving Whites, Jews and recent Asian immigrants. "I mentioned [that] back in the '40s and '50s, some of the merchants who were Jewish ... drew from the black community. And later they were replaced by Palestinians and other Arab merchants, then by the Vietnamese and Koreans. These are people who generally take from the [black] community but don't give back." "The real evil in America is ... called white supremacy." "There's still two Americas, one black, one white, separate and unequal." On more than one occasion Farrakhan has asserted that the drug epidemic in the ghetto is a conspiracy by the white majority, including the Federal government, to enslave the black race and prevent it from breaking free of its social conditions.

Farrakhan argues that the real problem in America is not that Blacks hold themselves back nor that Whites oppress Blacks, but the fact that both processes are happening simultaneously. High crime and imprisonment rates reinforce the stereotype of the black male and the stereotype then encourages high crime and imprisonment rates and so on and on in a self-perpetuating cycle. At one time the root of racism in the USA was simple bigotry which was virulent and widespread. Whites believed that Blacks were inferior and ought to be kept in their place. Then prejudice was driven by hatred or contempt, but today it is driven by fear. Whites fear for their property values when Blacks move into the neighbourhood. A white woman feels fear when a black man steps into the lift; she crosses the street when she sees a black man walking behind her. The black man knows why she is afraid. He is a stereotype—a stereotype built on the statistics which show that black

Louis Farrakhan flanked by his bodyguards.

men are responsible for a disproportionately high rate of murder and mugging.

The Fruit of Islam are Farrakhan's bodyguards and front line workers who are easily identified by their white shirts and black bow ties. This militia is credited with cleaning up several inner city housing complexes which asked the group to eradicate drugs and violence from their neighbourhoods and, despite some failures, the group has gained much approval from these efforts. They also work amongst addicts, criminals and prostitutes and make many converts to their organisation. This direct action earns the NoI significant respect in the black community because other leaders and organisations do not seem to be having the same impact on people's lives.

While the media has focused on Farrakhan and the fact that he seems to have eclipsed other black community leaders, it would be wrong to see Farrakhan's separatist philosophy as the prevailing mood of black America.

One year on from the Million Man March, *The Washington Post* con-

ducted a survey within the black community to gauge the impact it had had on the lives of the people. It found that 49% of black men and 53% of black women felt that the march had had no direct impact on their communities, whereas 44% of black men and 36% of black women felt there had been a positive impact. This implies that there is no overwhelming endorsement for Farrakhan and his philosophy throughout the black community. Nevertheless, his growing popularity and influence is symptomatic of the deep resentments in the black community at the failure to address the underlying social and economic conditions and the discrimination which persists in US society. Currently, the majority of Blacks see the need to remain an integrated part of US society because it is that society in its totality which creates the wealth of which they wish to win a greater share. However, should the dominant white society continue to exclude Blacks, then the integrationists may lose the hearts and minds of the majority and the demand for segregation could become overwhelming, tearing at the fabric and shaking the foundations of US society.

The Rainbow Country

6 South Africa

South Africa has emerged from its painful experience of rigid white dominance into a nation which treasures the diversity of its people as a force for reconciliation and economic reconstruction. As Nelson Mandela, President of the Republic of South Africa, stated in 1996, "After South Africa's first ever democratic elections in April 1994, the world has been witnessing the birth and growth of a new nation; a rainbow country which in spite of its diversity has become a symbol of unity and good will."

Any study of South Africa must include the impact of the apartheid years (1948–1994) during which the white minority denied the black majority their political, social and economic rights. A legacy of vast inequalities between the races in terms of income, living standards, health care, education and employment opportunities remained. Nation building and reconstruction are the goals of this young nation inspired by the leadership of Nelson Mandela.

THE LAND AND THE PEOPLE

South Africa is five times the size of the United Kingdom with a population two-thirds that of the UK. Thanks to its size, it has different climates and landscapes in different parts of the country. Much of the west of the country is desert, while the south,

around Cape Town, has a Mediterranean climate.

Its population of 41 million is made up of numerous ethnic groups and this is reflected in the recognition of 11 official languages. Blacks make up 76% of the population, a figure which will continue to increase given the higher birth rate among Blacks. (See Table 6.2.)

The 'old' South Africa was made up of four provinces and designated areas (Homelands) for Blacks. This has been replaced with nine new provinces. (See page 48.) As the profile indicates, South Africa is extremely rich in mineral wealth and has a sophisticated economy and

an efficient civil service. However, vast inequalities exist between the races, a fact which is reflected in South Africa's ranking in the world's standard of living indicators. If the white 12% of the population constituted a separate country, its standard of living would rank 24th in the world, only a little behind that of Spain. Black South Africa, by contrast, would rank 123rd, just above the Congo.

Extreme inequalities in society and the existence of wide-scale poverty is a common feature of many developing countries, as is illustrated in Table 6.3. Significantly, countries in Africa take the three top spots, reflecting the decline in living standards and economic growth experienced by African states from the early 1980s onwards.

SOUTH AFRICA'S ECONOMY

South Africa has the strongest and most developed economy in the continent of Africa, dominating its neighbours. During the apartheid era, South Africa used its economic and military might to weaken countries such as Angola and Mozambique. Today, however, it is possible to travel from the Indian Ocean coast in Mozambique to the Atlantic Ocean coast in Namibia without passing through a single war zone. (Namibia only received its independence from South Africa in 1990.)

Population of South Africa, 1995

	Number (million)	%
Blacks	31.5	76
Whites	5.3	13
Coloureds	3.3	8
Asians	1.2	3
Total	41.3	100

Table 6.1

Birth Rates

	Blacks	Coloureds	Indians/ Asians	Whites
1970	40.0	34.1	32.3	22.9
1980	37.0	30.8	25.5	16.7
1985	36.0	27.0	24.1	16.5
1994	25.3	21.7	18.1	13.7

Table 6.2 Source: October Household Survey 1994

How Poor is South Africa?	
Percentage of the population living on less than $1 per day. Selected countries, 1992.	
Guinea-Bissau	87
Zambia	84
Niger	64
India	51
Zimbabwe	48
China	38
Brazil	35
South Africa	30
Mexico	25

Table 6.3   Source: World Bank

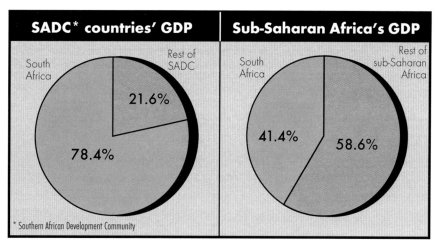

Figure 6.1   Source: Africa Institute of South Africa (1993 data)

South Africa's manufacturing sector dominates African manufacturing statistics. (See Figure 6.1.) South Africa acts as a magnet for job seekers across the region, adding to the problem of unemployment. Its strength is based on mining, manufacturing and large-scale commercial agriculture.

Mining

South Africa's industrial prosperity is based on the wealth of its mineral deposits. Although the country has only 0.08% of the world's land surface, it is a leading producer of the most useful and valuable minerals used by industry and consumers, as shown in Table 6.4.

South Africa is the world's largest producer of gold. However, the last few years have seen a decline in world gold prices and this is reflected in the fact that the industry has shed 180,000 jobs since the mid-1980s—a third of its work force. South Africa's gold lies deep beneath the ground and this makes it expensive and dangerous to mine. Over 300 gold miners die each year in South Africa's mines.

Agriculture

South Africa has a dual agricultural economy—a well-developed commercial sector and a subsistence-based sector in the traditionally settled rural areas. Improved farm management has more than doubled agricultural production during the past 30 years and South Africa is self-sufficient in virtually all major agricultural products. This is an excellent achievement given that only about 12% of the land is suitable for cultivation, rainfall is unreliable and the country as a whole suffers from periodic droughts. While still a major industry, agriculture contributes a substantially smaller proportion to the Gross Domestic Product (GDP) than it did in the past. It accounts for about 5% of GDP compared to 15% in 1955.

In the less fertile areas pastoral farming dominates with sheep-rearing and cattle-ranching particularly strong. The climate, varying from sub-tropical through Mediterranean to semi-desert, allows almost any crop to be grown. Maize is the most important crop, but wheat, sorghum, groundnuts, tobacco, cotton, dry beans, sugar cane, sunflower seeds and fruit are also grown.

SPORT

South Africans of all races love their sport and they suffered greatly during the apartheid years when they were banned from participating on the world stage. Sport was also divided on racial lines with only Whites taking part in the 'national' sport of rugby. Today South Africa participates in the Olympic Games and qualified for the 1998 Football World Cup. While athletics and football have representatives from all races, rugby is still regarded as an exclusively white sport.

Sport is part of the nation-building exercise where Blacks and Whites can compete and support each other. The 1995 Rugby World Cup, which South Africa hosted, marked a high point of reconciliation. Nelson Mandela turned up at the final dressed in the Springbok jersey (formerly regarded by Blacks as a symbol of white supremacy). Blacks and Whites united to roar on their team as it gained vic-

South Africa's Mineral Wealth

	World Production		World Reserves	
	Rank	%	Rank	%
Gold	1	23	1	45
Vanadium	1	51	1	45
Chrome Ore	1	36	1	69
Alumino Silicates	1	34	1	37
Manganese Ore	3	12	1	81
Platinum	1	48	1	56
Vermiculite	1	43	2	40
Antimony	4	12	2	5
Diamonds	5	11	2	21
Fluorspar	4	6	3	12
Titanium	2	20	2	17

Table 6.4 Source: Official Yearbook of the RSA, 1997

PROFILES OF THE PROVINCES OF SOUTH AFRICA

PROVINCE/Capital GAUTENG/Johannesburg

Principal Language Afrikaans (25%), English (16%), isiZulu (18%)

Population 7 million (17% of total)

Area Km² 18,810 (1.6% of total)

% of GDP 38

Agriculture & Industry Gauteng is South Africa's engine room, where about 40% of the country's GDP is generated. Gauteng means 'place of gold' and this is a highly urbanised and industrialised area. It is a magnet area for a large inflow of migrant labourers who settle in the townships and shanty towns.

Comment Pretoria, the administrative capital of South Africa, is situated in the province. The sprawling townships, such as Soweto, are struggling to overcome the social and economic legacy of apartheid. According to the Gauteng Economic Policy Document, 19% of the people live in shacks.

PROVINCE/Capital NORTHERN CAPE/Kimberley

Principal Language Afrikaans (66%), isiXhosa (6%), Setswana (19%)

Population 0.7 million (1.8% of total)

Area Km² 361,800 (29.7% of total)

% of GDP 2

Agriculture & Industry Extremely rich in mineral wealth with Kimberley being the diamond capital of the world. Other major minerals are copper, manganese and marble.

Comment It covers the largest area of South Africa and has the smallest population. It is a semi-arid region with low summer rainfall and is the home of the San (bushmen) people who live in the Kalahari area of the Northern Cape.

PROVINCE/Capital WESTERN CAPE/ Cape Town

Principal Language Afrikaans (62%), English (20%), isiXhosa (15%)

Population 3.7 million (9% of total)

Area Km² 129,379 (10.6% of total)

% of GDP 14.8

Agriculture & Industry Food basket of South Africa with a harvest of top grade fruits, vegetables and meats. Head offices of many South African businesses are in Cape Town. 95% of its population is urbanised.

Comment Cape Town is the legislative capital of the country. Western Cape has the highest literacy rate in the country.

PROVINCE/Capital FREE STATE/Bloemfontein

Principal Language Afrikaans (15%), isiXhosa (9%), Sesotho (57%)

Population 2.7 million (6.7% of total)

Area Km² 129,480 (10.6% of total)

% of GDP 6.8

Agriculture & Industry 'The granary of the country' with 31% of the potentially arable land of South Africa. Its main economic base is mining.

Comment It lies in the heart of South Africa and is the third largest province. Its agricultural sector has been affected by the drought experienced in the late 1990s.

PROVINCE/Capital NORTH WEST/Minabatho

Principal Language Afrikaans (9%), isiXhosa (6%), Setswana (59%)

Population, millions 3.3 (8.1% of total)

Area Km² 116,190 (9.5% of total)

% of GDP 5.5

Agriculture & Industry Main economic base is mining with its major agricultural products being maize and sunflowers. High unemployment levels in the province contribute to the poverty experienced by many of its citizens.

Comment At present it has no major airport. It is developing its tourist industry through national parks.

PROVINCE/Capital EASTERN CAPE/Bisho

Principal Language Afrikaans (10%), English (4%), isiXhosa (82%)

Population 6.4 million (15.6% of total)

Area Km² 169,600 (13.9% of total)

% of GDP 7.6

Agriculture & Industry Not rich in minerals but includes rich agricultural and forestry land. The urban areas of Port Elizabeth and East London are based primarily on manufacturing.

Comment Includes the former Homelands of Transkei and Ciskei.

PROVINCE/Capital NORTHERN PROVINCE/ Pietersburg

Principal Language Sepedi (57%), Tshivenda (12%), Xitsonga (23%)

Population 5.3 million (13% of total)

Area Km² 123,280 (10% of total)

% of GDP 3.7

Agriculture & Industry Extremely rich in minerals including coal, copper, asbestos, iron ore and platinum. Produces sub-tropical fruit and its Bushveld is cattle country. Unemployment is high. The per capita income is by far the lowest in the country. Contains the three former Homelands of Venda, Gazankulu and Lebowa.

Comment The province is the country's gateway to the rest of Africa as it shares borders with Botswana, Zimbabwe and Mozambique. This province has the Savannah Biome, an area of mixed grassland and trees (Bushveld).

PROVINCE/Capital MPUMALANGA/Nelspruit

Principal Language isiNdebele (11%), SiSwati (30%), isiZulu (24%)

Population 3 million (7% of total)

Area Km² 78,370 (6.4% of total)

% of GDP 8.1

Agriculture & Industry Produces sub-tropical fruits and its tree plantations supply half of the country's total timber needs. It is rich in coal reserves and the country's three biggest power stations are based in the area.

Comment Mpumalanga (formerly Eastern Transvaal) means 'place where the sun rises'. The province attracts migrant labour from neighbouring states, especially refugees from Mozambique. Suffers from extreme levels of poverty and low levels of literacy.

PROVINCE/Capital KWAZULU-NATAL/ Pietermaritzburg/Ulundi

Principal Language Afrikaans (2%), English (16%), isiXhosa (79%)

Population 8.7 million (21% of total)

Area Km² 92,180 (7.6% of total)

% of GDP 14.9

Agriculture & Industry Rapid industrialisation in recent times. Durban is one of the fastest growing urban areas in the world. Huge gap between the urban and rural per capita income.

Comment The only province with a monarchy specifically provided for in the 1993 Constitution. Ulundi is the traditional capital of the Zulu monarchy.

Northern Province

Gauteng

Mpumalanga

North West

Free State

LESOTHO

Kwazulu-Natal

Northern Cape

Eastern Cape

Western Cape

SOUTH AFRICA

48

tory. "Amabokoboko" —our Boks— cried *The Sowetan*, the best selling black newspaper, as it proclaimed the unity of the nation. Mandela reinforced this spirit of reconciliation by retaining the rugby team's springbok emblem.

Not all non-Whites share Mandela's view. Trevor Manuel, the coloured Finance Minister, admitted cheering on the victorious New Zealand team at a July 1997 match in Johannesburg. While 60,000 people, almost all of them white, witnessed this defeat, 100,000 people, almost all black, squeezed into Soweto's football stadium to watch the local football derby between the Kaiser Chiefs and the Orlando Pirates.

The South African Rugby Football Union (SARFU) is trying to change the racial composition of the sport. It is spending 15 million rand for the next three years on 'development' (ie. black) rugby. One non-White has played for the Boks and there are a few in the national youth teams. Unfortunately events in 1998 damaged this spirit of reconciliation. Louis Luyt, the President of the SARFU, used the courts to prevent Nelson Mandela from setting up a commission to investigate the activities of the SARFU. The National Sports Council called on Luyt to resign, accusing him of racism, nepotism and bad management. The threat of boycotts and demonstrations against the summer tours of South Africa by England, Ireland and Wales forced Luyt to resign in May 1998.

Sport has also been used as a vehicle for national pride. While South Africa was not chosen as the venue for the 2004 Olympic Games, it was one of the five finalists. South Africa's ambition is to become the first African nation to host the event. The Cape Town bid caught the imagination of the nation and reinforced the use of sport as a force for unity and optimism.

CAPE TOWN

It was no coincidence that President Mandela played host to an International Olympic Committee Team at Cape Town as the latter evaluated possible countries for the Olympic Games of 2004. Cape Town, nestling below Table Mountain, represents the new South Africa of prosperity, growth and self-confidence. Since the end of apartheid the city has become an international mecca—'Africa's little Rio'.

Charl Adams of the Cape Chambers and Industry proudly states, "In relation to the rest of South Africa, we are a success story. We produce 14% of GDP with only 9% of the population." The housing industry is booming as incomers from Johannesburg and other cities are attracted by Cape Town's low crime rate, pleasant environment and job opportunities with the influx of high-tech industries.

Cape Town is also fast becoming Africa's Hollywood. In 1997 seven foreign features were made, 182 foreign commercials shot and 32 foreign documentaries were made. Cape Town offers more than a dozen different types of scenery within a 100 mile radius. Its craggy mountains can stand for Scotland or Ireland, its winelands can make do for France or Italy, and the Karoo desert can double for the American Wild West.

However, the legacy of apartheid has created segregated residential patterns with the majority of people, once defined as Coloureds, confined to the inland wastland called the Cape Flats. There is no evidence of a fledgling black professional class emerging.

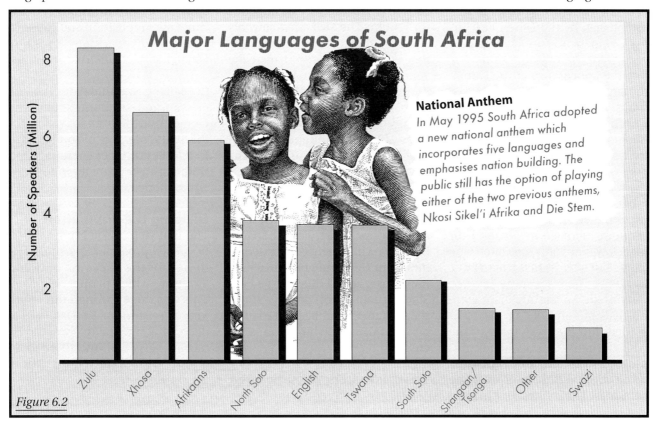

Major Languages of South Africa

Number of Speakers (Million)

Zulu — Xhosa — Afrikaans — North Soto — English — Tswana — South Soto — Shangaan/Tsonga — Other — Swazi

National Anthem
In May 1995 South Africa adopted a new national anthem which incorporates five languages and emphasises nation building. The public still has the option of playing either of the two previous anthems, Nkosi Sikel'i Afrika and Die Stem.

Figure 6.2

The Apartheid Years 1948–1991

7

In 1948, South Africa embarked upon the development of a unique political, economic and social structure which became known as apartheid—an Afrikaans word meaning 'separate development'. The policy of apartheid was developed by the Whites, one of the groups within South Africa, with the other groups forced to accept it. The fact that the Whites, a minority of South Africa's population, could take such a decision and continue to enforce it into the early 1990s, tells us where the economic and political power lay by 1948.

BOERS, BRITISH AND AFRICANS

White settlers came to Southern Africa in the 17th century to establish a settlement which would be part of the trade route to India and the Far East. In 1652 a settlement was established by the Dutch East India Company to supply fresh provisions for their trading ships. Before the appearance of the Dutch, the land had been inhabited by two main tribes, the San and the Khoikhoi—often referred to as Bushmen and Hottentots respectively. The San were mostly hunters who led a nomadic life, whilst the Khoikhoi were herders. Inevitably the Dutch settlers began to expand their numbers with a consequent increase in demand for land. It was not only the Dutch who came, but also French Huguenots, Germans and even some Scottish Calvinists. As the Africans were pushed out, some of them were absorbed into the work force of the white farmers. This was the beginning of a social structure which was to develop and deepen over the centuries. The Whites, in the form of the Dutch farmers, were the masters and the Africans the labourers.

By 1806 the British government had decided that control of Cape Colony was the key to controlling the trading routes to India and consequently took it over. The resultant increase in immigration from Britain established two distinct white communities—the Afrikaners (Boers) and English speaking Whites (Anglos). Their attitudes to the Cape were quite different. The Anglos saw it as a colony of the British Empire but the Afrikaners saw it as their home and country.

The British control of the colony was deeply resented by the Afrikaners and this resentment was fanned by the British decision in 1833 to abolish slavery throughout the Empire. The Afrikaners saw this as an attack on their values, namely that Europeans were intrinsically superior and meant to be masters. Between 1836 and 1846, therefore, thousands of Boers left Cape Colony and Natal in the Great Trek to establish the independent republics of Transvaal and the Orange Free State.

Britain left these Afrikaner Republics alone as they had no strategic or economic value. This changed, however, with the discovery of diamonds in 1867 and gold in 1886 in the Transvaal and the Orange Free State. Britain proceeded to annexe the Afrikaner republics and friction between the two white groups increased.

This eventually led to the Boer War 1899–1902 in which Boer hostility towards the Anglos was fuelled by the British use of concentration camps and a scorched earth policy. Alienation continued after the war when the British adopted an Anglicisation policy whereby only English was to be spoken in schools and in economic life. The Afrikaners' humiliation was complete when many of them were forced into waged labour as their farms failed.

THE UNION OF SOUTH AFRICA

In 1910 the four colonies were united under one government elected by the Whites. At first the Whites were divided between two parties—the South Africa Party, which looked for unity between the English and Afrikaners as the ruling class, and the National Party, which was predominantly Afrikaner in composition and support, and aimed for a Boer Republic which had no British associations.

In 1948 the National Party won the election and set about establishing Grand Apartheid as its vision for the final settlement of South Africa. In 1961 South Africa cut its ties with Britain and became an independent republic.

Dividing the population

The first step in the National Party's development of apartheid was to define the races or national groups to which people belonged. This was done through the *Population Registration Act* (1950) which decreed that all people were to be racially classified into three main groups with subdivisions. These are shown in Table 7.1.

Thus the majority African population, categorised according to language, features and/or ancestry, was divided into eight tribal groups. The Coloureds were made up of two main groups. There were descendants from miscegenation between Whites and the original African inhabitants of the Cape, the San and Khoikhoi. These constituted Cape Coloureds. Also there were the Asians, or Indians, descended from Indian workers who were indentured from India to work, especially in Natal, in the nineteenth century.

This piece of legislation was the foundation stone upon which apartheid was built. Having defined the population, the government acted to maintain its 'purity' by passing the Mixed Marriages Act (1949), which banned marriage between Europeans and non-Europeans, and the Immorality Acts (1950, 1957) which made inter-racial sexual relations illegal.

Dividing the Land

Having divided the population, the National Party began to divide the land to define where the different groups could live and exercise their individual and political rights. The 1950s saw the creation of the Homelands policy which defined the territory which Whites saw as the traditional land of the Africans living in South Africa. It was in these Homelands that the Africans would be entitled to exercise citizenship rights.

The legislation establishing the Homelands, however, was based on the Native Lands Acts passed in 1913 and 1936. The 1913 Act established that all existing African reserves were not to be sold to non-Africans and made it illegal for any African to be on European land unless he or she was a hired servant. Under the 1936 Act, Africans were to be allowed to own only approximately 13% of the land. It was on this figure that the apartheid governments constructed the Homelands policy. The aim was to develop the Homelands into inde-

pendent countries with governments elected by Africans recorded as citizens of the Homelands.

The 1970 Bantu Homelands Citizenship Act delivered an essential element in the implementation of Grand Apartheid. Under this Act, all Africans were to be allocated a Homeland as their 'country of origin'. They would be regarded as citizens of that Homeland and as foreigners in other parts of South Africa. Thus, when Transkei became 'independent' on 26 October 1976, every African with 'Xhosa' stamped in his or her passbook lost his or her South African citizenship. The same thing happened to those labelled 'Tswana' when Bophu-

thatswana became 'independent' on 6 December 1977. The 'independence' of these two Homelands led to over 6 million Africans, many of whom had never seen their new 'countries', losing their South African citizenship. By 1985 two other Homelands, Venda and Ciskei, had also become independent. (The four Homelands were collectively known as the TBVC countries.)

APARTHEID IN ACTION
Establishing the Homelands did not cater for all the non-Europeans in South Africa for two main reasons. Firstly, the economy required a permanent supply of black labour, many of whom could not travel daily from their Homeland.

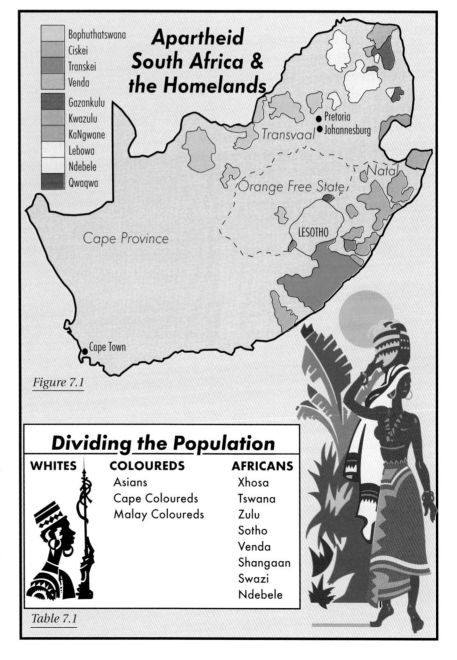

Apartheid South Africa & the Homelands

Bophuthatswana
Ciskei
Transkei
Venda
Gazankulu
Kwazulu
KaNgwane
Lebowa
Ndebele
Qwaqwa

Pretoria
Johannesburg
Transvaal
Natal
Orange Free State
LESOTHO
Cape Province
Cape Town

Figure 7.1

Dividing the Population

WHITES	COLOUREDS	AFRICANS
	Asians	Xhosa
	Cape Coloureds	Tswana
	Malay Coloureds	Zulu
		Sotho
		Venda
		Shangaan
		Swazi
		Ndebele

Table 7.1

Secondly, the coloured population was not included in the Homeland policy. Both of these groups would be permanent in 'white' South Africa and so alternative arrangements were made for their settlement and control within the white areas.

Coloureds in White Areas

The principle of land segregation was applied to both Whites and non-Whites in 'white' South Africa through the *Group Areas Acts* (1950, 1957, 1966). It applied principally in urban areas and established areas which would be for the exclusive occupation of each racial group.

Establishing these urban divisions required the forced removal of families who had, before the Acts, been settled in areas which were now designated by the authorities for occupation by another racial group. By 1980 over 116,000 families, mainly Coloured and Indian, had been removed under this policy. The Acts resulted in non-Whites being forced into the outskirts of the towns and cities. This was demonstrated in Pageview, an Asian area in the centre of Johannesburg. In 1981 the government flattened it for use by Whites and moved the Asian families to Lenasia, an Indian suburb well outside Johannesburg. Lenasia became very overcrowded and so many Asians who had come from Pageview had to rent rooms in the 'white' areas. These Acts also prevented Blacks from buying land, trading or owning businesses within a so-called 'white' Group Area. As the business districts of most towns and cities were invari-

EDUCATION

Education was used by the government to shape people to fit the apartheid mould. The Afrikaner view on the role of education was made quite clear by a future Prime Minister, Hendrik Verwoerd, in 1954 when he said, "The native must be taught from childhood that equality with Europeans is not for him. There is no place for him in the European community above the level of certain forms of labour." To the Africans it was simply a case of "the Boers wanting to indoctrinate African children into being perpetual slaves of the white man."

The subjects taught in schools reflected white dominance. One of the main aims was to condition the different groups for the roles they were supposed to play in South African society. Joyce Sikakane summed up how Blacks viewed their education:

"Bantu Education meant being taught of a tribal identity. In their history books, it meant that the white man 'discovered' the 'savage' African and civilised him. The derogatory word 'Bantu' was used instead of African.

It meant being taught that our national heroes like Tshaka and Hintsa were brutal murderers yet they were African patriots who fought against the white invasion of our country. ...It meant being taught that the white man is superior to a black man. Above all it meant the unquestionable acceptance of the philosophy of apartheid."
(From *A Window on Soweto* Joyce Sikakane)

In 1959, segregation was extended to university education, with separate universities being established for Whites, Coloureds, Indians and Blacks. Access to universities was unequal, as demonstrated by the 1980 student roll which had 160,000 Whites, 16,000 Indians, 12,000 Coloureds and 10,500 Africans.

REPRESSIVE LAWS

One of the difficulties faced by opponents of apartheid in South Africa was the legal restrictions placed on their activities by the government. These legal restrictions were known collectively as the 'Security Laws' under which the authorities had the power to:

● detain people without trial,
● ban people, organisations and meetings,
● break up meetings, and
● imprison people.

The government had developed these repressive laws since 1950, reacting to any new threat to apartheid with a new repressive law. This allowed the legal system to deal with the threat.

The Pass Laws

The most notorious and widely used regulations for controlling the movements of Blacks were the Pass Laws. These were introduced in 1952 and required all Africans to carry a set of documents which proved their identity to any representative of white authority and to show whether they were legally entitled to be in the 'white' area. Every African over 16 had to carry either one of these passes, or else a 'passport' if he or she was defined as a citizen of an independent Homeland. If the pass was not in order, he or she could be arrested and subsequently fined, imprisoned or 'endorsed out' to his or her Homeland. Between 1948 and 1981 over 12.5 million people were arrested or prosecuted for pass law offences.

ably in 'white' areas, this greatly limited the opportunity for Blacks to develop successful businesses.

THE HOMELANDS

Comprising no more than 13% of the total land in South Africa, the Homelands were expected to support almost 73% of the population, or 21 of the 28 million people living in the country. On the most fertile soil and with the most modern farming techniques this would be an awesome task.

Land Erosion and Overpopulation

The quality of even the best land in the Homelands was diminished by the demands placed upon it as more and more Africans were forcibly resettled there. Most Africans in the Homelands were subsistence farmers and as more people were forced into the Homelands, the demand for land increased. This, in turn, eroded the land. In 1954 the Tomlinson Commission found that 30% of all the land in the Homelands was already "badly eroded".

Quality of the Land

The quality of the land allocated to the Homelands varied. The largest, Bophuthatswana, had a very large amount of desert and semi-desert, with only 6–7% of the land considered suitable for arable farming; the rest was too dry for anything other than livestock grazing. A similar picture existed for the small, northern Homelands in the Transvaal—Venda, Gazankulu, and Lebowa—which have limited rainfall and periodic droughts and were unsuitable for arable farming.

Fragmentation of the Land

The Homelands were fragmented, with pockets of land cut off from the rest of the Homeland by 'white' areas. This weakened the economic viability of the Homelands. In the first place it was more expensive to develop the infrastructure such as transport and housing. Also, people living in one part of the Homeland had much further to travel if industry was situated in another part. Furthermore, access to the

Homeland authorities was more difficult. Finally, the borders were arbitrarily drawn to satisfy white requirements. This ensured that most major towns, industrial and mining developments were kept out.

Search for Work

Due to the shortage of land and employment many Africans had to seek work outside the Homeland. It was estimated that at any one time 35% of all employable males were absent from the Homelands and over 70% of the economically active population was involved in the migrant labour system. Thus the Homelands were left with a disproportionately large number of children, women, elderly and sick, ie. those who were of no productive use to the 'white' economy. The most disturbing consequence of this was the effect it had on African families in the Homelands. With wives only able to visit their husbands on a 72-hour pass, the links which bind families together were often broken and children in the Homelands were left fatherless.

Homeland Standard of Living

Some people in the Homelands had a very good standard of living, for instance, those who were elected 'representatives' in the Homeland legislature. For the vast majority of the population, however, living standards were very poor by any criterion.

Standard of living depends on income levels and in the Homelands these were very low. A study of incomes in the Transkei in 1978 found that 95% of all households had an income of under R50 per month, which was well below the subsistence level; 50% had under R12 per month. The low level of income is also demonstrated by the fact that the Homelands accounted for only 3% of the Gross Domestic Product of South Africa.

Health standards were very poor by all accounts, although the government did not issue statistics on these, unlike other areas of Home-

land life. In 1972, one survey of Ciskei and Transkei found severe malnutrition. As a direct result of this, 50% of surviving children in the Ciskei were stunted in growth. Common childhood diseases such as measles and whooping cough became killers under such conditions and the infant mortality rate was very high.

THE TOWNSHIPS

Most Africans who qualified to stay in 'white South Africa' under Section 10 regulations were housed in one of the many townships. These were housing areas for the African labour force which was required by local industry and they were usually situated on the outskirts of an urban area. Soweto, situated 12 miles southwest of Johannesburg and housing well over one million Africans, was an example of one such township.

By the 1980s, Soweto had 26 locations inside its boundaries. There were over 108,000 houses and, although some were modern and even relatively luxurious, the majority had no bathroom or indoor toilet. They were built to accommodate the labour required by Johannesburg's industry and commerce, but the number built was always inadequate with an average of six to seven people living in each house. Most homes used candles, paraffin or gas lamps for lighting and coal stoves for cooking. Water was supplied to most houses by an outside tap from which residents carried supplies. Only 3% had running hot water and 7% had a bath or shower. Electricity was not common in houses.

Soweto mothers were not encouraged to stay at home. The system had created townships to house workers; normal family life was not part of the plan for Africans in the 'white' areas. Also, the low level of wages forced women to try to supplement their husbands' incomes. Child care was difficult to find. There were few nursery facilities and young children were catered for in a number of ways. A granny

Section 10 Regulations

A Black was only allowed to live in an urban area if he or she:

1 had lived in an urban area continuously since birth;

2 had held the same job in the area for at least ten years;

3 was the wife or dependent child of someone qualifying under one of the first two rules;

4 was employed on contract in the urban area, his or her permanent residence then being in a Homeland.

hold contributing to the cost of water, refuse disposal and education services. It evolved its own laws and elected a 30-member committee to run the area. Crossroads reflected an African demand to live a normal life and a rejection of the single-sex hostels which were built to house migrant workers while their families were banished to the Homelands to face starvation.

INTERNAL OPPOSITION TO APARTHEID 1948–1988

Black opposition was a recurring feature during the apartheid years. The outlawing of mass organisations since 1960 and the repressive acts of the regime drove the liberation movement underground. The African National Congress (ANC), the Pan Africanist Congress of Azania (PAC), the Black Consciousness Movement (BCM) and the United Democratic Front (UDF) were all declared illegal. Political activity among black South Africans spanned a broad spectrum. It ranged from groups working within the system, such as the ethnic Zulu organisation and black trade unions, to the banned ANC.

Early Years of Resistance 1948–1970

It would be incorrect to imagine that African opposition to white dominance was a feature only of the post-1948 era. The ANC was formed in 1912 with the goal of forging national unity among Africans in their struggle for civil rights. The entrenchment of the apartheid system in the early 1950s turned the ANC into a mass movement. Despite the brutality of the regime, the ANC continued to preach and argue for non-violent, non-revolutionary change. Its leader from 1952 to 1960, Chief Albert Luthuli, was a dignified reformist in the mould of Martin Luther King.

Freedom Charter to Sharpeville

A significant factor in unifying and strengthening the non-white opposition was the adoption of the Freedom Charter by the African, Col-

or unemployed neighbour would be used in the first instance. Joyce Sikakane recounts that when no 'grannies' were available more extreme measures were taken. "Our mothers were forced" by circumstances "to leave us locked alone in a room. They would remove anything dangerous, leaving us with a plate of mealie pap, a mug of water and a chamber pot. Peeping through the drawn curtains and closed windows with window bars was the only enjoyable game. We did it in turns. Otherwise we had fights, cried and slept ... By the age of six our parents regarded us as responsible. We could be left with a house key so as to unlock the house to go to the toilet or to go out and

play. ... When left alone like this, days used to drag and drag on and on. You would cry for your mother until you fell asleep."

THE SHANTY TOWNS

The main response to both the housing shortage and the attack on African family life by migrant labour policies was for Africans to live illegally in squatter camps, or shanty towns, in the urban areas. Probably the best example of this was Crossroads, a vast squatter camp of about 4,000 'illegal' families, a few miles outside Cape Town. In such camps Africans were willing to flout apartheid's regulations in order to maintain family life. The camp flourished, with each house-

oured and Indian Congresses (The Congress Alliance). The Charter called for a non-racial, unitary, democratic state based on the socialist principle of nationalisation of key industries and services.

The solidarity of black opposition suffered a blow in 1959 when a splinter group from the ANC formed the Pan Africanist Congress. Its supporters emphasised the need for Africans to act alone without the support of white liberals. Robert Sobukwe, the first President of the PAC, described its aims as "Government of the Africans, by the Africans and for the Africans."

It was a PAC campaign against the pass laws that led to the Sharpeville massacre of March 1960, when police shot dead 69 demonstrators. The authorities declared a state of emergency and savagely crushed the peaceful black organisations.

Over 20,000 people were detained, both the ANC and the PAC were banned and their leaders tried and sentenced to long years of imprisonment.

The ANC went underground in 1960 and initiated an armed struggle. In 1964 Nelson Mandela, leader of the ANC, was sentenced to life imprisonment for attempting revolution by violence. For more than a decade, black opposition lay crushed and dispirited. However, in the 1970s the struggle was taken up by a new generation and by 'the children'.

'The Children Awake'

In 1976 and 1977, over 700 Africans died in what were referred to as the 'Soweto Riots'. The significance of these events was not the brutality of the regime but the resistance offered by the children of Soweto. This new generation had watched

their parents retreat into sullen submission to the system: "You look at your parent and see a worn-out hopeless person."

The seeds for this reappearance of African pride and self-respect can be traced to the emergence in the 1970s of a new layer of organised opposition which worked within the framework of apartheid. Its leader, Steve Biko, was a charismatic figure who unified the people and revived the African spirit.

The riots started on 16 June 1976 when high school pupils began to march on Phefeni Junior Secondary school. This was the focal point of the protest against the introduction of Afrikaans as a medium of instruction in African schools. The protest march of up to 1,000 students began peacefully. They carried banners with slogans denouncing the use of Afrikaans.

STEVE BIKO   & THE BCM

To many Blacks, especially the young, Steve Biko was South Africa's Martin Luther King. He was born in King William's Town on 18 December 1946 and for a brief period studied medicine at the University of Natal. His involvement in the struggle for black civil rights led to his expulsion from the university and in 1968 he founded the (Black) South African Students Organisation (SASO). Biko travelled around the country to spread the gospel of Black Consciousness, instilling self-confidence, pride and dignity in the young.

The authorities arrested him for the fourth and last time on 13 August 1977. Their purpose was to discredit Biko by forcing him to confess to acts of terror-

ism. On 12 September, Biko died. His death shocked the world and an international outcry forced the Republic of South

Africa to conduct a judicial inquiry. The Inquest Inquiry gave a disturbing insight into the workings of the Security Police. Biko

was the 46th detainee to die in police custody. He was kept naked, chained to a grille and tortured. Finally, on 11 September, he was put into the back of a Land Rover and driven 750 miles to a military hospital in Pretoria, where he died almost on arrival. The Inquest Inquiry lasted three weeks, with no charges being brought against any of the interrogators.

In 1978, the rebirth of Black Consciousness occurred with the formation of AZAPO (Azanian People's Organisation). Its leaders were arrested immediately, but its loose federation of various interested groups ensured its survival. However, over the years it lost much of its appeal and support, many of its former supporters returning to the fold of the ANC.

The tragedy which followed was predictable. The police opened fire when the students started stoning them. The riots quickly spread throughout Soweto and to other townships. The Soweto Students Representative Council (SSRC) was set up to coordinate resistance. The school boycott was extended to a work boycott.

Although the school boycott ended in 1979, schools in Soweto never fully regained their previous enrolment levels. By Christmas 1977, open resistance had been crushed. The government outlawed 18 movements and banned the newspaper *The World*. Three months earlier, Steve Biko had died in police custody. Resistance had been crushed but the embers of black pride, dignity and high aspirations could not be totally smothered. Steve Biko had not died in vain.

TRADE UNION ORGANISATION

In 1979 PW Botha, the Nationalist leader, legalised black trade unions. It was also an attempt to bring black trade unionism within the limits of white industrial discipline. It failed miserably. The 1980s witnessed a rapid expansion in trade union membership and an increased militancy among black workers which was reflected in the rash of strikes that became an everyday feature of the industrial scene. In December 1985, the dream of a national trade union organisation became a reality. Thirty six South African trade unions, with a total membership of 500,000, formed the Congress of South African Trade Unions (COSATU). The trade unions played a crucial role in organising black opposition during the states of emergency in the 1980s and 1990s.

INKATHA

Inkatha, founded in 1974, is predominantly a Zulu movement, although it claims to be a national organisation. It straddles rural and urban areas with some 30,000 paid-up members and 700 registered branches. Inkatha rejected violence as the best means of bringing about racial change and favoured non-violent tactics such as consumer boycotts. Inkatha's leader, Chief Mangosuthu Buthelezi, always denied that he was a puppet of Pretoria. In 1976 he stated that "the Zulu people have rejected the policy of independence. I know I am vilified as a 'collaborator' for my cooperation with the government. But we have up to a point, not because we believe in apartheid but because since there was no alternative allowed, it was in the interest of a peaceful settlement of South Africa's problem."

Inkatha and the ANC were once fraternal organisations and initially Buthelezi was encouraged by the ANC to build up his movement. However, the ANC President, Oliver Tambo, accused Buthelezi of using Inkatha as a personal power base and of collaborating with the government.

ARMED STRUGGLE— RE-EMERGENCE OF THE ANC

The Soweto Riots of 1976 and the demise of the Black Consciousness Movement rekindled the fires of the ANC. The 1980s witnessed a steady escalation of the acts of sabotage perpetrated by the military wing of the ANC (Umkhonto We Sizwe). The group's leader in exile was Oliver Tambo, who fled South Africa at the time of Nelson Mandela's arrest. Tambo's headquarters were in Lusaka, the capital of Zambia, and he had built up an estimated force of 6,000 men and women trained as saboteurs and urban terrorists.

Tambo insisted that armed struggle was the only way of ending apartheid. In 1983 he stated, "Never again are our people going to do all the bleeding. We have offered the other cheek so many times that there is no cheek left to turn."

Botha's state of emergency curtailed the activities of the ANC. Nevertheless, acts of sabotage against military and industrial targets were a common feature of the period 1986–88. Despite the ANC's decision not to engage in a terror campaign against civilian targets, bombs were set off in town and city centres, causing civilian casualties or injuries. However, these were isolated incidents which were deplored by the National Executive Committee of the ANC.

Significantly, the ANC's status as a legitimate organisation gained worldwide acceptance. Leaders of the ANC met with government officials in London and Washington. From a terrorist group in exile the ANC had been elevated to a government-in-waiting.

DISMANTLING APARTHEID 1978–1990

PW Botha became the new Nationalist Leader in 1978, replacing the disgraced Prime Minister John Vorster. "We must adapt or die" was his message to his white constituents as he embarked on a series of reforms. His purpose was to preserve the existing structure, not to destroy it—in short, to introduce apartheid with a human face. His intention was to create a larger non-black minority by extending the franchise to the Coloureds and Asians. He also planned to offer economic and political concessions to the expanding black middle class in order to split African solidarity. Furthermore, he hoped that change would promote a new image of a reformist South Africa, thus ending its status as an international pariah.

However, the outcome of these reforms was not peace and prosperity but the outbreak of massive black unrest and further action by the international community against South Africa. (See page 60.) Botha resigned in August 1989, a bitter and perplexed man. It was the new leader, FW de Klerk, who brought the apartheid system to an end and paved the way for the creation of a democratic society for all the citizens of South Africa.

Inkatha leader, Mangosuthu Buthelezi, ringing his Party bell to signal the end of campaigning in local elections in June 1998

Social Reforms

Botha continued Vorster's policy of eliminating petty apartheid, thereby improving the quality of life for the black élite. Hotels, restaurants and sports clubs could apply for international status which allowed them to serve alcohol to African guests. A permit also existed by which people of different races could attend live performances in certain theatres. In short, wealthy Blacks could emulate the lifestyle of the Whites.

The coloured community especially benefited from the relaxation of barriers between the races, although it was still illegal for Coloureds and Whites to live in the same district. Generally, if the white residents did not object to sharing an apartment building or beach with Coloureds then no notice was taken of the breach of policy. Significantly, the government finally decided to scrap the 'heartbreak laws'. In April 1985, after years of deliberation, Botha agreed to rescind the laws prohibiting mixed marriages and inter-racial sexual relations. In 1986 Botha abolished the hated Pass Laws.

Economic Reforms

The report of the Wiehahn Commission into labour legislation led to the recognition of black trade unions and to the end of job reservation. The Reikert Commission was more concerned with economic progress for Blacks. As a result of its recommendations they were able to purchase their own homes under a 99 year lease and some of the rules for setting up their own businesses were relaxed. Electricity and other amenities were going to be installed in the townships.

Political Reforms

In 1984 South Africa introduced a presidential system of government. At the same time the Whites-only parliament was replaced by a tricameral parliament consisting of three separate chambers, one each for Whites, Coloureds and Indians. Each House had a Ministers' Council composed of five members to govern its own affairs. Each House also nominated members to the President's Council which coordinated government policy under the direction of the executive State President.

Joint Standing Committees, comprising members of all three Houses, were appointed with the task of preventing deadlock and conflict between the Houses. If legislation affected only a specific population group, then that particular House passed its own laws without interference. Legislation on general or national affairs had to be approved by all three Houses in separate sessions before it went to the State President for approval. However, to ensure that the Coloured and Indian Houses could not block any government legislation, the President's Council, with its built-in white majority, could overrule their objections.

In short, the new constitution did not create power sharing between the Whites, Coloureds and Asians. The white assembly had an overwhelming majority (50 to 38) in the electoral college and so its choice of State President was predictable—the white Leader of the National Party.

DE KLERK'S REFORMS

"There is neither time nor room for turning back. There is only one road – ahead." FW de Klerk.

1990

2 February: De Klerk lifts the ban outlawing the ANC, the South African Communist Party and other political groups.

11 February: After 27 years in jail, Nelson Mandela is freed.

2 May: The ANC and the government hold their first formal talks and agree to negotiate a new non-racial constitution.

7 June: De Klerk ends the national state of emergency with the exception of Natal Province.

19 June: The Separate Amenities Act is repealed.

6 August: The ANC agrees to suspend its armed struggle.

31 August: The National Party opens its ranks to all races.

October: State of emergency lifted in Natal.

1991

1 February: De Klerk announces plan to repeal the Land Acts, Group Areas Acts and Population Registration Act—the remaining pillars of apartheid.

17 June: The three racially defined Houses of South Africa's Parliament vote to repeal the Population Registration Act.

OPPOSITION TO THE NEW CONSTITUTION

In 1982, Dr Treurnicht, a member of Botha's Cabinet and leader of the 'Verkrampte' (the right wing of the Nationalist Party), resigned and, along with 14 National Party defectors, formed the Conservative Party. Reform, in Treurnicht's opinion meant "that the Government has finally scrapped separate development. We will fight this fatal course on every terrain."

Botha faced strong opposition to his reforms from within the white community and this ensured that the concessions offered to the urban Blacks would be limited. The proposed reforms were also condemned by the black majority and created a split within the Coloured and Indian communities. Even black moderates, such as Chief Buthelezi, accused those who participated in the new Assembly of betrayal and treachery.

The new constitution expressly excluded the black majority. Its preamble stated "God gave South Africa to the Whites." Africans would be able to enjoy their "separate freedom in the land allotted to them." Some minor concessions were given to the Blacks at local government level. The townships were given control over local affairs through elected Community Councils and were referred to as "municipal homelands". Organised boycotts of the elections ensured that these councils were a dismal failure; only about 10% of the electorate voted and the council leaders were regarded as traitors. Black opposition ensured that the townships were ungovernable and unfortunately acts of violence such as 'necklace killings' were carried out by the 'young comrades'. Botha was forced to declare several states of emergency, and while order was restored by 1989, it was clear that the country was heading towards a savage war between the apartheid regime and its black opponents.

1990 – THE YEAR OF CHANGE

In August 1989 FW de Klerk became the new President of South Africa and he moved swiftly to obtain a mandate for reform by holding elections in September 1989.

Events in South Africa in many ways resembled the upheavals which took place in Eastern Europe in 1989. A state ideology—Communism in Eastern Europe and Apartheid in South Africa—was declared dead. In South Africa it was a giant step away from the past, with the government willing "to renounce its sole occupation of the heights of Government". De Klerk had crossed the Rubicon.

Reasons for De Klerk's Reforms

1 Even within the Afrikaner community the demand for reform was intensifying. Professor John Heyus, the leader of the Dutch Reformed Church to which most Afrikaners belonged, had called on the government to drop its insistence that the ANC renounce violence as a precondition for talks.

2 South African isolation from the outside world was affecting the economy, especially in the area of investments. The demand for further sanctions was growing, with the possible introduction of UN economic sanctions.

3 The State of Emergency provided both an opportunity and a warning to de Klerk. The township revolt had been crushed with even the ANC admitting that its ability to continue the 'armed struggle' was at a low ebb. Paradoxically, therefore, the restoration of law and order by Botha offered de Klerk the opportunity to negotiate from a position of strength.

4 Finally, the changes in the world balance of power and the resolution of conflicts in Southern Africa weakened the far right's claim that "communism would

Nelson Mandela celebrates his freedom at a rally in Soweto

take over South Africa". Perestroika in the USSR, global superpower cooperation, the collapse of communism in Eastern Europe, independence in Namibia and moves towards national reconciliation in Angola and Mozambique all combined to redefine South Africa's regional role. It was clear that the USSR wished to end apartheid through negotiations rather than by bloodshed. 1990, therefore, was to be the year of change in South Africa.

Opening of Parliament

In February 1990, De Klerk stunned MPs by announcing that the ANC and other black nationalist movements would be legalised immediately and that Nelson Mandela would be freed. The reaction throughout the country was electric. Spontaneous celebrations broke out in the townships around the country. The ANC announced

an urgent review of the new situation which had emerged. The reaction from the Conservative Party and the far right was one of fury. The Conservative Party threatened a campaign of demonstrations and strikes to force de Klerk out of office. Treurnicht thundered, "If a government does not protect the rights of its people what can be expected but that the volk will protect itself." The neofascist Afrikaner Resistance Movement (AWB) (see page 62) sent hundreds of khaki-clad heavily armed marchers into Pretoria shouting, "Hang de Klerk, hang Mandela."

Walk to Freedom

On Sunday 11 February 1990, at 4.15 pm local time, Nelson Mandela walked out of the Victor Verster Prison Farm near Cape Town. The event, televised live around the world, was described by an announcer of the South African Broadcasting Company as "the mo-

ment that a majority of South Africa and the world had been waiting for." Archbishop Desmond Tutu summed up the mood of euphoria and expectation which swept through the black community. "We want to touch him and say 'Here he is', this man who has such a crucial role to play in the making of this new South Africa."

Mandela was well aware that the road to the creation of a new democratic South Africa would be treacherous and frustrating. It was obvious that the National Party would not simply hand power over to the black community. It was to take four long years of conflict resolution before the dream of all black South Africans was achieved. "Free at last" was the cry on 26 April 1994 when all of the people of South Africa went to the polls to vote. A 'rainbow nation' had been created from the storm clouds of violence, mistrust and injustice.

SOUTH AFRICA AND THE INTERNATIONAL COMMUNITY

The United Nations, the Commonwealth and the European Union each played an important part in orchestrating world opposition to the racist regime of South Africa.

In 1974 the UN General Assembly voted to reject the credentials of the South African delegation on the grounds that the government was not representative of the people of the country. In successive years, it had reaffirmed its recognition of the African National Congress (ANC) as the authentic representative of the people of South Africa.

The Assembly declared South Africa's occupation of Namibia illegal and refused to recognise the independence granted to the four Bantustans of South Africa. In 1977 the UN Security Council instituted a mandatory arms embargo against South Africa. The United Nations Special Committee Against Apartheid ensured a world sporting and cultural boycott against South Africa.

The Commonwealth, given its historic ties with South Africa, actively opposed apartheid. (South Africa withdrew from the Commonwealth in 1961.) However, Margaret Thatcher, the British Conservative Prime Minister, was reluctant to impose sanctions and only agreed to a limited programme of action: no further investment and a ban on the import of coal, iron, steel and gold coins from South Africa.

The European Union, South Africa's largest trading partner, imposed a similar range of sanctions against South Africa. It also adopted a code of conduct for subsidiaries of EU corporations operating in South Africa.

The USSR firmly supported the activities of the ANC and provided military and economic support to the front line countries of Angola and Mozambique. Prominent members of the ANC such as Joe Slovo and Chris Hani were also members of the South African Communist Party.

In contrast, the USA was a reluctant convert to the imposition of sanctions. Its policy in the early 1980s was one of constructive engagement with South Africa (reform and progress in South Africa could only be achieved by open dialogue with Pretoria). However, American domestic opinion and the campaigns of disinvestment ensured that the US government would impose its own sanctions. The number of US companies with direct investment in South Africa declined from 330 in 1983 to under 130 by the end of 1989. The 1986 Congress passed the Comprehensive Anti-Apartheid Act. This Act banned all US imports of South African iron, steel, coal, uranium, textiles and agricultural products. It also forbade new US loans and investments in South Africa.

Creating the Rainbow Nation

It was obvious that a series of obstacles would have to be removed before the new constitution could be agreed and elections held. With reluctance the National Party realised that it could not impose a settlement which would retain built-in veto powers to protect racial or group rights. The events of 1992, when the country seemed to be on the verge of meltdown with an escalation of violence combined with discord between Mandela and de Klerk, marked the turning point in negotiations.

CONSTITUTIONAL BREAKTHROUGH

The reformists within the National Party gained control and forced the Party to accept that its vision of building an election-winning anti-ANC alliance with Inkatha, the other Homeland leaders and the Coloured and Indian parties was an illusion. Their new strategy was to distance themselves from Buthelezi, end the destabilisation campaign and form a coalition with the ANC instead.

Two months of talks followed between the Constitutional Affairs Minister, Roelf Meyer and the ANC's General Secretary, Cyril Ramaphosa. The mechanism was to be put in place to prepare the country for elections in 1994 and for the ANC to share in the decision making process in the run-up to these elections. (The Convention for a Democratic South Africa was to be replaced by the Multi-Party Negotiating Process.)

The tragic assassination of Chris Hani, a prominent member of the ANC and the South African Communist Party, in April 1993 did not derail the peace talks. Chris Hani was killed by a right-wing Polish immigrant, Janusz Walus, and members of the Conservative Party were implicated. He was shot outside his house in Boksburg. He was the former leader of the military wing of the ANC and was a legendary hero among the comrades in the black townships.

In July 1993 the Negotiating Forum, which was set up as a result of the multi-party negotiating process, agreed on 27 April 1994 as the date for South Africa's first ever non-racial election. With 19 of the 26 organisations involved voting in favour of the resolution, this was regarded as "sufficient consensus" for it to be adopted. Both the Inkatha Freedom Party (IFP) and the Conservative Party subsequently announced that they were suspending their participation in the negotiations.

The new constitution created strong regional government in nine new provinces, but stopped short of creating a federation. There was to be a new national army which would incorporate ANC military units. Power sharing was assured for the lifetime of the interim government by guaranteeing cabinet seats to any party winning at least 5% of the national vote.

In response to the ANC/National Party 'partnership', the parties opposed to the multi-party negotiating process formed the Freedom Alliance. Established on 7 October 1993, it consisted of the Afrikaner Volksfront, the Inkatha Freedom Party, the Bophuthatswana and Ciskei administrations and the Conservative Party. All rejected the constitution deal and promised to boycott the 1994 elections. "Today is the beginning of confrontation," warned neofascist leader Eugene Terre Blanche of the AWB.

Countdown to Election

The run-up to the elections witnessed the disintegration of the Freedom Alliance, with the turning point being the disastrous invasion of Bophuthatswana by the Afrikaner Volksfront in March 1994. Despite this break-up the threat of civil war remained, with violence in Natal escalating and Buthelezi's determination to boycott the elections still strong. Suddenly, and at the very last second, Inkatha agreed to participate in the elections and the country heaved a collective sigh of relief. The miracle had happened—Buthelezi had pulled back from plunging the country into civil war.

The farcical 'invasion' of Bophuthatswana by the AWB destroyed unity among Afrikaner separatists. General Constand Viljoen resigned from the Volksfront and criticised the AWB for ignoring his orders, calling its commandos ill-disciplined and reckless. Viljoen, chief of South Africa's armed forces until 1985, had stepped forward in April 1993 to rally the Afrikaner people to fight for their homeland. (The leader of the Conservative Party, Dr Treurnicht, had died in April 1993

Eugene Terre Blanche, leader of the extreme right-wing AWB, leaving court in April 1998 after being convicted of atttempting to murder a former black employeee by assaulting him with an iron bar.

THE AFRIKANER VOLKSFRONT

There are numerous right-wing organisations in South Africa. Below is a summary of the major groups.

The Conservative Party

It was established in 1982 after 16 National Party MPs rejected Botha's reforms. In the 1989 Election it won 31% of the vote. It refused to take part in the constitutional talks and the 1994 Elections. This divided the Party, with many of its members supporting the Freedom Front. It supports the creation of an Afrikaner homeland.

Afrikaner Resistance Movement (AWB)

The most notorious right-wing organisation is the Afrikaner Resistance Movement (AWB). Its leader, Eugene Terre Blanche, is regarded as anti-semitic and an arch racist. The AWB was dismissed as a lunatic fringe in the 1970s but it experienced considerable growth after the reforms in the 1980s.

It has its own paramilitary forces and its members have carried out numerous acts of terrorism and murder. The AWB's emblem resembles the swastika and it is committed to the re-establishment of the old Boer Republics of the Transvaal and the Orange Free State as an Afrikaner homeland (Volkstaat). It does not contest elections and works as a pressure group.

Its influence has declined since the invasion of Bophuthatswana in 1994 and the further disunity within the Volksfront. Eugene Terre Blanche's own political influence declined after he was accused of flogging to death one of his black servants.

The Freedom Front

This was set up by Constand Viljoen to rally the moderate Afrikaners and to fight the 1994 Elections. Viljoen dreamed of a homeland that would encompass 15% of South Africa and 12% of its Gross National Product. The Freedom Front is active in the Volkstaat Council set up to investigate the concept of a nation state for Afrikaners. (See page 80.)

and the new leader, Ferdi Hartzenberg, lacked his political authority.)

Viljoen resigned from the Freedom Alliance on 14 March 1994, set up a new party, the Freedom Front, and submitted a list of candidates for the elections. He took with him eight Conservative Party MPs, including the presidents of the Transvaal and Orange Free State agricultural unions, and most of the Conservative Party's Natal Executive.

As the elections approached, violence and intimidation, especially in Natal, continued. By that time the death rate from political killings had jumped to 10 a day and de Klerk was forced to act. He declared a state of emergency in Natal and deployed the army. "Law and order will be maintained and elections will take place on the scheduled date," he stated.

Buthelezi denounced the state of emergency as a frontal assault against the Zulus. A mediation mission by Henry Kissinger and Lord Carrington on 13 April ended in failure. On 19 April, the Inkatha Freedom Party (IFP) agreed to participate in the elections. At this late hour, it was not possible to reprint the estimated 80 million ballot papers. The Independent Electoral Commission stated that a sticker, bearing the full details and logo of the IFP, would be placed at the bottom of the printed ballot papers by the electoral officers. Buthelezi's late capitulation—in return for some constitutional powers for the Zulu king in Inkatha's home base of KwaZulu—ensured that a relatively peaceful election would take place.

REASONS FOR INKATHA'S PARTICIPATION

1 Since the elections were going to take place whether the IFP participated or not, Inkatha and Buthelezi would have lost most of their influence in the new South Africa. More importantly,

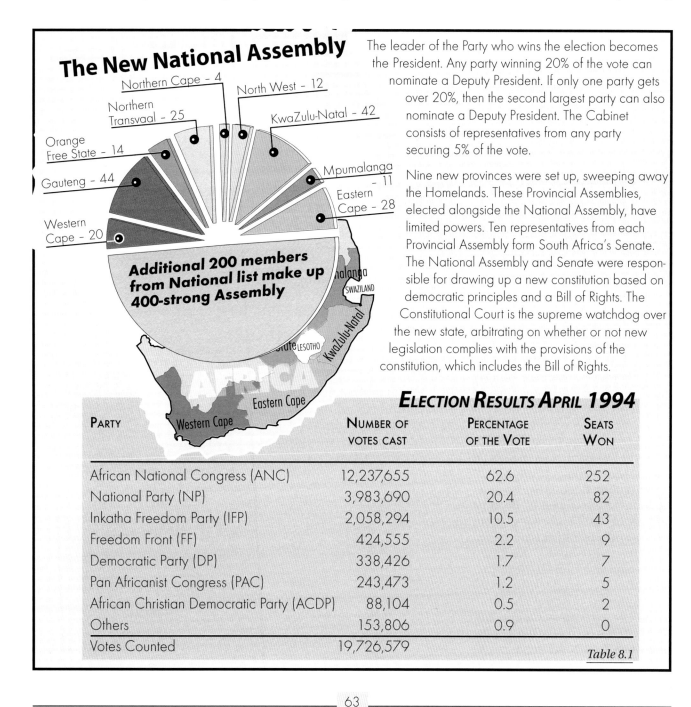

The New National Assembly

Northern Cape - 4
North West - 12
Northern Transvaal - 25
KwaZulu-Natal - 42
Orange Free State - 14
Gauteng - 44
Mpumalanga - 11
Eastern Cape - 28
Western Cape - 20

Additional 200 members from National list make up 400-strong Assembly

The leader of the Party who wins the election becomes the President. Any party winning 20% of the vote can nominate a Deputy President. If only one party gets over 20%, then the second largest party can also nominate a Deputy President. The Cabinet consists of representatives from any party securing 5% of the vote.

Nine new provinces were set up, sweeping away the Homelands. These Provincial Assemblies, elected alongside the National Assembly, have limited powers. Ten representatives from each Provincial Assembly form South Africa's Senate. The National Assembly and Senate were responsible for drawing up a new constitution based on democratic principles and a Bill of Rights. The Constitutional Court is the supreme watchdog over the new state, arbitrating on whether or not new legislation complies with the provisions of the constitution, which includes the Bill of Rights.

ELECTION RESULTS APRIL 1994

Party	Number of Votes Cast	Percentage of the Vote	Seats Won
African National Congress (ANC)	12,237,655	62.6	252
National Party (NP)	3,983,690	20.4	82
Inkatha Freedom Party (IFP)	2,058,294	10.5	43
Freedom Front (FF)	424,555	2.2	9
Democratic Party (DP)	338,426	1.7	7
Pan Africanist Congress (PAC)	243,473	1.2	5
African Christian Democratic Party (ACDP)	88,104	0.5	2
Others	153,806	0.9	0
Votes Counted	19,726,579		

Table 8.1

Inkatha's power base in KwaZulu would have been swallowed up by the new province of KwaZulu/Natal.

2   The collapse of the Freedom Alliance left Inkatha isolated, with its only 'allies' being the extreme right-wing fanatics. Such a partnership offered only humiliation and ridicule for Buthelezi.

FREE AT LAST – APRIL 1994 ELECTIONS

The outcome was never in doubt, but the euphoria of voting for the first time in their lives ensured a massive turnout of Blacks. "Today is a day like no other before it," Mandela said as the voting began. His 20 million fellow Africans stood in long lines which stretched across the open African landscape. (See The Voice of the People opposite.) They walked patiently and peacefully, sometimes standing alongside their white neighbours. In Ventersdorp, an Afrikaner stronghold, white farmers brought their black workers to the polling stations by the lorry load.

The only major violence occurred before the voting began. Bombs, apparently set off by White extremists, killed 21 people in Johannesburg and Pretoria. The police reacted immediately and arrested 34 members of the AWB.

Overall, the conduct of the election was free from intimidation and fraud. However, evidence quickly emerged of strange happenings in KwaZulu-Natal. A confidential report to the Independent Electoral Commission stated that the ballot boxes in KwaZulu-Natal had been stuffed with bogus votes; dozens of pirate polling stations had been set up in areas controlled by Inkatha; and voting cards had been given to 13-year-olds by officials of the old Inkatha-controlled KwaZulu Homeland government. Nevertheless, the ANC leadership urged their followers to accept the result in the interests of peace and stability. The IFP gained 41 of the 81 seats in the KwaZulu-Natal Province un-

der the power sharing agreements for the first five years. Inkatha will find it impossible to rule alone in the Province. The results elsewhere in the country reinforced the status of the IFP as a regional party rather than a national player. In the 8 other provinces its combined vote was only 214,000.

The National Party gained 20.4% of the votes, largely at the expense of the Democratic Party which gained only 1.7% of the votes. Its best performance was in the Western Cape where it won the provincial election. Early opinion polls (they were banned in the run-up to the election) clearly indicated that the Coloured and Indian votes were ebbing away from the ANC. This offered the National Party the opportunity to win the Western Cape where Coloureds are in the majority—a remarkable achievement by de Klerk. It should not be forgotten that it was the National Party which stripped the Coloureds of their right to vote and forcibly evicted tens of thousands of them from neighbourhoods reserved for Whites.

The extremist parties fared badly: the Pan Africanist Congress gained 243,000 votes and 5 seats in the National Assembly, well behind the Freedom Front which gained 424,000 votes and nine seats.

The ANC overall won 12.2 million votes (62.6%) and 252 seats in the National Assembly. It also won control of 7 of the 9 Provincial Assemblies. However, it failed to gain the two-thirds majority which would have allowed the ANC to rewrite the Constitution.

THE GOVERNMENT OF NATIONAL UNITY

The first session of the National Assembly was held on 9 May 1994 and Nelson Mandela was elected as the first democratic President of South Africa. On 10 May President Mandela was sworn in as South Africa's first black president and in a speech of great solemnity and passion the 75-year-old President pledged to create from the darkness of apartheid a rainbow nation at peace with itself. Helicopters flew overhead trailing the new flag and fighter planes painted the sky in the flag's six colours.

At the same ceremony, Mr Thabo Mbeki was inaugurated as the First Deputy President and Mr FW de Klerk as the Second Deputy President. Cyril Ramaphosa, the ANC's General Secretary and the architect of negotiations with the National Party, had high hopes of being the Deputy President and, significantly, he refused a seat in the Cabinet.

The South African Cabinet, which met for the first time on 11 May 1994, consisted of 27 members: 18 ANC, 6 National Party and 3 IFP. At this first meeting 12 deputy ministers were also appointed, including Winnie Mandela. The National Party had been hoping that Pik Botha would be appointed to Foreign Affairs, but this post was given to Alfred Nzo, the former ANC General Secretary. Instead, their six ministers received the posts of Provincial Affairs and Constitutional Development, Environment Affairs, Mineral and Energy, Welfare and Population Development, Agriculture, and Finance. Chief Buthelezi received the post of Home Affairs.

The peaceful handing over of power took place in eight of the nine Provinces. (The National Party retained power in the Western Cape.) Of the seven ANC premiers sworn in, all had either returned from exile or were released from jail after 1990. Power had been transferred to the majority while respecting the rights of the minority. The symbol of the new South Africa was the new ANC MP, Melanie Verwoerd. Her grandfather-in-law was the architect of apartheid, Dr Hendrik Verwoerd.

Extract from Nelson Mandela's Inauguration Speech, 10 May 1994

The time for the healing of the wounds has come. The moment to bridge the chasms that divide us has come.

The time to build is upon us.

We have, at last, achieved our political emancipation. We pledge ourselves to liberate all our people from the continuing bondage of poverty, deprivation, suffering, gender and other discrimination.

We succeeded to take our last steps to freedom in conditions of relative peace. We commit ourselves to the construction of a complete, just and lasting peace.

We have triumphed in the effort to implant hope in the breasts of the millions of our people. We enter into a covenant that we shall build a society in which all South Africans, both black and white, will be able to walk tall, without any fear in their hearts, assured of their inalienable right to human dignity—a rainbow nation at peace with itself and the world.

We are both humbled and elevated by the honour and privilege that you, the people of South Africa, have bestowed on us, as the first President of a united, democratic, non-racial and non-sexist South Africa, to lead our country out of the valley of darkness.

We understand that there is no easy road to freedom.

We know it well that none of us acting alone can achieve success.

We must therefore act together as a united people, for national reconciliation, for nation building, for the birth of a new world.

Let there be justice for all.

Let there be peace for all.

Let there be work, bread, water and salt for all.

Let each know that for each the body, the mind and the soul have been freed to fulfil themselves.

Never, never and never again shall it be that this beautiful land will again experience the oppression of one by another and suffer the indignity of being the skunk of the world.

Let freedom reign.

The sun shall never set on so glorious a human achievement.

God bless Africa.

Legacy and Reconstruction

THE LEGACY OF APARTHEID

When the final structures of apartheid were dismantled in 1991, the social and economic inequalities between the races still remained. This was and is the challenge which faces the Government of National Unity as it embarks on its journey towards its goals of Justice, Reconciliation and Prosperity. Nelson Mandela is well aware of the expectations of the people. He stated in 1994 that "a roof over one's head and reasonable living conditions are not a privilege. They are a basic right for every human being." The extent of the challenge facing the new government can be seen in the broad statistical summary of the economic and social indicators below and on page 67.

Black income per head is one-tenth of white income. Unemployment stands at 40% in the formal job market. Some 7 million Blacks live in the squatter camps (informal settlements) which are little more than forgotten cesspools of despair; 12 million have no clean water; 14 million cannot read. One major obstacle to economic equality is population growth. Forty percent of the black population of 28 million is under the age of 16. It is estimated that the present population will double over the next 30 years.

> *Apartheid has left a ghastly legacy. There is a horrendous housing shortage and high unemployment; health care is inaccessible and not easily affordable by the majority; Bantu education has left us with a massive educational crisis; there is a gross maldistrubution of wealth and an inequitable sharing of the resources with which South Africa is so richly endowed. Some 20% of the population owns 87% of the land. Then there is the hurt and anguish of those who have been victims of this vicious system, those who were forcibly removed from their homes, nearly 4 million people. Those whose loved ones were detained without trial or banned, or who died mysteriously in detention, such as Steve Biko, or at the hands of death squads.*
>
> *There is need of healing, of rehabilitation, of confession, of forgiveness, of restitution and reconciliation. Our beautiful land yearns for healing.* (Archbishop Desmond Tutu, 1994)

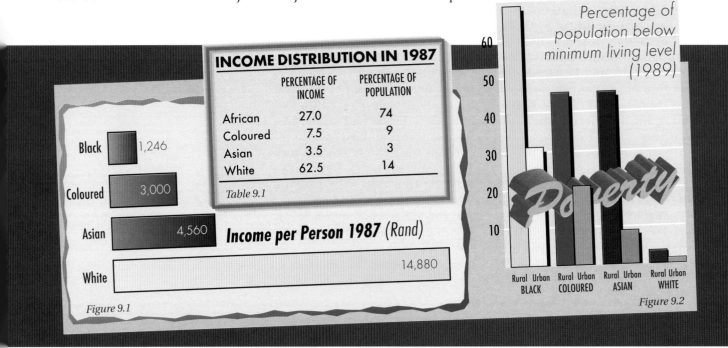

INCOME DISTRIBUTION IN 1987

	PERCENTAGE OF INCOME	PERCENTAGE OF POPULATION
African	27.0	74
Coloured	7.5	9
Asian	3.5	3
White	62.5	14

Table 9.1

Income per Person 1987 (Rand)

Black	1,246
Coloured	3,000
Asian	4,560
White	14,880

Figure 9.1

Percentage of population below minimum living level (1989)

Poverty

Rural Urban BLACK · Rural Urban COLOURED · Rural Urban ASIAN · Rural Urban WHITE

Figure 9.2

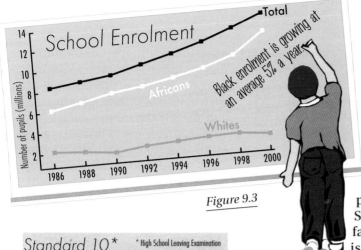

Figure 9.3

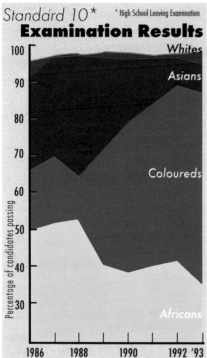

Figure 9.4

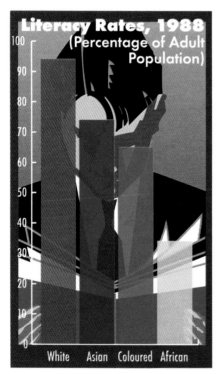

Figure 9.5

Education

Central to the future development of South Africa is the creation of a skilled work force. The paradox which South Africa faces at present is that, while it has an unemployment rate of 40% it is desperately short of skilled and educated Blacks. In 1996 there were 8.8 million black schoolchildren (see Figure 9.3) with this rising to 12.3 million by the year 2000. This demographic timebomb is one reason why the government spends 7% of Gross Domestic Product on education (see Figure 9.6). This is twice the level spent by developing countries of comparable wealth.

The culture of violence and the alienation of youth are still features of education in South Africa today, contributing to the poor performance of black students. When Nelson Mandela told students to throw their pangas into the sea and go back to school, some of them showed their displeasure by cutting his face off their T-shirts. According to Dr Hartshore, Consultant to the Centre for Continuing Education, schooling of black South Africans has reached crisis point. "It has produced people who do not know how to learn and who do not want to learn."

A clear indication of the impact Bantu education has had on the educational achievements of Blacks can be seen in the matriculation (examination) results, literacy rates and previous state spending (Figures 9.4 – 9.6). Overcrowded classrooms, few resources and a history of underinvestment have left many black students with little chance of developing the skills needed to move on to Higher Education.

Health

It was only in 1990 that hospitals were opened to all population groups. The inequalities in hospital provision led to the absurd situation of Johannesburg Hospital being underutilised, with whole wards closed down, while in Baragwanath Hospital in Soweto, a black township on the outskirts of Johannesburg, patients slept under as well as on top of beds.

The depressing statistics (see Table 9.2) illustrate the vast gulf between the 'First World' health care of the Whites and the 'Third World' health service administered to the Blacks. The statistics also highlight the contrast between urban and rural African health provision. A major factor in this disparity of health provision between the races is their contrasting lifestyles and socio-economic position. Poverty, which normally means inadequate housing and sanitary conditions and poor diet, is the major culprit.

Significantly, private health care is a growth area in South Africa. At present it provides 20% of hospital beds and 90% of the white community relies on private rather than on state funded medical care. Private hospitals have been open to all races for some time, but their high fees ensure that very few Blacks can

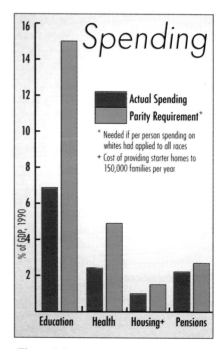

Figure 9.6

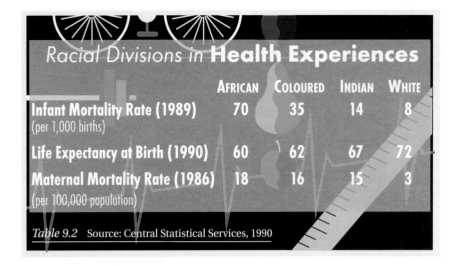

Racial Divisions in Health Experiences	AFRICAN	COLOURED	INDIAN	WHITE
Infant Mortality Rate (1989) (per 1,000 births)	70	35	14	8
Life Expectancy at Birth (1990)	60	62	67	72
Maternal Mortality Rate (1986) (per 100,000 population)	18	16	15	3

Table 9.2   Source: Central Statistical Services, 1990

afford to be treated in the private sector. In short, a two-tier health system, based on racial lines, exists in South Africa.

Land

As Archbishop Desmond Tutu highlights, almost four million non-Whites were forcibly removed from their homes by the apartheid regime. The Homeland and Township systems (see Chapter 7) created squatter camps, shanty towns and sprawling townships such as Soweto where the majority of dwellings lacked basic amenities such as electricity and proper sanitation. In the rural areas many Blacks were forcibly settled in arid lands which could not sustain them. The outcome was malnutrition, disease and abject poverty. Although de Klerk abolished the Group Area Acts and Land Acts of 1913 and 1936, this did not change the realities of ownership or the terrible consequences of 13% of the country's land being given to 80% of its people.

Cyril Ramaphosa, then ANC General Secretary, stated in 1993 that "unless we settle the land question we tear South Africa to pieces." As part of the 1994 peace agreement between de Klerk and Mandela, the white farmers were guaranteed that their land would not be taken from them through nationalisation or expropriation policies.

Legacy of Violence

The apartheid years created a culture of violence in South Africa both at the political level, with the ongoing antagonism between the ANC and Inkatha in KwaZulu, and at the domestic level with an explosion of violent crime. Leaving aside the issue of political violence, the crime wave which has engulfed South Africa can, ironically, be partly blamed on the dismantling of the rigid controls imposed by the security forces. The association of law enforcement and the rule of law with the apartheid regime has created a lack of respect within the black community for the police and the judiciary. E Webster, a South African sociologist, explains, "the capacity of key institutions like the police and judiciary to apply sanctions is weak because they have been discredited. That creates a no-man's-land where the old society is dead and the new not born and where people cease to distinguish between right and wrong and where normal rules of behaviour fall." (See pages 77–78.)

RECONSTRUCTION AND DEVELOPMENT PROGRAMME (1994–96)

This was an imaginative but over-ambitious attempt to bring about a rapid improvement in living standards for Blacks. The strategy of setting up a separate agency with its own Minister, Jay Naidoo, was seen as an innovative attempt to sidestep bureaucratic inertia and

inter-departmental competition. The Finance Minister withheld roughly 5% from the budgets of each of the spending Departments and placed the money into a Reconstruction and Development Fund. Each Department had to draw up a business plan showing how the money would be spent and, more importantly, how it would help the poor.

However, the new government underestimated the timescale involved in setting up a new national ministry alongside the nine new provinces and local government structures. The result was patchy. By the end of 1995 only 12,000 RDP houses had been built, 6% of the number the ANC had promised each year! (The apartheid government had built 40,000 homes in its final year.) The success stories have been in the arrival of electricity and water to the remote townships. Here the credit lies not with the RDP but with EsKom, the state-owned power supplier, and with the Water Minister, Kader Asmal.

The government announced in March 1996 that it was closing down the RDP agency and transfering financial control back to the Treasury. Nelson Mandela insisted that the aim of the RDP had not been abandoned, just absorbed. However, the RDP had been the flagship of the new nation and to many its ending was seen as a desertion of the poor.

GEAR

The new policy, Growth, Employment and Redistribution (GEAR) committed the government to the privatisation of state-owned enterprises and the phased removal of foreign exchange controls. Its budget for 1997 was applauded by the business markets and foreign investment increased, reacting to the 3.1% growth in the economy in 1996. The government wishes to encourage the black enterprise culture; 'wealthy, black and proud of it' is the goal of the government. The government recognises that white skills and capital have a key

> "A roof over one's head and reasonable living conditions are not a privilege. They are a basic right for every human being." (Nelson Mandela)

> "We want jobs. I support the ANC because I hear things will be better. Houses will be built and then we'll be working." (Michael Myengeza, unemployed father of 4 in the Harmony squatter camp)

> "They want a chicken in every pot, a job and clean water from the tap." (A Community Worker)

The Reconstruction and Development Programme 1994

	CHALLENGE	TARGET
Land	➤ Between 1960 and 1990 the government forced 2.5 million people from their homes. ➤ The best land was in the hands of agri-businesses and white farmers.	➤ Redistribution of 30% of agricultural land within 5 years. ➤ A pilot scheme to be set up allocating land to the rural poor and returning land to the dispossessed. ➤ No expropriation of land without proper compensation.
Employment & the Economy	➤ Over 50% of young Blacks are unemployed and are part of the 'lost generation' with no skills who put Revolution before Education. ➤ 220,000 young Blacks enter the job market every year. ➤ 4.7 million Blacks are unemployed. ➤ There is a shortage of foreign investment. ➤ There is a decline in key industries such as gold mining. ➤ There is a shortage of skilled and highly educated black workers.	➤ Establishment of a national public works programme to improve the infrastructure of the country through job creation. ➤ Create 300,000 jobs per annum within 5 years. ➤ Give preference to black job applicants (affirmative action). ➤ Black economic empowerment through enterprise and partnership between private and public providers.
Housing	➤ Some 13 million people live in sub-standard housing, lacking clean water and electricity. ➤ Only 14% of rural dwellers have access to adequate sanitation. ➤ 220,000 houses need to be built each year to keep up with the growth in population.	➤ Building 1 million low cost homes by 1999. ➤ Piped water for 1 million people. ➤ Electricity for 2.5 million people.
Health	High levels of malnutrition and under-nourishment among rural children. Only 7% of Blacks covered by medical schemes compared to 69% of Whites.	Free health care for children under 6 years of age and pregnant women. 172 clinics to be built or upgraded by 1996. Free 'nutrition' sandwich a day to 4.5 million primary school children in over 8,000 schools. Expansion of primary care services to all South African citizens.
Education	➤ About 6 million adults are illiterate. ➤ Problems of low attendance, poor examination results and breakdown of school discipline.	➤ To create a culture of learning. ➤ The phasing in of 10 years of free and compulsory education. ➤ No class to exceed 40 by the year 2000.

role to play in wealth creation for all of its citizens. The ANC leadership is promoting black economic empowerment, but to its radical wing this is dangerously close to economic enrichment for a privileged black élite.

Reasons for RDP's limited success

Thabo Mbeki apologised to the nation in 1996, "Everybody has felt a sense of frustration that we could not move as fast as we wanted to. But it turned out to be more complicated than we had thought."

1   Creation of new government structures at both the national and provincial levels prevented immediate and decisive action. Northern Transvaal, for example, had to integrate 3 former homelands, each with its own capital and civil service. Venda, one of the 4 'independent' homelands, had all the trappings of nationhood: a foreign ministry, an army, a bloated civil service and a fleet of limousines!

2   At the national level the first priority in Education and Health was to create national ministries. 14 separate education systems had to be dismantled and replaced with a National Department of Education.

The reform of the Armed Forces entailed the construction of a South African National Defence Force (SANDF) from the old South African Defence Force, the black homeland forces and the military wing of the ANC.

3   Civil servants, overwhelmingly white and Afrikaners, were given job security or received generous early retirement offers in order to make way for black replacements.

4   Local government elections did not take place until 1996. This delayed the reforms and also enabled white controlled local authorities to ignore the national government.

Housing, a responsibility of the provincial governments, was sadly

found wanting. The grand targets of the RDP remained on the architects' drawing boards.

5   The continuation of political instability in KwaZulu-Natal and the hostility between the National Party and the ANC over the new constitution frightened foreign investors and weakened the energies and direction of the Government of National Unity.

Health

One of the first actions of the Reconstruction and Development Programme was to restructure the country's health system. The fourteen former departments of health were amalgamated into a single National Health System, with one national and nine provincial health departments. The new NHS includes both public and private providers of goods and services.

South Africa also has a very strong private health sector which inevitably reflects a racial imbalance in favour of Whites. There are 207 private hospitals and 75 unattached operating theatres representing a total of 26,400 beds.

The RDP regards the extension of primary care to all South African citizens as its main goal. (See page 65). An impressive beginning has been made. Alongside the much publicised free health care programme for children under six and pregnant women, a clinic building

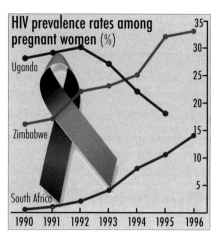

Figure 9.7

and upgrading programme has been implemented. 1,500 mobile clinics have been set up to take primary health care into the isolated rural communities where poverty causes undernourishment which stunts the growth of young children. A survey conducted by the Department of Health among children aged 6 to 71 months discovered that 33% suffered from a deficiency of Vitamin A and 23% were stunted in their growth.

The long-term goal is for all South Africans to obtain free health care at primary health centres, partly through the creation of a National Health Insurance system. In 1991 only 7% of Blacks were covered by medical aid schemes compared to 69% of Whites. Free treatment is provided only by state facilities or hospitals which receive state subsidies for more than half of their expenditure. All provincial hospital

PROVINCIAL DISTRIBUTION OF HEALTH PERSONNEL PER 100,000 OF THE POPULATION			
Province	Doctors	Nurses	Dentists
Eastern Cape	23.3	292.1	3.5
Mpumalanga	21.4	223.1	4.4
Gauteng	92.5	402.1	24.8
KwaZulu-Natal	44.5	412.4	5.6
Northern Cape	73.9	283.3	8.3
Northern Province	9.6	306.5	1.5
North West	18.3	212.1	3.3
Free State	34.7	344.2	5.3
Western Cape	77.3	476.2	23.2

Table 9.3   Source: Department of Health 1995

HEALTH CARE FACILITIES IN SOUTH AFRICA				
	PRIVATE SECTOR		PUBLIC SECTOR	
PROVINCE	Hospitals	Clinics	Hospitals	Clinics
Eastern Cape	10	3	95	614
Mpumalanga	19	3	29	146
Gauteng	78	44	34	443
KwaZulu-Natal	31	3	69	179
Northern Cape	14	0	32	44
Northern Province	4	0	43	322
North West	17	4	37	298
Free State	14	7	33	254
Western Cape	30	10	61	304

Table 9.4   Source: Department of Health 1995

Life expectancy at birth by province, 1991	
Eastern Cape	60.7
Mpumalanga	62.4
Gauteng	66.0
KwaZulu-Natal	61.6
Northern Cape	62.7
Northern Province	62.8
North West	59.7
Free State	61.9
Western Cape	67.7

Table 9.5

Source: Department of Health 1995

patients, with the exception of children under 15 and pregnant women, pay for examinations and treatment on a sliding scale in accordance with their income and number of dependants. If an individual or a family cannot pay they will still receive treatment.

A major problem facing South Africa is the spread of HIV/Aids. There has been an explosion in the number of people who are HIV positive in many countries in Central and Southern Africa since the 1980s, but in South Africa the virus is a relatively new arrival. The ending of South Africa's isolation in the post-apartheid era has led to its rapid spread.

It is estimated that 2.4 million people are infected with HIV. Since 1991 the percentage of HIV among pregnant women has rocketed from 1% to a startling 14%. (See Figure 9.7.) The government is aware of the problem and has set up an Aids Unit and an educational awareness programme. The extent of the problem is partially concealed by attributing death to other diseases. South Africa is currently undergoing an epidemic of tuberculosis—in 1995 over 3,000 people died from this disease. However the statistics fail to indicate that over a quarter of TB deaths are related to HIV infection.

The challenge facing South Africa is to maintain its worldwide repu-

PRIMARY HEALTH CARE

The Primary Health Care programme offers a comprehensive range of services delivered by health professionals and associated organisations such as school and nutritional services along with water and sanitation services, both of which have an obvious connection to health.

The strategy embraces health education, nutrition, family planning, immunisation, screening for common diseases, HIV/Aids education and counselling, maternal and child health, oral health and the provision of essential drugs.

Projects such as the National Primary School Nutrition for needy primary schoolchildren have improved educational achievement as well as health standards. Every day more than 5 million children in over 12,000 schools munch on a 'Mandela sandwich'. This has increased attendance at school and improved concentration and alertness levels.

Immunisation against tuberculosis, whooping cough, diphtheria, polio and measles is available free of charge to all children under the age of six.

tation for specialist care while providing quality basic (primary) care for the millions of South Africans, especially in the rural areas, who are denied proper treatment and services. South Africa annually spends 6.4% of its Gross National Product (GNP) on health care. This is above the 5.5% recommended by the World Health Organisation as sufficient for health care expenditure. Part of South Africa's problem is that resources and health personnel are concentrated in the wealthier provinces and that there

is an imbalance in provision between the races.

The fact that maldistribution rather than an actual shortage of doctors, nurses and dentists is the main problem can clearly be seen in Table 9.3. There is a heavy overconcentration of health personnel in Gauteng and the Western Cape. This inequality in provision is also evident if we look at health care facilities and life expectancy. (See Tables 9.4 – 9.5.)

Already standards of care in former white hospitals are suffering from a massive influx of black patients. The realities of poverty, poor diet and primitive sanitation place a tremendous burden on the over-stretched Health Service.

Racism Lives On

The fine line between protecting one's language and culture and open racism disintegrated in the village school in Potgietersus, situated in the Northern Province. The Afrikaner school governors provoked a national outcry when they refused to admit black pupils in January 1996. White parents organised a daily vigil to ensure that the black children could not enter. Even when the action was declared illegal by the Constitu-tional Court, a hardline group of white parents held out. They set up a 'private' school where ten teachers taught the children in their spare time. They even attempted to take chairs and desks from the primary school but were forced to return school property.

On 11 March there was an arson attack on the school principal's office and this forced the provincial government to take control of the school. The government wished to send a clear message to other reactionary schools that it would not be possible to maintain white or Afrikaner state schools and that 'cultural rights' could not be used to maintain or to legitimise segre-gated schooling. The ruling of the Constitutional Court means that schools cannot refuse to admit any child on the grounds of "race, ethnic or social origin, culture, colour or language".

The Afrikaner parents claim that they are not racist. They say that

- Ten years of free and compulsory education for pupils aged 5 to 15 (to be phased in).
- A further three years of 'post compulsory' educa-tion when students will work towards a National Higher Certificate (target 2006 onwards).
- The expansion of early childhood 'educare'.
- A national adult basic education programme.
- Curriculum reform starting in 1994 (now 1998).
- A Higher Education Commission to consider the reform of university education.
- Upgrading the qualifications (and salaries) of thousands of teachers from disadvantaged communities.
- To address the acute shortage of teachers in rural schools through redeployment of staff.
- To work towards equal spending on white and black students.
- To reduce class sizes to a maximum of 40 in primary schools and 35 in secondary schools.
- To create a culture of learning and for schools to become centres of learning.

The RDP Proposals for Education

Standard 10 Matriculation Examinations

At first glance the results of the 1996 school leaving examinations were impressive. The pass rate for Blacks in many of the prov-inces had gone well above 50% and in some provinces such as Gauteng and KwaZulu-Natal the figures were over 60%. The worst results were in the Northern Province which only had a 38.7% pass rate.

However, it be-came clear that other factors had been taken into considera-tion and that an informal policy of positive discrimina-tion had been imple-mented in some of the provinces. Upward adjustments of marks were made for students coming from disadvantaged communities in an attempt to address the inequalities between the races.

The Department of Education recom-mended a figure of 10% upward adjust-ment as being appro-priate.

Inevitably the Whites, Coloureds and Indians, while accepting some standardisation, were concerned that this could lead to a lowering of standards and that it was further evidence of preferential treat-ment for Blacks.

they only wish to protect the Afrikaans ethos of the school. The demographic reality of South Africa haunts the Afrikaners. At present the language of instruction is decided by parents and the community. In the short term Afrikaans will be used

in Potgietersus Primary. However, as more black pupils are admitted the day will surely arrive when the white children will be the minority. What future for Afrikaans then?

A new history of South Africa

In January 1998 schools started to introduce a new curriculum which will sweep away the values and traditions of the apartheid system. The emphasis will be on a culture of learning with schools becoming centres of learning.

The new curriculum will be phased in over six years, starting in the first years of primary and secondary schools and then moving up the levels until all years are covered. This staggered approach allayed the fears of teaching unions worried over workload and in-service training issues.

The new curriculum will focus on what pupils can do and on their levels of understanding at the end of the course, rather than on acquiring a specific body of knowledge. The History curriculum has been rewritten. The detailed history of white settlers has been reduced and the history of the pre-colonial natives, the San and the Khoikhoi, included. The new textbooks will include the struggle against apartheid and its ultimate overthrow.

Education

The legacy of Bantu education, described on page 52 creates a major challenge for the Government of National Unity. It faced the initial problem of having to dismantle fourteen separate education systems, replacing them with a National Department of Education and 9 Provincial Education Departments. Education and training are crucial in the creation of economic prosperity. There is a shortage of skilled and highly educated black workers, yet an abundance of poorly educated, unskilled Blacks who face a lifetime of formal unemployment.

The goals of the Reconstruction and Development Programme are being implemented, albeit over a more realistic timescale. The creation of a culture of learning, a new curriculum, investment in new classrooms and resources and an upgrading of teaching standards are all central to improvement. Racism is still a problem (see 'Racism Lives On') as is the alienation of many young Blacks as evidenced by their poor matriculation results.

Painful adjustments have to be made by the white community. The target of reducing class sizes to 40 in primary schools and 35 in secondary schools will, in the long run, have an impact on all state schools. Staffing levels will be funded on these figures, thus benefiting the overcrowded black schools which will gain more teachers. The mixed schools (formerly white) will have to shed staff and increase class sizes. In theory, the surplus teachers will go to schools in the townships or in the rural community. However, the imbalance is also between provinces and most teachers will not be prepared to move house and live in another province or in areas of multiple deprivation. Although equal spending on black and white pupils will be ensured, the question arises, where will the teachers come from?

A second issue has also infuriated the teaching unions. Salaries in South Africa are dependent on qualifications and while 100% of Whites have the minimum new standards, only one-third of black teachers fall into this category. The government solution is to accelerate black qualification through open learning courses and recognition of prior achievement. This will ensure an increase in salary for black teachers. The shortage of highly qualified Blacks in industry (with the resultant high salaries) makes a career in teaching a poorly paid option. The best qualified Blacks are eagerly recruited by the business sector on a salary which is double that which they could earn as a teacher.

Land and Housing

The government is aware of the enormous task it faces in order to provide for its citizens adequate housing with access to decent services. In 1994 the late Joe Slovo, as Minister of Housing, said in Parliament that there was a total housing backlog of 1.4 million houses. Planact, a pressure group, estimates that countrywide about 13 million people do not have proper homes. The statistics provided by the October 1994 Household Survey highlight the racial divide. (See Figures 9.8 – 9.9.)

In the initial euphoria after the 1994 Election the government promised to deliver one million fully serviced brick and mortar homes over a five year period. This figure has been retained, but now extends over a ten year period with much of it being 'starter homes' rather than fully completed units. The government is prepared to work in partnership with the large construction companies, but recognises that many black South Af-

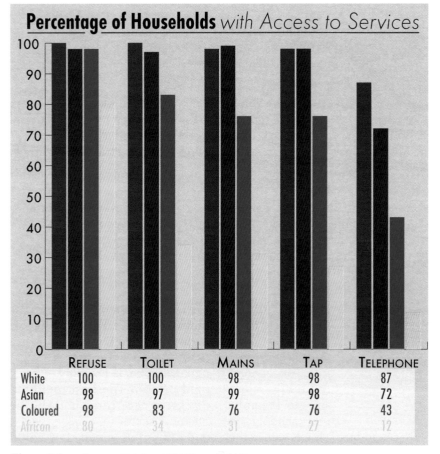

Percentage of Households *with Access to Services*

	REFUSE	TOILET	MAINS	TAP	TELEPHONE
White	100	100	98	98	87
Asian	98	97	99	98	72
Coloured	98	83	76	76	43
African	80	34	31	27	12

Figure 9.8   Source: October 1994 Household Survey

ricans do not have the financial means to acquire a house of their own. Financial institutions are willing to lend to low income families in return for mortgage guarantees from the government. The banks have pledged to provide 50,000 loans a year to low income groups.

Progress has been made in providing basic amenities such as electricity and running water. In 1995 Eskom linked up 3,000 homes in poor black areas to the national grid. The social impact is tremendous: little dwellings where schoolchildren huddled round woodburners doing their homework by candlelight have been transformed with fridges, television and electric heaters and lights.

A serious problem facing the government is how to end the culture of non-payment. One form of protest against the apartheid system was for black residents to boycott the payment of rent and amenities charges. The government claims that the climate is changing and

that, for example in Soweto, payment for electricity has moved from 20% to 65%.

Land reform, especially in the countryside, is a major issue. A new Department of Land Affairs was created in 1994 with the responsibility of developing and implementing a policy of land reform. The policy has seven main points.

● Compensation for those who lost their land because of apartheid laws.

● Redistribution of productive land to those who were disadvantaged.

● New land holding rights to be established.

● Compensation to be paid to those whose lands are redistributed through the Settlement/Land Acquisition Grant.

● Creation of an independent Commission on Restitution of Land Rights as well as a Land Claims Court. Any claimant will

have to prove that he or she was dispossessed after 1913 without financial compensation or alternative land being provided.

● The setting up of the Land Reform Pilot Programme to "establish mechanisms for state-assisted entry into the land market for the most disadvantaged sectors of rural society".

● The right for tenants to buy the land on which they farm and protection from eviction. This became an Act of Parliament in November 1995 despite opposition from the white farmers.

The Afrikaner farming community is also concerned about the attacks made on white farms. Since 1994, when the ANC came to power, the South African Agricultural Union (SAU) has recorded some 2,250 attacks on farms resulting in the deaths of 521 farmers and their workers. These attacks, according to the SAU, are not just the action of criminals but are politically motivated. Their aim is to drive the Whites from their farms in a campaign of terror. Some of the attacks have been particularly brutal and have included torture of the victims. Some of the assailants are reported to have boasted that they were members of the ANC's military wing, others that they belonged to the Azanian People's Liberation Army.

The Afrikaners are convinced that there is a coordinated black conspiracy to drive Whites from the land. Events in May 1998 reinforced this viewpoint when 80 attacks took place leaving 19 farmers and their families murdered. The government has reacted by setting up a Rural Safety Plan which promotes cooperation between local communities, the police force and the army. Inevitably the Freedom Front and the Conservative Party have made political capital out of the government's failure to protect the white farmers. The demand for an Afrikaner Volkstaat has been rekindled. (See pages 62 and 80.)

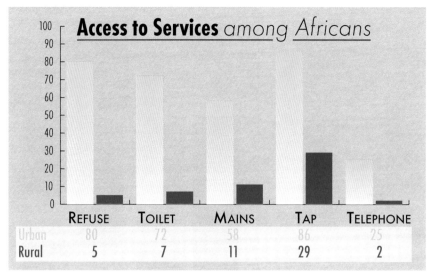

Access to Services among Africans				
REFUSE	TOILET	MAINS	TAP	TELEPHONE
Urban 80	72	58	86	25
Rural 5	7	11	29	2

Figure 9.9   Source: October 1994 Household Survey

The government's view is that there is no organised conspiracy against the white farmers. However, after years of harsh treatment at the hands of their Boer masters, a desire for revenge among dispossessed Blacks is one possible explanation. In 1998, a white farmer shot dead a black child who had wandered onto his property and this further increased tension between the races.

Urbanisation

One problem faced by all developing countries is the movement of people from the countryside to the towns. Since 1990 most towns and cities in South Africa have experienced a great influx of rural people. The situation has been worsened by the large number of illegal foreigners from Mozambique and Zimbabwe.

The three major metropolitan areas of Gauteng, Greater Cape Town and Durban account for 40% of the total population and 68% of the country's total manufacturing output. This influx of workers to these areas maintains the squatter dwellings and high crime rates.

The RDP set up 14 Special Integrated Projects on urban renewal to improve housing and basic amenities in selected areas such as Katorus in Gauteng.

EMPLOYMENT

Affirmative Action

South Africa has not passed legislation to compel employers or institutions to discriminate in favour of Blacks as happened in the USA through a policy of affirmative action. Nevertheless, through the creation of a directorate for affirmative action in the Employment Ministry which will "guide and monitor" progress in the hiring and promotion of Blacks, clear signals have been given that the employee profile in "each institution reflects the true character of our country".

The government gave a clear lead when it offered early retirement packages to its civil servants, who were predominantly Afrikaners. (All civil servants were guaranteed their jobs by the new government.) Most of the 11,000 'new' posts advertised were filled by non-Whites (a staggering 1 million non-Whites had applied). Business is eager to hire a proportion of Blacks at each level, but the problem is a shortage of highly educated black workers. The irony is that these new young managers can demand high salaries because of their scarcity value. The extent of the problem is illustrated by the fact that there are 14,000 white chartered accountants but only 65 black ones.

The policy has created some resentment among the Whites who claim that they are being discriminated against because of their race. They also argue that less highly qualified Blacks are leap-frogging their white colleagues. One example was a recent row over the appointment of a black adviser without a university degree to a well-paid civil service job which required a degree. White teachers are also concerned that the status of their profession is being eroded with the move towards equal salaries regardless of qualifications.

The Black Enterprise Culture

Adverts in the South African press show a smiling Cyril Ramaphosa, former General Secretary of the ANC and now Chairperson of Johnnic, a black controlled holding company, inviting the black community to "share our interest in beer, food, property and newspapers". The share plan has been marketed under an African name— Ikageng, which means self-developed. The aim of the National Empowerment Consortium, says Ramaphosa, is "to get people from historically disadvantaged communities to become more meaningfully involved in the South African economy." Small investors are able to pay the cost of buying 50 shares over three years with the hope that 300,000 Blacks will buy. Their target is people who have lower incomes.

Significantly, trade unions have participated in investment plans. The National Union of Mineworkers, of which Ramaphosa was once General Secretary, now owns a 5% share in Johnnic and over a dozen other unions control almost 15%.

From almost nothing, Blacks now control 10% of the Johannesburg Stock Exchange. To its supporters this is Black Empowerment; to its critics 'black enrichment'. Not only are Blacks investing in business, the white corporate world is desperate to have black faces in junior and senior management and in the boardroom. For the skilled and col-

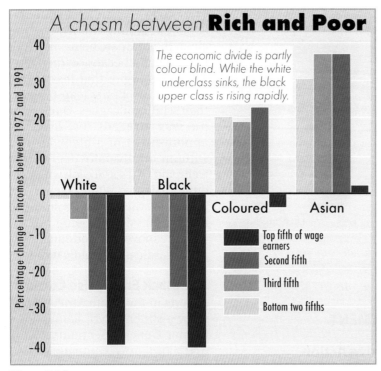

Figure 9.10

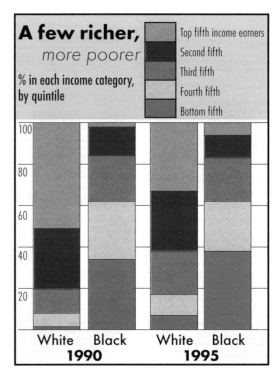

Figure 9.11

lege educated Blacks the sky is the limit in this new rainbow nation. The paradox is that while millions of unskilled Blacks are unemployed, there is a desperate skills shortage in South Africa. This is why education is crucial to the future development of South Africa with the Bantu education system being the culprit for the present tragic situation.

Black Flight from the Townships

Evidence of the emergence of a black élite can be found in the number of Blacks now living in the wealthiest suburbs of South Africa's cities. Houghton, the grandest suburb in Johannesburg, has among its growing number of black residents Nelson Mandela and former Regional Premier Tokyo Sexwale. There is even a new television comedy, 'Suburban Bill', about a black family which moves next door to a white one with mutual misunderstanding and confusion.

This emerging black middle class has enrolled its children in the schools in the suburbs rather than in the township schools. The loss of such talent, wealth and role models further impoverishes life in the townships. In America, through Affirmative Action Projects, this pattern has accelerated the further decline of the inner cities where drug barons and criminals have become the role models for the black youths. This could also happen in South Africa's townships. Mr Mugadi, the editor of the black magazine *The Tribune*, is aware of the impact of the flight of the black élite. One Sowetan wrote to *The Tribune* accusing "black yuppies" of "scurrying away into the comfort and safety of white suburbia" rather than using their talents "to liberate their people". However Mr Mugadi does not blame the black élite. "You can't glorify and have a sentimental attachment to the townships as if they were our creations: they were imposed on us by apartheid."

Soweto continues to have its 'Beverly Hills' and can boast that Winnie Mandela still lives there. Nevertheless, the majority of the new élite are leaving—black success means leaving the townships and comes at a cost to those left behind.

Poor Whites

The days when Whites, especially Afrikaners, were guaranteed full employment, a home and welfare as part of the package which came with being white, are gone forever. For the first time in 60 years poverty in South Africa has crossed the race barriers and white beggars are appearing on the streets. Whites are now competing against Blacks for low paid and unskilled work.

Poor Whites have also had to adjust to the influx of black families into what were once White only neighbourhoods. John Mbeki illustrates the advancement of the black, skilled workers. He has moved with his wife and four children from a squatter house and has bought a house in what was once a white area. As a turner and fitter, his prospects are better than those of many of his new neighbours. John is shocked by the way many poor Whites live, but he has little sympathy. As he states, "I suffered to get where I am, but for them there's no excuse. They've had all the opportunities. It's not that I don't feel compassion. It's just that it's our time now. They've had theirs."

It is of no comfort to the unemployed Whites that their present plight reflects the transition of South Africa to a more equal society. As Figure 9.10 shows, the Whites as a whole are getting poorer while an emerging black, coloured and Indian middle class is becoming significantly better off. This statement must be viewed in the context of South Africa being one of the world's most unequal countries.

Figure 9.11 confirms the continuation of black middle-class advance alongside the further impoverishment of unskilled Blacks. Between 1990 and 1995 the percentage of Blacks classified as being among the richest fifth of the country tripled from 2% to 6%; the proportion of Blacks in the poorest fifth of the population grew from 34% to 38%. Further evidence shows that recent economic growth has not led to an increase in jobs. The huge, mainly black, underclass is developing. Its statistics are depressing—17 million people out of a population of 34 million Blacks.

A growing white underclass is also emerging. The share of Whites in the bottom category increased from just over 1% in 1990 to 7% in 1995. In contrast, 51% of Whites belonged to the country's richest fifth in 1990, but this figure had fallen to 33% by 1995, reflecting the slow movement to a more equal society.

CRIME EXPLOSION

Crime used to dominate the conversation of the middle classes. However, it has become an issue of national importance for all South Africans with the publication of the latest crime statistics. It is now official that South Africa has one of the highest murder rates—87 per 100,000—in the world. (See Figure 9.12.) This amounts to 71 people being murdered every day in 1996. Car hijacking, rape and armed robbery are rife. This crime epidemic has serious implications for the political and economic stability of South Africa. As Ken Warren of the South African Chamber of Business states: "Almost without exception, visiting trade delegations and fact-

Major Crimes in South Africa

(per 100,000 of the population)

	1994	1996
House breaking	916.6	988.9
Car theft	440.4	456.8
Attempted murder	93.4	93.6
Murder	85.4	87.2
Common Assault	755.0	810.7
Arson	32.9	30.1

Table 9.6   Source: South African Police Services

finding missions pose the following question: 'How safe will my staff be in South Africa?'" When one adds the continuation of violence in KwaZulu-Natal—it is estimated that since the April 1994 Election over 1,800 people have been killed in political killings—then it is clear that South Africa faces a crisis.

In his February 1996 address to Parliament Nelson Mandela admitted that the cuts introduced to the police budget since 1994 had been a mistake, but he blamed the present crisis on the legacy of apartheid. The Police and Security Forces were identified in the past as agents of white domination and the whole ANC strategy in the 1980s and early '90s was to make the townships ungovernable. Organised rent boy-

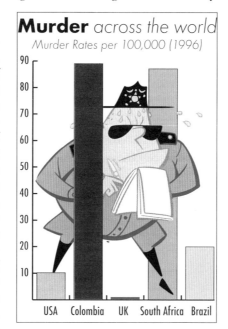

Murder *across the world*

Murder Rates per 100,000 (1996)

Figure 9.12

cotts and defiance of the police were badges of honour. While there is talk of white flight, the major problem is the influx of illegal immigrants sweeping into the country from the North and the appearance of organised crime syndicates from as far afield as Colombia. According to the ANC activist Sally Motlana, there are around 1 million illegal immigrants in Soweto alone.

All sections of society are affected by the rising crime rate—taxi drivers in Soweto have 'shotgun assistants' to protect them and their customers. Ironically, the Minister of Justice, Dullah Omar, had to leave his Cape Town home as it was situated in a high crime area. Corruption and inefficiency in the police force are high and there is little respect for law and order. In May 1997 the government admitted that of the 1,800 members of the police VIP protection service, no fewer than 198 were facing criminal charges, 22 of which were for murder. Vigilante groups have emerged, especially among the muslim community of Cape Town. In August 1996 PAGAD (People Against Gangsterism and Drugs) openly shot and set on fire a leading drugs gangster.

In May 1997 the government appointed Meyer Kahn, Chairperson of South African Breweries, to head the national police force. Prior to his appointment it was clear that the public were demanding action. Banks across the country closed for two hours as their employees marched in protest at the number of armed bank robberies—in a four month spell there had been 184 in which 14 people had been killed. A Johannesburg newspaper created a 'wall of remembrance' in the city centre. Within days it was covered in hand painted portraits of murder victims.

A 1997 survey by the World Economic Forum ranked South Africa alongside Colombia and Russia as countries in the grip of organised crime. The ending of an authoritarian regime in a society of vast inequalities has attracted hundreds of international criminal gangs which have flourished. The police force needs to be reformed with higher salaries and a higher calibre of recruit. A consultancy survey found extensive evidence of poor management. At one police station 80% of the police cars were unavailable for police duties. At another, a quarter of the police force was 'off sick' at any one time. At yet another, only one policeman in ten was out on the beat; the rest were doing 'administrative work'.

It is ironic that the law and order issues which dominated the 1994 Election, namely the fear over white extremists and over civil war in KwaZulu, have been overshadowed by the basic issue of social and political stability—the issue of crime and how safe are the streets. In order to attract foreign investment, to protect the value of the rand, to lessen the white flight and to retain the body politic of a healthy and confident society, law and order must be restored. This cannot be done in isolation but must be linked to the social and economic policies of the government.

WHITE FLIGHT

White flight is not simply the exodus out of the country—8,000 emigrated in 1996—it can also refer to the fortress mentality as many Whites move into self-contained high-security housing estates.

Organisations such as 'Opportunity Australia', a specialist emigration service founded in 1991, have expanded rapidly. For a fee of £1,500 this organisation promises to get Australian residence permits and to support people in their move. Its director claims that it sees about 500 prospective customers each week at the introductory seminars. (They are 100% Whites.) Debbie du Plessus is moving to Australia with her husband and two children: "We used to have the good life here," she said, "but not any more. The country has changed; it will never be the same again. It's hard enough for us to get a job now—imagine what it will be like for our children. All the jobs are for Blacks now."

The rising crime rate has created employment opportunities for the private security industry and the specialised builders. There are more private security guards in South Africa than there are officers in the 146,000 member South African Police Service. New housing estates like Mount Edgecombe outside Durban offer an "electrified palisade fence" which encloses the estate and "24 hour security and access control". Ronnie Van de Walt, a 41-year-old locksmith, sums up the frustration of the white community. "The government has no control. Ordinary people are living behind bars and criminals are walking the street. You tell me how this is right."

The Rainbow Government

THE EARLY YEARS 1994–96

This period marked the high point of cooperation between the National Party and the ANC within the Government of National Unity (GNU), a position which ensured political and social stability. The GNU's commitment to a mixed economy, combined with its policy of reconstruction reassured both domestic and international business communities. The guarantee of jobs to the mainly white civil service ensured that they would support and cooperate with the new black group of Ministers who had no experience of running a country.

One of the first major tasks for the Constitutional Assembly, under the leadership of Cyril Ramaphosa, was to prepare a new constitution which would come into force in 1999. Although de Klerk held the office of Deputy President and his Party had nine posts in the Cabinet, his influence on decision making was limited. The role of 'junior party' angered and frustrated the National Party. It became clear that it could not protect what it called the "cultural identity" of the Whites (although the ANC thought that these were "privileges").

Symbols of the new order were the demotion of Afrikaans to minority language status on the broadcasting services and the opening of rural white schools to all races. Prior to February 1996, the national state-owned television had offered to share time equally between English and Afrikaans and this decision was seen as an attack on the Afrikaans language. It had also become clear that Nelson Mandela, while agreeing to set up a Volkstaat Committee within Parliament, had no intention of supporting an independent Afrikaner Homeland (Volkstaat). The National Party had also failed to win any concessions during negotiations over the new constitution. Power sharing at the national level would not continue beyond 1999. Power would remain with the National Government, the nine provinces having limited powers. Furthermore, cultural identity could only exist within the concept of the Rainbow Nation and not as an excuse to maintain white privileges.

Relationships with Inkatha and Chief Buthelezi were especially difficult. Al-

Cyril Ramaphosa—architect of the new constitution

CENTRAL GOVERNMENT

EXECUTIVE

- President
- Deputy President
- Cabinet Ministers

PARLIAMENT (Legislature)

- National Council of Provinces
- National Assembly

Complimentary Institutions

Council of Traditional Leaders

Volkstaat Council

THE SOUTH AFRICAN CONSTITUTION
(adopted 1996)

PROVINCIAL GOVERNMENT
Nine Provinces each have a state government

EXECUTIVE AUTHORITY
- 9 Premiers
- 9 Executive Councils

LEGISLATIVE AUTHORITY
- 9 Provincial Assemblie

LOCAL GOVERNMENT

House of Traditional Leaders
(in 5 of the 9 Provinces)

THE SOUTH AFRICAN CONSTITUTION:

● maintains unitary government.
"The Constitution of South Africa shall provide for the establishment of one sovereign state, a common South African citizenship and a democratic system of government committed to achieving equality between men and women and people of all races."

● supports cultural identity.
"The diversity of language and culture shall be acknowledged and protected, and conditions for their promotion shall be encouraged."

● offers limited powers to the Provinces. The powers granted to the Provinces are to be used to improve the well-being of their inhabitants in accordance with the policies and priorities of the National Government.

Parliament

Parliament consists of a National Assembly and the National Council of Provinces. The Council plays two roles—that of an upper house and as a body with special responsibilities to protect provincial interests. Each provincial legislature appoints a delegation of ten to the National Council of Provinces.

Council of Traditional Leaders

Provincial governments have the right to set up a Council of Traditional Leaders (Tribal Chiefs) and these have been set up in the Eastern Cape, KwaZulu-Natal, Free State, Mpumalanga and the North West. In April 1997 a National Council of Traditional Leaders was set up. Each Provincial House of Traditional Leaders nominates three members to represent it on the Council.

Volkstaat Council

The Volkstaat Council consists of 20 members elected by the MPs who support the establishment of an Afrikaner Homeland (Volkstaat). In 1996 it made its submission on self-determination for the Afrikaner people. It proposed an Afrikaner Homeland or majority area incorporating parts of Gauteng, North West, Mpumalanga and the Free State—1% of the total South African land surface.

Provincial Government

All provincial constitutions and laws must correspond with the National Constitution as confirmed by the Constitutional Court. Provinces have legislative powers over agriculture, cultural affairs, education except Higher education, environment, health services, housing, local government, police, traditional authorities welfare services, urban and rural development.

---

though Inkatha was a member of the Government of National Unity, it spent much of its time boycotting Cabinet meetings and the drafting of the new constitution.

APPROVAL OF THE NEW CONSTITUTION 1996

May 1996 was marked by the passing of the country's post-apartheid constitution and the end of the National Party's involvement in the Government of National Unity. The Party had failed to win any concessions and only voted for the new constitution after the ANC threat-

ened to call a national referendum if de Klerk vetoed the proposals.

De Klerk made the best he could of his Party's retreat from government. He was determined to set up

"a strong and vigilant opposition necessary for the maintenance and promotion of genuine multi-party democracy". By giving up its nine cabinet posts and the post of Deputy President in June 1997, the

National Party could begin to prepare an electoral challenge to the ANC in 1999. The difficult task of expanding its base among black voters was to become an impossible task when events unfolded in 1997 to weaken the National Party further .

While de Klerk condemned the new constitution as sounding the death knell for multi-party participation in decision making, and as "majority domination", the ANC were jubilant. Mandela addressed the Special Constitutional Assembly with the following words:

> "And so it has come to pass that South Africa today undergoes her rebirth, cleansed of a horrible past, matured from a tentative beginning and reaching out to the future with confidence."

Predictably, Inkatha's 48 Members of Parliament boycotted the occasion and 10 members of the Freedom Front abstained from voting. Inkatha were not to follow the ac-

tions of the National Party, however, and they remained in the Government of National Unity.

THE DECLINE OF THE NATIONAL PARTY

In August 1997 de Klerk resigned as leader in a futile attempt to enable the National Party to reinvent itself. The remorseless disclosures from the Truth and Reconciliation Commission (TRC) – see pages 84 and 86 – of government-sanctioned atrocities by de Klerk and his colleagues (despite their denials) had turned de Klerk into a liability. In May 1997 the National Party rejected the findings of Roelf Meyer (a Minister in the last apartheid government) whom de Klerk had appointed as head of a task team to redesign the Party for the future. Meyer's radical vision was for the National Party to disband and emerge within a new multi-racial party. Meyer left the Party and pledged to carry through his vision of a new political party.

De Klerk was praised by Mandela, attacked by white extremists and remembered by the world as South Africa's Gorbachev who began a reform process which swept him from power.

Significantly, Hernus Kriel who was the premier of the Western Cape (the only Province controlled by the National Party) did not seek the national leadership. The Kriel faction within the Party had been instrumental in the rejection of Meyer's vision of a new beginning. Kriel was content to retain political control at the provincial level and to preside over a province which is the success story of South Africa. Its economy reached a level of 6% growth in 1997, well above the national average of 2.5% and its unemployment figures were one-third of the national average.

FORMATION OF THE UDM

In September 1997 Roelf Meyer carried out his promise and announced the formation of a new political party, the United Democratic Movement (UDM), in part-

nership with Bantu Holomisa. The latter had been the military leader of the Transkei after he seized power in 1987. He won favour with the ANC by allowing the organisation to operate in his Homeland and his reward in 1994 was a senior position in the ANC executive and a cabinet post, Deputy Minister of Environmental Affairs. He heavily criticised some of his ANC colleagues for their extravagant lifestyles and for their delay in providing services for the rural areas. In 1996 he was expelled from the Party "for bringing it into disrepute with his unfounded allegations".

The slogan of the UDM is 'Convergence, Unification and Progression'. The Party has chosen policies which are popular with the electorate and which the government has failed to control, namely crime and unemployment. They wish a referendum on the death penalty— public opinion favours its reintroduction. While the new party might attract Whites and Coloureds who voted for the National Party but are not inspired by Marthinus Van Schalkwyk (de Klerk's successor) or those who supported the Democratic Party, it can only succeed by attracting the ANC's black supporters. The extent of the UDM's task can be judged by the fact that the electorate votes along racial lines— only 2.7% of Blacks favoured the three traditionally white parties and just 3.7% of Whites supported the ANC. In the short term the creation of another party can only weaken the opposition to the ANC.

THE DEMOCRATIC PARTY

Events in 1998 further weakened the National Party and even led to some political commentators questioning its future survival. High profile figures such as former Health Minister, Rina Venter, and one of the chief negotiators in the constitutional talks, Tertius Delport, left to join the Democratic Party. To add to the National Party's troubles, its Leader, Marthinus van Schalkwyk was investigated over a sex scandal.

The Democratic Party, under the dynamic leadership of Tony Leon, hoped to benefit from this decline and replace the National Party as the main opposition party after the 1999 General Election. Leon's strong criticism of the government's affirmative action policy and of the self-enrichment of many of the new African élite gave him a high national profile. The government responded by setting up a Commission under Judge William Heth to investigate corruption in public life. The Commission's early findings indicate that £2.5 billion of public money has been 'lost' since 1994.

The Democratic Party represents the white liberals who led the white opposition to apartheid and, therefore, retained the moral high ground. The end of apartheid enables white liberals to enjoy the privileges of their lifestyle without the guilt. They still have their black maids and their swimming pools. However, the 'Africanisation' policies of Thabo Mbeki and the rise in crime disturb their future. It is significant that the majority of Whites who are leaving South Africa tend to be English speaking. The Afrikaners regard themselves as Af-ricans with no home across the ocean. "We've trekked, we've fought and this is our country," sums up their attitude and determination. According to the Central Statistical Services (CSS) in Pretoria, 40,000 South Africans emigrated between 1994 and 1997.

DEMANDS FOR AUTONOMY

One of the great success stories in the new South Africa has been the acceptance by the Afrikaners of black majority rule and the recognition by many that an Afrikaner homeland is simply a pipe dream. Right-wing terrorism still exists. In December 1996 a series of bomb blasts killed four people in Worcester near Cape Town. While the far right movement could claim membership of 25,000 prior to the 1994 Election, four years on even the leader of the Boerstaat Party, Robert van Tonder, admits that 3,000 would be an optimistic figure. Eugene Terre Blanche, leader of the AWB, has been discredited after being found guilty of killing his servant.

The key to this change of heart has been the actions of Nelson Mandela and his policies of eco-nomic moderation and national reconciliation. Before the 1994 Election, white farmers such as Mannie Maritz were prepared for a last stand to rescue South Africa from certain ruin. The apocalypse never came. This white separatist regards Nelson Mandela as "an exceptional man". He admires, for example, the unifying effect of Mandela wearing a Springbok rugby jersey when South Africa won the 1995 World Cup.

While Mr Maritz would move to a volkstaat if one were created, he accepts that it is an unlikely dream. Along with his fellow Afrikaners he is determined to protect the unique culture of a special people. "We are not really a religion but a royal national group of a unique race," he declared. His goal and that of the Freedom Front (see page 62) is to protect the right of their children and grandchildren to be educated in Afrikaans. He supports the actions of the people of Orania (see below) and would like to see more communities such as this emerge.

The challenge facing Thabo Mbeki when he becomes President is to maintain the support of the major-

Apartheid survives in Orania

Apartheid lives on in Orania, an exclusive haven for Afrikaners who reject the new South Africa.

The Whites only town of Orania is situated in the vast open semi-arid desert of the Northern Cape. It takes a seven hour drive from Johannesburg to reach the isolated community of 500 inhabitants. One of its citizens is Tammie Verwoerd, the widow of the architect of apartheid, Hendrik Verwoerd.

Orania is a private community where the Afrikaners have an opportunity to ignore the realities of the new South Africa. The community is a former ghost town bought by the right-wing Freedom Front.

'Strictly private' warns a sign nailed at the entrance to the fenced town. The town museum displays relics of Afrikaner glory and the Boer flag of the old Transvaal Republic flies on top of the hill.

Life is frugal and harsh—there are no opulent houses, tennis courts or private swimming pools. Orania is self-sufficient and resourceful; its citizens grow their own food, clean their own streets, educate their children and worship together in the community hall. Orania has no black servants, gardeners or coun-cil workers to carry out the manual tasks.

Its citizens deny that they are racists. Lida Strydom Kontreiwinkel, a mother of three small children, and her husband John gave up their farm in Northern Natal because of the constant threat from thieves. "We were thinking of emigrating to Canada and then we stopped over in Orania. It was very peaceful. People did not talk about crime. We don't belong to the Freedom Front. I have three children and when they are so small you have to protect them." Lida and John now live in a caravan on the plot of land they bought to farm pecan nuts.

Annamaria Boshoff, an elderly lady, is happy to end her days in Orania and dreams of a Boerstaat. "I don't feel at home in the new South Africa. It's not my country any more. It's not our government, the culture is different, the religion is different. We can't have the whole country, that is impossible; we're too small a nation. We just want a country of our own."

Thabo Mbeki was born on 18 June 1942 in the Eastern Cape. His father, Govan, was a close comrade of Nelson Mandela and was in prison with him on Robben Island. The young Thabo joined the ANC Youth League at the age of 14. In 1962 he went into exile in Britain and took an Economics degree at the University of Sussex. This was followed by a spell in Moscow where he joined the Communist Party and underwent military training. On his return to Africa he went to Zambia where he became a prominent member of the South African Communist Party and Secretary of the National Executive of the ANC.

The death in 1993 of the national Chairperson Oliver Tambo and the assassination of Chris Hani enabled Mbeki to become the leader of the radical wing of the Party. With the support of Winnie Mandela, Mbeki became ANC national chairperson in 1993. He was appointed Deputy President in the Government of National Unity in 1994 and with the support of Nelson Mandela he drove his main rival, Cyril Ramaphosa, ANC General Secretary and Chairman of the Constitutional Assembly, into the political wilderness.

In 1996 Nelson Mandela began the transition of power by announcing that Mbeki would be in charge of day-to-day affairs. In December 1997 Mbeki inherited the leadership of the ANC when Mandela stepped down.

It will be hard for Mbeki to replace a legend and to maintain the nation building which was characterised by Nelson Mandela. Critics are concerned that he has ruthlessly removed his political rivals in the Party— Cyril Ramaphosa and Patrick Lekota in 1996 (Lekota was forced to resign as Premier of the Free State) and Tokyo Sexwale, the Premier of Gauteng, in 1997.

Despite his communist past, Mbeki is committed to a market economy and to work in partnership with private enterprise. He is aware that the patience of the black majority will not last forever but the present policy has restored international confidence and maintained the support of the non-Blacks. Mbeki with his radical past and connections represents both wings of the Party.

A DELICATE BALANCE

Thabo Mbeki is aware that he must tread the delicate line between black hopes and white fears. However, if a black rebellion is to be avoided he must improve the living conditions of the black majority over the next five years. Below is an extract of what he said in November 1997.

"The reality is that the legacy of Apartheid still defines present-day South Africa. The white population I don't think has quite understood the importance of this challenge ... If you were speaking of national reconciliation based on the maintenance of the status quo, because you did not want to move at a pace that frightens the Whites, it means you wouldn't carry out the task for transformation. You would not produce reconciliation on that basis. It might look so to the people who benefited from Apartheid—everybody's forgiven us, nobody's after our swimming pools. It isn't, because you have the anger that would be boiling among the black people. So, you've got to transform the society. Affirmative action isn't a philosophy, it's not an end in itself. It's an instrument to get to a more equal society, broadly representative of South African demography."

ity of the Afrikaners. The white extremists are waiting in the wings. Robert van Tonder is still convinced that an Afrikaner rebellion will take place. "The ANC bombed themselves into government and we will do the same," he declared. "The masses are out there just waiting to be mobilised. When they hear the call, they will rise up and help us reclaim Boer land for the Boer people. Whatever means are necessary, we will use them."

The escalated attacks on white farms in 1998 (see page 74) strengthened the Afrikaners' demand for a homeland. The constitutional arrangement of 1994 set up a Volkstaat Council to explore Afrikaner self-determination. However, its 1996 proposals were largely ignored by the government.

The Freedom Front proposes a modest Homeland in the Northern Cape in a semi-arid and under-populated corridor of land bordered by the Orange River in the North and the Atlantic Ocean in the Southwest. It wishes to expand and duplicate communities such as Orania and is buying land in this area to support its policy. While this will not create an independent Volkstaat, it would provide a limited form of self-determination and a home for the Afrikaner language and community. General Constand Viljoen recognises that the ANC government will never set up an

independent state for Afrikaners. Their long-term dream is that 500,000 Afrikaners will take part in the last 'Great Trek' into freedom and will thus escape from the hostile black world around them.

INKATHA

The period 1994–96 marked the continuation of ill-feeling between Chief Buthelezi and Nelson Mandela at the national level and the continuation of killings in KwaZulu-Natal. In the 18 months which followed the May 1994 Election, a thousand 'political' killings took place in the Province.

Inkatha supports a federal system of government with more power being given to the provinces. In February 1995, Buthelezi pulled his Party out of Parliament. He accused Mandela of breaking his promise that he would bring in foreign mediators to resolve the question of the status of Goodwill Zwelithini, the Zulu King. The boycott had a negative effect because it ensured that Inkatha had no input into the new Constitution which offers little devolved power to the provinces. Nevertheless Inkatha, unlike the National Party, did not resign from the Government of National Unity and remained in the Cabinet.

The Municipal (local government) Elections were finally held in July 1996 and the outcome confirmed the urban–ANC, rural–Inkatha split

in KwaZulu. In a 44% turnout, with both sides accusing the other of cheating and intimidation, the ANC gained control of cities such as Durban and Pietermaritzburg, while Inkatha retained control of the scattered villages and Kraals.

A precarious balance of power exists. Inkatha controls the Provincial Government and is responsible for schools, health, housing and public transport within the policy guidelines set down by the ANC in the Government of National Unity. There is now hope in KwaZulu-Natal that future disagreements between Inkatha and the ANC will be debated and resolved in the political arena. In 1996 a breakthrough took place when, after secret meetings, the two parties agreed to work for peace.

The National Party's withdrawal from the Government of National Unity enabled the moderates within Inkatha to soften Buthelezi's hard-line opposition to the ANC. Buthelezi had felt excluded from the relationship created between the National Party and the ANC both before and after the 1994 Election. Inkatha has remained in the Government of National Unity and the ANC has given the Party greater respect and consideration. This was reflected in the informal talks which took place between the ANC and Inkatha to try and agree an electoral pact for the 1999 Election.

CRY FREEDOM, CRY HONOUR

In the same week that Colonel Harold Snyman and four others at last admitted the truth that they had murdered Steve Biko, the nation finally honoured his memory twenty years after his death.

Nelson Mandela came to East London where Biko had been imprisoned to unveil a large bronze statue of Biko in front of the city's town hall and to rename the main bridge spanning the Buffalo River after him. The ANC

had finally acknowledged the crucial contribution which Biko and his Black Consciousness Movement had made to the fight for liberation. It was Biko's death in September 1977 which shocked the international community into action against South Africa.

George Bizos, the lawyer for the Biko family at the Truth and Reconciliation Commission, was unimpressed by Snyman's claim

that it was not their intention to kill Biko. "Torturing helpless detainees for the purpose of extracting information from them ... to the point that they finish up dead is not a political objective in any civilised society," Bizos told the hearing.

Unfortunately the ugly side of white racism surfaced with the statue being defaced by racist slogans only days after the official recognition. It is obvious that the extreme

right within the white community do not believe in reconciliation, justice and truth.

ARCHBISHOP DESMOND TUTU

In June 1996 Desmond Tutu, then 66 years old, retired after 10 years as Archbishop of Cape Town and head of the Anglican Church in South Africa. Tutu had played a central role in the fight against apartheid through his eternal optimism, good humour and determination. Faith, hope and charity were his watchwords. It was therefore fitting that Nelson Mandela appointed him Chairperson of the Truth and Reconciliation Commission charged with investigating and revealing the country's brutal past.

Desmond Tutu entered the ministry as a means of opposing apartheid. His spell at medical school ended when his parents could not pay the fees and so he became a teacher. "I was a schoolmaster for four years before they introduced Bantu Education (1957) ... I just couldn't collaborate with this dreadful thing." Consequently, Tutu entered the Church. In 1977 he was appointed as Secretary of the South African Council of Churches and in 1986 he became Archbishop of Cape Town. Thanks to his struggle against apartheid he became South Africa's most famous cleric.

Tutu is well aware of the criticism made of the Truth and Reconciliation Commission. He gently reminds his critics that the offer of amnesty was a central part of the 'peace settlement' achieved with the Nationalist Government. Tutu believes that standing up and admitting acts of atrocity is in itself a form of punishment. He also believes that many of the victims and witnesses have received restorative justice: "They have had the opportunity of telling their story and the nation is able to say we acknowledge your pain". He has shared the tears of the witnesses, bowing his head and participating in their grief. Nevertheless he is optimistic about the future. "Yes we have problems now but we are proud now that we can say we have a Government that we have chosen, we have a President who was elected by us. I have no doubt South Africa is a scintillating success waiting to happen."

VIEWS ON THE TRUTH AND RECONCILIATION COMMISSION

"Only by knowing the truth can we hope to heal the terrible wounds that are the legacy of apartheid. Only the truth can put the past to rest."
(Nelson Mandela)

"We were taught that the Blacks would subvert our culture and deny us the land our forefathers fought and died for. We believed that our cause was just and we believed our leaders. Where are our leaders now?"
(Greg Deegan, former police officer)

"I want to find out just where my husband is buried, even if it's just his remains, even if it's just the ashes or the bones."
(Ncediwe Mfeti, whose student husband disappeared in 1987)

"I am a Christian. One day every man will have to kneel before Him in judgment. I will kneel before nobody else."
(PW Botha, former President, explaining his refusal to appear before the TRC)

"The truth is going to hurt."
"Some say 'let us forget the past', while others say 'we want revenge'. We are saying we do not want to forget, but we do not want revenge."
(Desmond Tutu)

"Some see the amnesty process as letting the killers off the hook. One critic said it would be awful to see Steve Biko's killers go free. Free of what? They will be forever tainted."
(Donald Wood, white liberal and friend of Steve Biko)

At the local level there are still acts of violence carried out by local warlords, but these reflect the violence common to all parts of South Africa.

THE TRUTH AND RECONCILIATION COMMISSION, 1997–98

In January 1997, the 17 members of the Truth and Reconciliation Commission, chaired by Desmond Tutu, finally held its first session in the Eastern Cape. As its title suggests, the purpose of the Commission was to create unity and reconciliation rather than simply to achieve justice. In its 18 months of activity the Commission aroused much controversy. Many convicted and suspected killers achieved freedom simply by admitting their guilt and by claiming their crime was a political act.

The widows of black heroes such as Steve Biko and Chris Hani felt betrayed by the Commission and demanded justice. Other ordinary people had an opportunity to share their grief with the nation and to discover what had happened to their loved ones. The perpetrators of the evil acts were forced to relive their 'crimes' and to face the spotlight and condemnation of a nation. Ordinary Whites could no longer pretend that apartheid was simply a bad system which made 'mistakes'. The hearings, aired on television, shocked and horrified the nation. The revelations damaged the National Party and created 'a crisis of faith' among some of its members. (During the hearings de Klerk resigned as Leader of the National Party.)

The remit of the Commission was to establish as complete a picture as possible of the "causes, nature and extent of the gross violation of human rights committed between 1960 and 10 May 1994." The first phase of the Commission during its tour around South Africa was to hear the accounts of victims of atrocities and to offer modest com-

pensation. This phase also included general investigations and spokespersons for the political parties were invited to participate. De Klerk admitted endorsing "extraordinary" measures against the ANC during the 1980s but denied rubber-stamping murder, assassination or any other criminal activity.

Thabo Mbeki, representing the 23 strong delegation from the ANC, stated that the struggle for liberation was a just war. He admitted that the ANC had been guilty of gross human rights violations which he described as the "excesses" of the struggle. The ANC's submission came in two volumes, over 300 pages long, with names, dates, times and locations of incidents, abuses and atrocities including 34 executions.

This phase was followed by a rush of applicants, already found guilty by the courts and with nothing to lose. Colonel Eugene de Kock, who had been found guilty of six charges of murder, appeared before the Commission, admitted his guilt and then accused senior members of the security forces and leaders of the National Party of being involved in secret operations to 'destabilise' the ANC right up to the 1994 Election. While the courts had acquitted Magnus Malan, the former Defence Minister, along with 17 of his colleagues of carrying out acts of murder, it was clear that the evidence freely brought by de Kock, Coetzee and others conflicted with de Klerk's version of history in which he said that he had never authorised "assassinations, murder, torture, assault or the like".

The amnesty applications of Clive Derby-Lewis and Janusz Walus who killed the ANC leader, Chris Hani, in 1993 created the greatest controversy. The wounds inflicted by the murder were still too fresh for the Hani family to contemplate a release from jail for these individuals. Derby-Lewis explained to the Commission that their act was a

political one—a deliberate attempt to undermine the peace process and to precipitate a civil war. (It should not be forgotten that Hani's popularity in the townships was second only to Nelson Mandela's.)

The investigation into the death of Steve Biko was even more significant. Most of the applications for amnesty had been made either by people already convicted or by security police who could argue that they were acting on orders. In this application, the security policemen voluntarily confessed to having killed Steve Biko. They had come forward to avoid possible legal charges. (See page 84.)

The appearance of Winnie Madikizela-Mandela before the Commission in December 1997 attracted the attention of the international media. A procession of her ex-friends and foes appeared before the Commission to testify against the Mother of the Nation and to accuse her of a reign of terror in Soweto township during the late 1980s. The former 'coach' of the Mandela United Football Team, Jerry Richard, who was now serving life imprisonment for Stompie Seikei's murder, declared to the Commission, "I killed Stompie under the instruction of Mamie (Winnie Mandela). She never killed anyone but she did give instructions to kill a lot of people."

Over the five days of evidence, former supporters told the TRC that she had ordered at least six murders and had herself assaulted a pregnant woman during her reign of terror. When Winnie Mandela took the stand she displayed no remorse, only denial and defiance. The evidence presented against her was "pure fabrication" and was part of the campaign engineered by the apartheid regime to discredit her and was now being used by a faction within the ANC to destroy her political career. She left the hearings surrounded by her supporters and acting as if she was the victim, not the perpetrator of evil acts.

WINNIE MADIKIZELA-MANDELA

In March 1995, when Winnie Mandela was sacked by her then husband Nelson Mandela from the Cabinet, she defiantly stated that "this is not the South Africa I ruined my life for". Her comments struck a chord among the black majority who supported her accusations that the Government was bending over backwards to reassure business, investors and the white minority. To many in South Africa, Mamie Mandela is the Mother of the Nation and represents the voice of the downtrodden and impoverished residents of the townships, especially the country's disaffected youth.

Her involvement in the murder of Stompie Seikei, accusations of corruption and evidence of her extravagant lifestyle may have damaged her political career but they have had little impact on her popularity among the ANC rank and file. During the township unrest prior to the collapse of apartheid she supported the 'young comrades' in their actions against the security forces and collaborators. In a controversial speech she seemed to support the brutal excesses of the 'young comrades' when she declared, "Together, hand in hand, with our boxes of matches and our necklaces, we shall liberate this country." After the death of Chris Hani in 1993, Winnie Mandela and the radical wing of the ANC gave their support to Thabo Mbeki and ensured his election as Chairperson of the Party. Her hatred of Cyril Ramaphosa was one factor in his retirement from politics. With Thabo Mbeki the heir apparent and next President of South Africa, Winnie Mandela set her sights on the post of Deputy Leader of the Party. Her appearance before the Truth and Reconciliation Commission weakened her political credibility. However, the legend of Winnie Mandela will ensure that she will play a 'wild card' role in South African politics and will continue to offer an alternative economic policy.

While the ANC leaders have moved to the white suburbs, Winnie remains in her Soweto villa, close to her people. She has turned her former home in Orlando, West Soweto, into a museum and is selling little bottles of 'Heroes' Acre' soil from the garden to tourists. The certificate which accompanies the bottled soil modestly states: "It was from this house where she led the resistance struggle that would ultimately liberate a nation." In her own words, "This is where it all happened."

1934	Born in Bizana, Transkei.
1956	Qualified as country's first black social worker.
1958	Married Nelson Mandela.
1964	Nelson Mandela's life sentence marked the beginning of Winnie's 27-year campaign to free him and of her persecution by the security forces.
1969-70	Placed in solitary confinement.
1976	Declared a 'banned person'—in force until 1986.
1977	Banished to Brandfort in the Free State, 250 miles south of Soweto.
1986	Returned to Soweto, exile over.
1989	Involved in the death of 14-year-old Stompie Seikei who was killed by her chief bodyguard, Jerry Richard.
1990	Nelson Mandela freed; Winnie appointed head of ANC's social welfare department.
1991	Winnie sentenced to six years for kidnapping and assaulting four youths abducted by her bodyguards, the 'Mandela United Football Team'. After appeal, she was granted a suspended two year sentence.
1992	Officially separated from Nelson Mandela.
1994	Nelson Mandela elected President. Winnie in Cabinet as Deputy Arts and Culture Minister.
1995	Dismissed from the Cabinet for her criticisms of the Government. Her home raided over housing corruption inquiry.
1996	Divorce of Nelson and Winnie Mandela.
1997	Winnie Madikizela-Mandela re-elected as President of ANC Women's League.
1997	In December appeared before the Truth and Reconciliation Commission and denied any involvement in acts of murder and brutality including the death of 14-year-old Stompie Seikei in 1989.

Winnie Madikizela-Mandela and her lawyer pray at the Truth and Reconciliation Commission hearings into charges that she was involved in the murder of young black activists.

The outcome was less than satisfactory. "We have heard lies, half-lies, half-truths, the whole spectrum," said a frustrated Deputy Chairman of the Commission, Alex Borame. The Commission's final judgment on all its deliberations was to be published at the end of 1998.

The ANC was not prepared to wait for this. Sports Minister Steve Tshwete called her "a liar and a wayward political charlatan". Her appearance before the Commission weakened her political credibility and it was no surprise when she announced that she would not stand for the post of Deputy Leader of the ANC at the December 1997 Party Conference.

Further controversy occurred in January 1998 when P W Botha, the last hard-line apartheid President, was threatened with prosecution and a possible jail sentence if he refused to appear before the Commission. He declared, "I have nothing to apologise for and I have nothing to be ashamed of. I was fighting against communists, anarchists and terrorists. I believe I contributed towards developing this country. Why should I apologise?"

THE ANC TODAY

The ANC is a broad organisation made up of Christians and communists, trade unionists and free marketeers, tribal chiefs and town councillors. All were united in the past by their opposition to apartheid, and in the present their unity springs from a determination to build a new South Africa based on justice, reconciliation and prosperity. In such a grass roots organisation, it is important that the leadership maintains strict discipline and control.

While it is an over-simplification, two distinct factions can be defined within the ANC. The Rainbow National majority are committed to economic growth through private and public partnership, whilst the minority Africanist group led by

President Nelson Mandela

Winnie Mandela wish to see greater state intervention and redistribution of wealth.

1997 PARTY CONFERENCE

This was an emotional conference as it marked the first stage in Nelson Mandela's retirement from political life. He stepped down from the post of President of the ANC. Candidates for three of the top four posts were elected unopposed, showing the strength of unity and discipline within the Party. Thabo Mbeki was elected President, Jacob Zuma as his Deputy and Kgalema

Mothanthe as General Secretary.

The appointment of Jacob Zuma was significant. He is a Zulu and counters arguments that the ANC is Xhosa dominated. Zuma played an important role in bringing peace to the troubled KwaZulu-Natal province in 1996. Mr Mothanthe gave up his post as General Secretary of the National Union of Mineworkers. The one surprise was the election of Patrick Lekota as Party Chairperson. His political future had seemed to end when he was forced to resign as premier of the Free State in 1996. Mr Lekota had criticised some of his colleagues for their extravagant lifestyle and this explains his popularity within the rank and file of the ANC. Lekota's political comeback has delighted those in the Party who are unhappy with the style and policies of Thabo Mbeki.

Nelson Mandela's Farewell

In a five hour marathon, Mandela delivered an aggressive speech which condemned "the enemies of change". He warned the delegates that the revolution was not over and that sinister forces were bent on undermining South Africa's young democracy. He attacked the media, big business and the opposition white parties. Whites were too complacent and suffered from a collective delusion that they had done enough by "allowing majority rule". He declared: "Whenever we have sought real progress through affirmative action, the spokespersons of the advantaged have not hesitated to cry foul, citing all manner of evil—such as racism, violation of the constitution, nepotism, dictatorship, inducing a brain drain and frightening foreign investors."

TRANSFORMATION POLITICS

The new mood among Blacks is that the shift of power which has occurred in the political field must cover all aspects of economic and social life. Control of the media, the universities, the stock exchange and industry must, in the long run, be in the hands of the majority. Affirmative Action is one mechanism which can be used to redress the balance. Even Desmond Tutu is critical of the white response. He has also criticised three multi-national oil companies—Shell, BP and Mobil—for their close links with the former apartheid government. Archbishop Tutu wishes these companies and others to admit responsibility and to make reparations. "It would be wonderful if representatives of these business giants would say they wished to donate, say R10 million to the President's Fund which seeks to aid the victims. It would go a long way to showing you want to be part of the healing process," he told businessmen.

"Four years after they elected a government our people still wake up in their shacks with no services of any sort. They go to work mainly for white people in nice houses with clean water, lights and salubrious circumstances. And at night they return to squalor. … The white community at this moment is doing a great deal of moaning about the state of South Africa. I say to them, 'What have you done to promote reconciliation?' "(Desmond Tutu)

One public corporation, Eskom, the state owned power supplier, apologised in November 1997 for its actions during the apartheid years. It admitted it had been discriminating and had done nothing to improve the plight of Blacks.

There is a strong feeling within the ANC that big business should contribute to economic reconstruction. Professor Terre Blanche, a professor of economics, has claimed that several corporations "grew spectacularly rich working hand in glove with the apartheid government". He has proposed that a wealth tax be levied for the next 20 years on those corporations with assets worth more than R2 million.

The People's Republic of China

11

China is the third largest country in the world, by area, after Canada and the Russian Federation. It is bordered by eleven countries. The 1,133,682,501 citizens of China (1990 census) make up one-quarter of the world's population, making it the most populated country in the world.

China is important because of its economic potential. It has deposits of most minerals including oil and gas and it is the world's biggest coal producer. The Chinese work force is the largest in the world. China has the potential to overshadow the economy of any other country, both as a consumer and as an industrial producer.

It is the largest remaining communist controlled country and its military might is awesome in terms of both nuclear weapons and a large conventional force. One of the permanent seats on the UN Security Council is occupied by China and it has influence well beyond its own borders.

China is a society undergoing great change. In the 1970s, factions within the leadership of the Communist Party of China (CPC) became acutely aware that economic

A TIME LINE OF CHINA'S HISTORY

2 AD	China counts 57,671,400 people in its first recorded census.
1086	China now has 108 million people governed by an elite bureaucracy chosen by competitive examination.
1215	Genghis Khan takes Yanjing (Beijing). His grandson Kublai rules all China by 1279.
1618	Manchu begins invading. Manchu Dynasty established.
1762	China has 200 million people.
1911	Wuchang uprising in SE China spurs 17 provinces to form a provisional government at Nanjing.
1912	Republic of China formed.
1921	Communist Party of China (CPC) formed.
1943	CPC makes the 'Long March' to Yenan to escape Nationalist Party (NP) or Kuomintang (Kt).
	On this march, Mao develops his ideas of revolution based on the rural peasants not the urban working class.
1949	Renewed civil war between CPC and Kt. Mao's victory leads to the establishment of the People's Republic of China.
1953	Mao launches first 5 year plan: boosts heavy industry but fails to increase farm productivity.
1958	Great Leap Forward—a disastrous attempt at collectivised agriculture. 30 million people die of starvation.
1966	The Great Proletariat Cultural Revolution seeks to purge 'revisionist' thought. Education suffers as schools are closed and intellectuals are sent to labour communes.
1976	Mao dies. The Gang of Four are arrested and put on trial.
1977–8	Deng Xiaoping, a moderate, consolidates power and becomes leader. Emphasis on Four Modernisations.
1979	USA establishes diplomatic relations with China.
1982	Population over 1 billion (1000 million).
1989	Protests in Tiananmen Square.
1997	Deng Xiaoping dies. Jiang Zemin becomes leader.

The People's
Republic of China

500 km

0   500 Miles

and social pressures might undermine and destroy their control. For this reason they embarked on reforms which involved loosening economic and social controls in the country while retaining their strong political grip.

By the late 1970s, the CPC had largely organised the provision of basic housing, health, food supplies, clothing etc. to the population. However, the people were now ready to demand a standard of living beyond the basics. If this was not forthcoming then it was feared that discontent would develop and threaten the leadership role of the CPC. The Chinese economy there-

fore had to be modernised in such a way that political control was maintained.

To understand events in modern day China it is important to place them in the context of its history.

History and background to Modern China

The political development of modern China has been influenced by four main factors. Firstly, it had a long history of centralised government dating back 3,000 years. This led to a second factor, the legacy of a social system which stressed working together and obedience rather than individualism and de-

mocracy. Thirdly, the lack of individualism prevented innovation which resulted in continued economic backwardness and the poverty of a mainly agricultural country. Finally, the backwardness of the country left it open to external pressure and invasion in the 19th and 20th centuries and to external influences and ideas.

To maintain its belief in its own superiority China became an enclosed society, refusing to allow western influences to intrude. The social structures remained rigid. Throughout the latter half of the 19th century and the early 20th century China's society came under

THE IDEAS OF COMMUNISM

KARL MARX

MAO ZEDONG

The philosophy (ideas) of communism were developed by Karl Marx, a 19th century German philosopher. Marxist theory states that the flow of history is inevitable. All countries pass through certain stages of economic, social and political development.

The initial stage is feudalism. Agriculture is important and land—"the means of production"—is the basis of wealth. Landowners have the economic power in the country and hence have political and social control over the peasants. Eventually industry will develop and become more important than agriculture. New groups will emerge. Capitalists own the industries—"the means of production". The peasants move to the cities to become an urban proletariat (the workers). After a struggle the capitalists replace the landowners as the ruling elite in the country. This is the capitalist stage of development.

As the capitalist state develops, the capitalists become extremely wealthy and the proletariat live in poverty. As the gulf in wealth increases, the proletariat realise that they are being exploited and finally overthrow the capitalists to take control of society. This final and ultimate stage of social development is communism in which all wealth will be evenly distributed and there will be no class distinction—a classless society. According to Marx this is inevitable.

Marx predicted that the first countries to experience communism would be the most advanced industrial countries in the 19th century such as the UK and Germany, but in 1917 Russia was the first country to undergo a Communist Revolution. It was led by Lenin who was a follower of Marx. Lenin argued that, with strong leadership and control from the Communist Party, Russia could by-pass the capitalist stage and move directly to the classless communist society. This was called Marxist-Leninist theory. The Chinese version of communism is a variation of Marxist-Leninist Theory.

MAOISM

Mao Zedong adapted Marxist-Leninist theory to suit conditions in China. He believed that the revolution would start in the countryside as poor peasants rose in revolt against the oppression of their landlords. Mao built up support in rural areas and established his People's Red Army whose job it was to lead the peasants in dealing with the landlords. In areas under their control, the Red Army established rural soviets (peasants' groups) to run affairs. This was to form the basis of Chinese communism. On 1 October 1949 the People's Republic of China (PRC) was proclaimed with Mao as its leader.

As the USSR (Russia) was the first communist state, it was used as the model to build communism in China. Initially, therefore, China concentrated on large-scale industrial projects to build up the country's strength. However, by the mid-1950s Mao had begun to develop his own model of communism based on the peasants.

MAO'S MASS LINE

Mao's Mass Line was his political model for the development of China. This tried to take account of the ideas of the population in China. The masses were to be led by the Communist Party which would be a strong, well-disciplined organisation, responsive to the ideas and wishes of the masses and accountable to the masses for its actions in an on-going process. It would take the thoughts of the masses and concentrate them into usable ideas for running the country and the government. These would then be given back to the people as Communist Party policies.

This process was meant to produce continual change in the running of China. Government policies would be relevant to the peasants' needs and would always be able to adapt to changing circumstances in China.

increasing pressure from countries such as the UK and the USA. The illusion of superiority was destroyed and the structures of Chinese society were undermined. External forces produced internal stresses and China's final dynasty (Manchu) was overthrown in 1911.

A number of organisations with a variety of ideas for reform began to emerge.

The years from 1911 to 1949 were a period of conflict between competing groups influenced by foreign ideas. The CPC eventually emerged victorious and introduced a new political system based on the ideas of Marxism-Leninism with a peculiarly Chinese twist. They imposed this new system on a society which had a long tradition of respect for authority and group control.

Politics in China

China functions as a one-party state in which all aspects of social, economic and political life are dominated by the Communist Party of China (CPC). The CPC provides ideas and leadership and oversees the work of the government. The structure of the government is laid out in the Constitution.

THE CONSTITUTION

Since the establishment of the People's Republic of China in 1949 the country has seen 4 different constitutions—1954, 1975, 1978 and 1982. The 1982 version of the constitution was revised in 1993. Apart from outlining the government structure

Primary Party Organisations (PPOs)

PPOs are set up in farming communities, factories, offices—in fact any place where there are more than 3 members of the Communist Party. Their job is to implement the decisions of higher Party Organisations, "guide and supervise" work places and pass on any reactions to Party directives. They are the eyes, mouth and ears of the CPC at local level.

County/Provincial Organisations

Above PPOs, CPC organisations can be found at every 'regional' level such as county (xian) and province (sheng). They have their own structure similar to that of the CPC nationally—congress, secretariat and standing committee.

National Congress of the CPC

This is, in theory, the highest organisation of the CPC. Members are elected to it from the lower organisations. The Congress should be held every 5 years but, in practice, terms have varied. The last one was in September 1997. There are about 2,000 members and it is really just a showpiece. It is supposed to elect the Party's Central Committee and approve any policy changes. However, any decisions it takes have already been approved by a higher authority. The main concern of the Congress is to generate good publicity.

Central Committee

This is elected by the Party Congress and meets at least twice a year. It has about 300 members who are mostly male and elderly. Its main jobs are to elect the Politbureau and to ratify policy decisions.

Politbureau

This is the 'cabinet' and is effectively in day-to-day charge of the country. It is composed of about 20 members who are elderly and experienced and who also occupy high positions in the state government and the military.

The Standing Committee of the Politbureau

Within the Politbureau there is an 'inner cabinet' called the Standing Committee. It is composed of 6 leading CPC officials including the CPC General Secretary (the Party's official head) and the Prime Minister. This group exerts overall control. The positions of greatest authority in the Chinese government are those of Prime Minister and General Secretary of the Party. Overall authority rests very much on the personalities of the individuals who hold these posts.

Secretariat

This is an adjunct to the Politbureau. The four members operate under the CPC's General Secretary. It provides administrative backup and support and plays a key role in formulating policies.

it also "guarantees the fundamental rights of every citizen, including the right to vote and stand for election, the freedoms of speech, of the press, of assembly, of association, of demonstration and of religious belief." It also states that, "the People's Republic of China is a socialist state under the people's democratic dictatorship led by the working class and based on the alliance of workers and peasants."

These two extracts appear to contradict each other. The first extract

THE STRUCTURE OF GOVERNMENT

State Council

National People's Congress

Provincial People' Congress

County People's Congress

Rural/Town People's Congress

The Great Hall of the People

Although the CPC dominates policy in China there is a parallel state structure of government which is in charge of the more routine work of administration. The state structure mirrors the CPC structure but it is the Party which controls the state organisations. There is some intertwining of the CPC and state structures.

Local People's Congress

In each province, county, town and rural area people over 18 vote for candidates for the local People's Congress. Voting is by secret ballot and the number of candidates standing exceeds the number of places available. The elected candidates then go on to vote for deputies to be sent to the higher level congresses. These Congresses each have a smaller group called a People's Council Standing Committee which carries out the day-to-day administration. These groups follow instructions from higher state councils and from Party committees.

The National People's Congress (NPC)

In theory, this is the Parliament for China and the highest organ of power. Elected for a term of 5 years, the 3,000 delegates meet at least once a year for 1 to 2 weeks to ratify policies and elect the President (a ceremonial post), the Vice President, Prime Minister and State Council members. In practice, the NPC is a 'rubber stamp' group which follows the wishes of the CPC.

State Council

This is the administrative cabinet and is composed of department ministers and other dignitaries with the Prime Minister (Premier) at its head. The State Council is the leading executive body in the state structure. It is in charge of day-to-day management of the country. It meets once a month but has an 'inner cabinet' of 14 who meet more frequently.

People's Courts

The state structure also includes the judiciary consisting of the Supreme People's Court, local People's Courts and special People's Courts such as military courts. A formal court system is fairly new to China. Since the 1978 Constitution was written, the Chinese system has moved towards developing a judicial structure which is recognisable to a western ob-

server. For centuries, order was the responsibility of the family, the neighbourhood and the local government. Courts were interested in understanding the reasons for an individual crime in an attempt to get redress for the victims. Procedures were alien and informal compared with those of foreign legal systems.

In civil cases the leading authority in an area would act as mediator. After 1949 this meant the local Communist Party officials. They were called on to resolve disputes, divorces, family arguments and minor thefts. This gave the CPC an enormous insight into, and influence over, the Chinese people.

Criminal cases at a higher level were often tried rapidly and went unreported. Trials effectively rubber stamped a criminal's predetermined guilt. People brought to trial were not given the opportunity of a defence because their guilt had already been decided after interrogation. All the accused was allowed was an admission of guilt. Public trials were held, but the function of these was to be instructive for the Chinese people.

describes "freedoms" and "fundamental rights" guaranteed to every citizen in China, but the second extract uses the phrase "dictatorship led by the working class." The official Chinese interpretation of this is that democracy is practised within the ranks of the people while dictatorship is exercised over the enemies of the people who are the masters of the country. In effect, the people of China can enjoy their wide-ranging "freedoms" and "fundamental rights" within the limits laid down by the CPC. These limits may vary from time to time.

The structures of the CPC and the state government and the relationship between the two (see pages 93 – 94) show how the CPC maintains its "democratic dictatorship".

THE PEOPLE'S
LIBERATION ARMY (PLA)

The PLA played an important role in the victory of the CPC between 1934 and 1949. It has retained its political significance ever since. It was 4 million strong in the 1970s and is still the largest army in the world with 3 million soldiers. A programme of modernisation has turned it from an ill-equipped peasant force into a well-equipped professional organisation.

However, the PLA is more than a fighting force. It has developed a wide network of businesses. There are 10,000 registered military enterprises producing everything from tanks to toothbrushes. Although originally intended to make the army self-reliant, 70% of the output of PLA-owned enterprises are consumer goods for the civilian market and for export. One PLA division enterprise trades as China North Industries Corporation (Norinco) and makes such diverse products as window glass, contact lenses, motor cycles and buses.

It is reported that the PLA made US $5 billion from its civilian enterprises in 1993. The process of restructuring the Chinese economy has enabled the PLA to become involved in a wide variety of joint venture operations with foreign investors and, it is reported, in several illegal enterprises. In Guangdong, the army owns many hotels, bars, discos etc. as well as illegal brothels and gambling dens.

The vast incomes generated by these enterprises are encouraging corruption on a grand scale. They are also creating a huge divide between the officer corps who are making large fortunes and the low paid ranks. Officers who are involved in business are diverted from studying the art of war. This, along with growing dissatisfaction in the ranks means that the PLA is not as efficient a force as it might be. Public respect for the PLA, which was once held in high regard, is rapidly diminishing.

THE CPC AND
THE GOVERNMENT

Political power in China is dominated by the Communist Party of China (CPC) which controls the government structure. At each level of the government structure almost all personnel are members of the CPC. At the lower levels a few government officials are not members of the CPC but they are approved by the CPC.

The most powerful organisation in China is the CPC's Standing Committee of the Politbureau which takes the final decisions on policy. The rank which someone has in this group determines the power and influence they enjoy. Yet power is not always apparent. For example, until his death in 1997, Deng Xiaoping was still considered to be the most powerful man in China although he had held no official position since his 'retirement' in 1989. Another example is the new Prime Minister Zhu Rongji. Zhu replaced Li Peng as Prime Minister but ranks behind him on the Politbureau. So Li Peng, who is no longer Prime Minister, remains more powerful than Zhu Rongji who has become Prime Minister.

The People's Liberation Army on display

Figure 12.1

THE COMMUNIST PARTY OF CHINA

The CPC is organised as a hierarchy. (See page 93) It is controlled from the top down through a system known as *democratic centralism*. This means that policies are meant to be democratically debated during their formulation stage but, once agreed, they must be implemented with disciplined obedience. Belief in the leadership and total support for policies is mandatory. Anyone who publicly questions their superiors, or a policy once it has been decided, is swiftly silenced.

Membership of the CPC is strictly controlled. It has always remained below 5% of the population. Each cadre (individual member) is carefully selected and has to serve a probationary period. In democratic countries, political parties are broad-based, mass movements which try to encourage as many people as they can to become members because they are attempting to win or retain power. However, the CPC already has total control over the government of the country and does not need to seek a mandate from the people to form a government. It claims to have the 'leading role' in guiding the people of China to their socialist goal. Therefore only those considered by the Party as worthy to participate in this 'leadership role' may be invited to join.

The leadership role was restated by Jiang Zemin's report to the 15th National Congress of the Communist Party on 12 September 1997 when he said, "Only the Communist Party of China can lead the Chinese people in achieving victories of ... socialism ... making the country prosperous and strong and improving the people's well-being."

Although, the Party remains fixed in its grip on power, it is not necessarily viewed with the reverence it would like by the mass of the Chinese people. Its separate structure for communication, command and discipline means that it operates as a secret and closed society. Its meetings are closed to non-members and information is a privileged secret for members only. The CPC ensures the promotion and advancement of its members and therefore earns the resentment of non-members. Some join the CPC because their jobs depend on membership, while others join because they want the connections.

Those who are cultivated for future membership or those who actively seek membership to secure their personal advancement are often despised by their fellow workers and neighbours. They are shunned for their toadying and for reporting on their colleagues and acquaintances. Aspiring members often face harassment. In one state-owned factory it was reported that the workers "didn't hate the Party leaders as much as the Party activists who reported on them." (Walder, *Communist Neo-Traditionalism*). In retribution, activists were 'sent to Coventry,' beaten or had their clothes burnt by their fellow workers.

Membership of the CPC is by invitation only which means that the current members control who can join their closed society. It is also riddled with nepotism, cronyism and factions. Those in authority seek to ensure that their friends and relations are advanced through the ranks to positions of power and influence. Their continuing authority may depend on ensuring that their faction retains control of power within the Party. Each member of the Politbureau has the support of the Party leaders in the province s/he came from or s/he would not have gained and kept a seat on the top body. Much of this goes on unseen.

Struggles between factions and groups are usually not obvious to the wider world. Those who carefully study the CPC may see subtle changes in the role or prominence of an individual or a group. Who is making an important speech or who appears to meet a foreign visitor? Whose name is suddenly being reported in the newspapers or who has ceased to be mentioned? Who has been given some medal or honour? Which minor officials are being promoted? These may be the only visible signs of a significant shift in the balance of power between the Party factions. Occasionally, though, power struggles do spill out into the open.

The most famous occasion was when Mao Zedong unleashed the 'Great Cultural Revolution'. He and the ultra-left group, 'The Gang of Four', used the PLA to rid themselves of political opposition and to secure their position and power. This struggle continued for 10 years until Mao died and a faction led by Deng Xiaoping was successful in removing the Gang of Four from their positions in the CPC.

Another glimpse of this in-fighting appeared after Deng died in 1997. It was between a faction led by Jiang Zemin, the Party General Secretary, who had been chosen by Deng as his successor, and critics from the moderate and liberal areas of the Party. They used the name of Zhao Ziyang as a focus for their cause. Zhao had been the General Secretary and Deng's favoured successor until 1989, but he was removed and placed under house arrest because of his sympathy for the protestors in Tiananmen Square.

Jiang Zemin led a group called the Shanghai-Jiangsu faction who took a conservative approach to the development of democracy in China

Chinese President Jiang Zemin casts his vote at the ninth National People's Congress. The NPC re-elected him to a second five-year term by an overwhelming 98% of the vote.

and the process of economic change. Zhao was reported to have written a "Letter to the Politbureau and the Preparatory Committee for the 15th Party Congress" in which he stated that the CPC had made a mistake in its handling of the events leading to the massacre in Tiananmen Square. The letter also accused Jiang of trying to reintroduce and fill the post of Party Chairman which Deng had abolished in 1982. The letter charged that to give so much power to a "core figure" in the Party was "contrary to the teachings of Deng Xiaoping, Mao and Lenin". The letter was, therefore, an attack upon Jiang and his faction.

The official CPC view was that the letter was an invention of the overseas media but it was worried enough to send out a document to high ranking and middle ranking Party officials refuting the accusa-

tions and trying to contain the damage. The People's Liberation Army and the police were also put on high alert in urban areas. Jiang was significantly worried by Zhao's influence and he refused him permission to attend Deng's funeral.

Since 1997, Jiang has consolidated his grip on the levers of power in China. He was able to achieve a balance of power among the Party's major factions and build a solid power base by introducing his supporters into the Politbureau and into the regional Party organisations. He secured the allegiance of China's military establishment through his chairmanship of the Central Military Commission. His position will depend on his management of the various factions within the CPC. There are also signs that the economic changes are undermining the power and influence of the CPC.

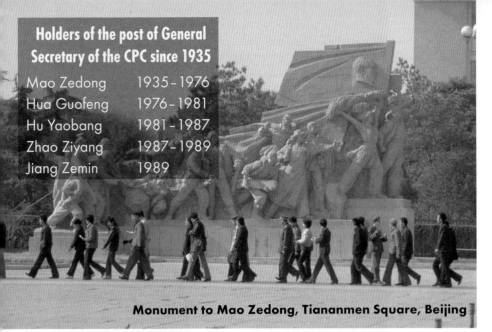

Holders of the post of General Secretary of the CPC since 1935

Mao Zedong	1935–1976
Hua Guofeng	1976–1981
Hu Yaobang	1981–1987
Zhao Ziyang	1987–1989
Jiang Zemin	1989

Monument to Mao Zedong, Tiananmen Square, Beijing

Collective leadership

Mao Zedong and Deng Xiaoping at the height of their powers had total control. They ruled without reference to any of their colleagues on the Politbureau. In 1980, Deng wrote *Regulations on Political Life in the Party* which stated that the Party was to be run in the future by a collective leadership and warned against the dangers of "the authoritarianism of one person." In 1982, Deng abolished the post of Party Chairman to indicate his opposition to the personality cult. After his death, Deng planned to hand over power to a collective leadership rather than to an individual.

In 1997, the Central Committee of the CPC issued a document which demanded that Party cadres at all levels should rally "tightly around the leadership with Mr Jiang as its core." This appeared to go against Deng's intended legacy of a collective leadership. 'Core status' implied that Jiang was more important than the other members of the Standing Committee. This 'core status' was the basis on which the Zhao letter criticised Jiang and the Party leadership for the direction the Party was taking. The moderates and the liberal wing of the CPC criticised the idea of a 'core' figure as being against the transition of power proposed by Deng and Mao. This, linked to the accusations that Jiang was trying to reinstate and occupy the post of Chairman of the Party, left him open to the accusation that he was trying to become the supreme authority in China with same power as Mao or Deng.

Despite the Chinese economy opening up to the world, its Communist leaders remain as secretive as ever. Those who study China closely agree that the CPC is in deep crisis. "Ideologically bankrupt, sapped and corrupted by the capitalist reforms it has set in motion, but held in place by a huge security apparatus, the Party commands fear but no adoration. Even its supporters believe its credibility is so low and the problem so daunting that it could be swept away within a decade."

One Beijing office worker is quoted as saying: "Communism is something the leaders use as a tool to unify the country. No one believes in it any more. People in their thirties grew up and believed in communism Chinese-style; now people in their twenties don't. Before, you had to join the Party if you wanted a good job or a house. All you need now is to know how to make money."

"The Party may be a dazed and ailing dragon but it can draw on reserves of strength and its claws remain razor sharp." In other words, the CPC may be struggling to convince the Chinese people that it continues to have the right to retain its central role in leading them towards socialism when, increasingly, they have no actual interest in socialism. Nevertheless, the CPC continues to command the means of control—the People's Liberation Army (PLA) and the police as well as the media. The rewards which power brings are too great for the CPC to give that power away so it will fight with all the means at its disposal to retain control.

However, Party members also say that time is short. Ning Sao, a professor of political science at Beijing University who has been a member of the CPC for 20 years, says that over the next 10 years "if the Communist Party solves its problems, its position will remain. If not, it will be removed."

Some analysts suggest that the Communists could reinvent themselves as a nationalist party, similar to the Kuomintang. This would give rise to an authoritarian regime promoting stable economic growth and forceful foreign policy but also carrying out some political reform from within.

The unease felt by the Party leadership over their control of the country is reflected in the changes which have occurred in the police over the past few years. Since Tiananmen Square the People's Armed Police has grown from 600,000 to over one million and it is set to double in size over the next few years. This is due to the growing social unrest in the country and the unwillingness of the PLA to become involved in internal unrest.

Increasingly, there are incidents of civil unrest and internal disturbances caused by economic and social change. There are several groups in China whose existence causes instability. There is a very large group of poor peasants who have seen their living standards fall. There are government workers in health and education who similarly have suffered from inflation and fixed wages. Then there is a large and growing number of unemployed workers in the coastal cities whose numbers are swollen by a large influx of poor migrants from the countryside seeking to improve their living standards. These people are increasingly desperate and angry.

It has been made clear that the PLA can only be used for "national defence". In other words they will only defend China from external threats. The PLA had difficulty in organising the assault on Tiananmen Square in 1989 because local units were unhappy at being ordered to fire on citizens from their own province. Troops had to be brought in from outside Beijing and this was one of the reasons for the delay in clearing the square. The use of 300,000 troops at that time caused a great deal of debate and controversy in the army and the commanders took the decision that their forces would not be used in the future to deal with internal disturbances.

The leadership of the CPC therefore had to set about building up the paramilitary police to deal with internal disruption. There has been a rapid increase in police manpower and equipment and they are controlled directly by Jiang Zemin through his chairmanship of the Central Military Commission. In this way the CPC has built its own heavily armed defence organisation to maintain its grip on power and its control over the people.

MAIN POLICIES OF THE CPC

The current Party line (basic policies) of the CPC was outlined in Jiang Zemin's address to the 15th Party Congress in September 1997 and was given the heading of "building socialism with Chinese characteristics." It involved establishing and developing a set of principles and policies covering "the economy, political affairs, foreign affairs, education, science and technology, cultural affairs, military affairs, the motherland's reunification and Party building." Through this process the CPC has been forced to depart from its initial ideals and take on capitalist methods. Yet it has maintained that these methods are a natural progression of socialism. This means

that it has had to change its philosophy to accommodate changing circumstances.

Economic Development

In the economy the 'central task' was economic development which involved altering the control and management of state controlled industries and continued the process of opening up China to foreign investment and trade. (See Chapter 13.)

Political Affairs & Democracy

The main tasks in political affairs "... are to develop democracy, strengthen the legal system, separate government functions from enterprise management, streamline government organisations ... and maintain stability and unity."

The CPC announced its intention of improving the system of democracy by holding democratic elections and making policy decisions "in a democratic manner" in order to extend "the scope of democracy at the grass roots". The system of People's Congresses would be improved and closer links would have to be established between the deputies and the people they represent. Democracy would be advanced by "ensuring that the people enjoy rights and freedoms endowed by law" and by "respecting and guaranteeing human rights."

These announcements are viewed with a great deal of scepticism by the Chinese people themselves.

Deng Xiaoping said, "when you open the window, some insects fly in." He was describing the opening up of China to the world with the introduction of market reforms. This process had allowed some 'nuisances' to be introduced into China and amongst these was democracy. Jiang's reference to the introduction of democracy at the grass roots level was a way of damping down disquiet at home and for the benefit of the international community. It was for appearance rather than reality and cannot be seen as a major shift in policy. Although the statement was "widely hailed overseas as signs of political reform in China", any actual change would be cosmetic.

Elsewhere in Jiang's address to the 15th Party Congress he said, "It is our Party's persistent goal to achieve socialist democracy...It is imperative that we should uphold and improve this fundamental political system, instead of copying any western models. This is of decisive importance in upholding leadership by the Party and the socialist system and realising people's democracy." In other words, there is to be no change. "Democratic centralism, instead of being weak-

Hong Kong is one of the world's most dynamic economies. In the early 1990s, its world trade was approximately double the value of China's. It has well-developed trade and transport links with China. Macao enjoys the same advantages but to a lesser extent.

ened, must be improved and developed."

It will not be a surprise that there is no sign of the CPC having any desire to extend democratic involvement beyond the limited experiments at village and town level. Indeed, there is every indication that they wish to keep things very much under their control as the case of Zhao Ghangqing reveals. Zhao tried to run for office in the local elections in 1998 but was arrested and charged with "endangering national security". Zhao had been a student demonstrator in 1989. He wanted to stand at the local elections to represent the factory for which he worked but the management of the plant said he was not qualified to stand. After a detention which lasted for a month he was released, but was promptly laid off from his job. Then he was arrested again.

"The peaceful reunification of the motherland"

The CPC wanted Hong Kong, Macao and Taiwan back under the control of Beijing and it has devised policies and strategies to have them returned. Hong Kong was handed over in 1997 because that was the end of the UK's lease on the colony. It was a peaceful hand-over because China saw the economic advantages in assuring the entrepreneurs of Hong Kong that there would be limited change. This was the policy of 'one country, two systems'. The Chinese government implied that the people of Hong Kong could carry on with a largely capitalist system while the rest of China continued along its socialist road. Macao is expected to be handed back under similar arrangements in 1999.

Taiwan is a more difficult problem. It has been a successful country with a powerful economy and has a strong ally in the USA. For years the USA used Taiwan as a military base in the Cold War and has forged a special relationship with the country. China has attempted to threaten Taiwan with military ma-

China has made a great deal of effort to change its role in world affairs. From the isolation of the 1960s and 1970s, China has become an influential player in international diplomacy. It has developed a new relationship with the United States and with neighbouring countries. Criticism has been made of its trade with Iraq and of its sale of nuclear material and weapons to countries like Pakistan and Myanmar (Burma). Nowadays it has a much more involved approach to foreign relations and takes far more notice of international criticism than previously. For example, in preparation for the visit of the President of the USA to the country it released some dissidents from long prison sentences and sent them to the USA in order to win over public opinion.

In the past, China has made threats and used hostilities as a means of extending its influence over its neighbours. It invaded and occupied Tibet in 1959—an event which China described as 'liberating' the country. Hostilities

China's Foreign Policy

developed between China and India in 1962 and with Vietnam in 1979 and in 1988. These events have caused many countries in the region to be suspicious and frightened of China's power and intentions.

Currently, China is pursuing a more diplomatic and friendly approach throughout the region. Its change in policy is a consequence of its wish to improve the economy. Jiang Zemin said in 1997 that "foreign affairs … (have) … created a favourable international environment for us to concentrate on our modernisation drive." China has successfully developed trading links with Japan, South Korea and several other neighbours it once considered to be major capitalist en-

emies. A number of senior Chinese leaders have toured the region stressing China's interest in trade and making no reference to territorial claims which were made previously.

In the past the USA, along with other large capitalist economies, has used the issue of human rights to criticise what China represents and to restrict the development of trade. China's open door policy has provided many potentially profitable economic opportunities. The USA at first insisted that China would have to improve its human rights record before the US would grant 'Most Favoured Nation' status to China. Eventually the US government was forced to accept that free trade might be better than sanctions in the long term for securing an improvement in human rights, so it granted China the same trading rights as other nations. The reality was that other trading nations were becoming involved in the vast Chinese market and US companies were in danger of losing out. China's policy of using its economic potential as a diplomatic carrot has paid dividends.

noeuvres on the nearby mainland and in the narrow straits which lie between the two. The USA has helped Taiwan by showing a military presence in times of crisis. However, the Chinese are playing a long game. They will not invade the island unless they can be assured of victory. This means isolating Taiwan from the USA and making relations with China of far greater importance to the USA so that it will not interfere if China ever tries to take over the island.

It also involves cultivating economic integration with the island. Much trade is routed indirectly through Hong Kong and Korea because Taiwan and China do not have direct trade relations. There is a considerable minority of the Taiwanese population who favour integration with mainland China. China is willing to wait, but it would be infuriated by the recognition of the independence of Taiwan by its inclusion as a full member of the United Nations.

Socialism with Chinese Characteristics

The CPC has adapted its basic philosophy in response to changed circumstances. It is switching from the command economy model introduced in the 1950s to a capitalist economic model, but it does not admit it. Instead it describes the economy as "socialism with Chinese characteristics". The leadership argues that Mao's achievement was to use the command economy model to lay down the necessary foundations for the Chinese economy to develop. They also claim that Deng's changes were not changes of direction towards capitalism but a progressive development laid on Mao's foundations. The "socialism with Chinese characteristics" is a socialist approach not a capitalist approach because of how it is managed.

Jiang, in his address to the 15th Party Congress in 1997, said that China "must keep to public ownership as the foundation of its socialist economic system" but that it must "develop diverse forms of ownership" to meet the "three favourables." (The three favourables are increasing production, developing China's strength and improving living standards.) "The joint stock system is a form of capital organisation … which is favourable for separating ownership from management and raising efficiency. It can be used under both capitalism and socialism." "We cannot say in general terms that the joint stock system is public or private for the key lies in who holds the controlling share."

Jiang therefore has altered the philosophy of the CPC to accept the joint stock system which is effectively the basis of capitalism. However, he now claims that the joint stock system is socialist and therefore not at odds with the basic philosophy of the Party. While Deng said that it did not matter whether the cat was black or white as long as it caught mice, Jiang is now saying that the colour is irrelevant because both cats are socialist anyway because of who owns them.

The Party has to ensure that every change of direction it makes appears to be part of its progression towards socialism. If the Party was ever to admit that it was in any way departing from the socialist road then its lead role in guiding the masses would be undermined and its autocratic position would be difficult to justify.

PROBLEMS FACING THE CPC

The CPC is aware of major political problems as it enters the 21st century. The Party is fully aware of the serious spread of corruption throughout the organisation and the power this gives to local officials. It is also aware that dissidents continue to question various aspects of its control and provide a focus and voice for discontent in the population at large.

Corruption in the CPC

In order to secure the loyalty of local Party officials and the military, the CPC has allowed each local Party boss, each department of the government and each unit of the armed forces the right to go into business for itself. Army units own discos, local Parties own property etc. In effect, these enterprises are run by the officers and the Party bosses, who negotiate contracts and keep the profits.

The system is closed—for CPC members only. The Party is able to siphon off vast amounts of wealth from the rapid economic development of the country and it is therefore a perfect opportunity for corruption. This is a source of anger and unrest among many of the ordinary Chinese citizens who are denied access to this wealth and who suffer from hardships as a consequence of the economic changes. The CPC remains firmly in control of the government, the military and the media, but it is losing credibility with the people in China because of this rampant corruption.

The CPC is attempting to take steps to deal with the corruption and to make itself appear more honest to the citizens of China. *The People's Daily* stated that "Corruption is the big problem which the Party faces." Jiang also addressed the problem of Party corruption at the 15th Party Congress. "The fight against corruption is a grave political struggle vital to the existence of the Party and the state … We should continue to make sure that leading cadres (Party members) are clean, honest and self-disciplined, investigate and deal with major cases and rectify unsound practices …"

Recently, the Party has recruited younger cadres and has publicly dealt with corrupt officials. In 1995, Chen Xitong, the Beijing Party chief and Politbureau member, was dismissed for running a corrupt administration. He was among 18 senior officials accused of embezzling as much as US $2.2 billion from city funds. Party cadres in Beijing also began to man a telephone hot line to take complaints about sloppy housing repairs, sanitation difficulties, shoddy goods and other problems.

With the problem being so deep-rooted it is very difficult for the CPC to deal with it. On the one hand, the Party must retain the support of its cadres and the armed forces. Should it lose their loyalty it would run the risk of fragmenting and losing power. On the other hand, if it allowed the corruption to continue unchecked it would risk a build-up of resentment and opposition from the Chinese people. Tiananmen Square illustrated that resentment can lead to dangerous levels of public opposition to the CPC.

Political Opposition

Democracy is alien to the political history and culture of China. In the West, democracy is seen as an essential element in binding the people of a country together into a free nation. Our western concept of democracy, in which separate parties with individual political programmes compete with each other for the votes of the electorate to get their turn to put policies into practice, is a totally alien concept to the Chinese people.

Traditionally, China was a union of provinces and regions, each with its own identity based on its separate language, tradition, food etc. Chinese people see themselves as members of communities based on their provinces of origin. They do not claim to be Chinese but to come from Beijing or Sichuan or Shanghai. Throughout history, these provinces were ruled by local warlords. Control by the centre was

Other Chinese political parties:

Chinese Revolutionary Committee of the Kuomintang
about 40,000 members

China Democratic League
about 105,000 members

China Democratic National Construction Association
about 50,000 members

China Association for Promoting Democracy
about 50,000 members

China Peasants' and Workers' Democratic Party
about 40,000 members

China Zhi Gong Dang (Party for Public Interest)
about 10,000 members

Jiusan Society
about 40,000 members

Taiwan Democratic Self-Government League
about 1,000 members

strong or weak depending on the relative strengths of the provincial leaders and the leadership in Beijing.

The concept of a national identity only began to develop with the communist takeover in 1949. The CPC developed a strong, centralised system but this did not replace the provincial focus of the people. Within the CPC, the struggle for power at the centre is based round

provincial factions vying with each other to control the Party. The concept of democracy binding China together has never taken root.

Although China has eight other political parties in addition to the CPC, these parties, which are collectively known as the democratic parties, do not exist in opposition to the CPC. They are members of the Chinese People's Political Consultative Conference (CPPCC) and, "together with the CPC, they share a policy of long-term coexistence" and "mutual supervision." They do not have separate political programmes to offer to the Chinese people, neither do they seek to build a mass membership to replace the CPC as the governing party. They work alongside the CPC and share many of its aims.

In 1997, a letter was sent to the democratic parties saying that the policy of "long-term coexistence and mutual supervision" would be "unswervingly upheld and the multi-party cooperation system under the leadership of the CPC will be adhered to and improved."

The power of the provinces

There are several pressures building in China which could severely weaken the control of the centre and drive the provinces apart. In Xinjian province, in China's north west, there are between 20 and 30 million Muslims. There are pressures for greater independence in this province and the Beijing government is worried that the area might seek independence from China. This is a wealthy province because there are large oil deposits. For that economic reason alone, Beijing wants to retain control over it. However, Beijing also wants to increase its trade and investment links with Muslim countries in central Asia. It therefore wants to avoid a crackdown on the Muslims in Xinjian.

Another problem is the economic and social divide which is emerging between rich and poor provinces. Regions with powerful local economies such as Guangdong,

Chinese people see themselves as members of communities based on their provinces of origin. They do not claim to be Chinese but to come from Beijing or Sichuan or Shanghai.

Sichuan, Yunnan and Fujian have already gained wide-ranging powers to conduct their own economic affairs. Now that economic power has been devolved to the provinces the pressure is building to devolve political power.

The economic changes have already shifted power to the provinces and increasingly there are reports that Party bosses in rich provinces are issuing orders which contradict decrees which have come from the central Party authority in Beijing. In the past, individual Party cadres were loyal to the Party and its leadership, but the tradition in China is to have allegiances to the province from which one comes. If there is a dispute between the two, bonds of loyalty are stronger to the provincial Party and its leadership than to the Party as a whole. The growing autonomy of local Party bosses means that Party cadres have become more loyal to these local bosses on whom they depend for access to promotion, influence and wealth.

The special relationship which Hong Kong enjoys will encourage other provinces to seek similar arrangements. If one area can be given a special relationship then why not all regions?

As the number of wealthy middle-class non-Party members continues to increase they will eventually demand more political freedoms. Chinese citizens are increasingly coming into contact with western business people, investors and experts who regularly visit China. They will learn how these people can influence governments to enhance their wealth and status. The Chinese middle class will want these political freedoms to give them the same advantages.

Foreign news and information services will also provide more information than the Beijing government can control. Satellite television, as well as international radio stations, will become increasingly available to the Chinese in the next few years. They will beam in information in such quantities and in such variety that it may undermine the Party line. Once the internet becomes more accessible the difficulty of restricting the information it contains will make it almost impossible for the authorities to prevent the transfer of ideas across China. Millions of people throughout China will be able to exchange ideas which the CPC will be unable to influence and control.

It may well be that if China is not to tear itself apart as the USSR did it will have to create a federal structure with weak ties binding the provinces to the centre. Either way the centralised CPC control will have to evolve to survive in the next century.

TIANANMEN SQUARE

Opposition to the Communist Party of China is not tolerated and neither is opposition to the currently approved Party line, but there have been times when criticism has been encouraged. During the 'Hundred Flowers Campaign' in 1957, Mao Zedong called for constructive criticism and free opinion. However, it led to a flood of protests, some directed against the communist system itself and the CPC. The process was quickly abandoned and many of those who had criticised the CPC were subjected to 'thought reform.'

Tiananmen Square in more peaceful times.

In the late 1970s, when Deng Xiaoping was involved in a power struggle with the centre-left of the CPC, he wrote the Four Great (or Big) Freedoms into the constitution. These were freedom of speech, press, meetings and freedom to write big posters.

Once again criticism began to be directed at the Communist system and once again Deng sanctioned a crackdown against the 'democracy movement'. He returned to the Four Cardinal Principles—socialism, proletarian dictatorship, Communist Party dictatorship and Marxist, Leninist, Maoist thought. The Four Great Freedoms were removed from the constitution.

However, many people had tasted the freedom to criticise aspects of the system, particularly students who had been brought up within the confines of ideals laid down by the CPC. Over the next decade the economic reforms brought many advantages to the people of China but they also brought inflation, unemployment and disparities between rich and poor.

Public confidence in the Party line weakened. Respect for the Party cadres was undermined as reports of involvement in corruption were slowly revealed. People could tune in to foreign radio stations on their newly bought radios and were made aware of alternative political systems. All this led to an undercurrent of economic and political disenchantment with the CPC and the protest of spring 1989 attracted substantial support from students and workers.

'Beijing Spring'

In late April 1989 students occupied Tiananmen Square in the heart of Beijing. The square stands in front of the Forbidden City which houses the government. The students were peacefully protesting for more openness in government and for democracy. Throughout May support grew. The Communist leadership showed no signs of giving in to the demands of the students, so a group of protesters began a hunger strike. On 31 May the students uncovered 'The Goddess of Democracy'—a statue based on the Statue of Liberty. It faced the Forbidden City and made the leadership very angry with its apparent challenge to them.

Throughout this period, the leadership was confused about how to handle the scale of the demonstration. They were not sure how the People's Liberation Army would react if it was ordered to open fire on the people. However, Deng remembered the Cultural Revolution and the disastrous effect that uncontrolled mass action had had on China and, in particular, how it had affected him personally. His anger was intensified when he lost face because the Premier of the USSR, who was on a state visit to Beijing, had to be smuggled into the Forbidden City by the rear entrance. Deng spent some time in discussion with several army commanders until he was sure that he could count on their loyalty and that of their troops.

On 4 June, the Chinese People's Liberation Army was ordered to attack the demonstrators and clear the square. Reports vary about how many were killed and injured. According to the official line only 200 civilians were killed, including 36 students, and a further 3,000 people were wounded, but this tally is a gross underestimate. Realistic estimates suggest that approximately 2,000 people were killed and 10,000 injured in the ensuing massacre.

Martial law was imposed until the following January. By that time, all political enemies of the CPC had been removed from key positions in the country. 350,000 Chinese people had been 'disciplined.' Of those, 2,500 had actually been arrested and about 24 had been executed. Many had been sent to the labour camps. These are the 'official' figures and are likely to be underestimated.

The students who occupied Tiananmen Square were not seeking to establish some form of western democracy immediately. Despite the symbol of the 'Goddess of Democracy', they were not there to attack socialism but to seek more openness and to denounce the corruption of the CPC. Two of the student leaders in Tiananmen Square said that "our aim is to make the people wake up. China is not ready for democracy yet, but people must start to think about it."

The workers who joined the students were not there to support some abstract revision of the political system but rather for economic reasons. They were demanding protection from the excesses of the capitalist reforms in the economy. This would involve them being protected from inflation which had eroded the salaries of public employees such as health and education workers. Furthermore, they were seeking protection from the spectre of unemployment and the uncertainties of the ending of the 'iron rice bowl' which had reduced their standards of living.

The aftermath of Tiananmen Square

Was this brutal crackdown on the pro-democracy movement necessary? The official Dengist interpretation of the events states that it was. From their viewpoint, the aim of the demonstrators was to overthrow the CPC regime and replace it with a western style political system. Therefore resorting to force was not only justifiable, it was necessary to protect the legitimate government of China.

Was the use of armed troops the best solution? In many countries, a similar challenge to the elected authority would be met with trained riot police and troops perhaps employing tear gas, water cannon and rubber bullets. China had not developed such a system of policing. Even if it had been available to the Chinese authorities, some commentators argue that armed troops would still have been deployed because leading members of the CPC wanted bloodshed as a means of asserting their authority.

Following the events in Tiananmen Square, the government instituted a crackdown to root out 'subversive elements' and to discourage the people from future involvement in anti-government demonstrations.

To stop future 'disloyalty', a series of public punishments began. Through a state media blitz, pressure was put on people, in accordance with Chinese tradition, to inform on those who had been involved with the demonstration. Within workplaces, employees were called upon to compose self-criticisms of their actions during May and June and encouraged to study important speeches of Deng. On the TV, regular pictures appeared of arrested 'young hooligans' who had been beaten up in custody. From the crowd photos taken in Tiananmen Square, the police rounded up the ringleaders including Wang Dan and Lui Gang. In late June, well-publicised, executions of the 'rioters' began. Many were held in custody awaiting trial and were tortured to gain 'confessions.' Many simply 'disappeared.'

At universities, students were made to study the 'communist basics' of Mao and Deng. In the case of Beijing University, the entire first year was sent to a military academy 160 miles away for one year for 'patriotic study.'

CASE STUDY—WANG DAN

At the age of twenty, Wang Dan became one of the student leaders in Tiananmen Square. In the aftermath he was at the top of the police list of 21 'most wanted' student leaders. He evaded capture for one month but was eventually caught trying to talk to the western media. He was jailed for "counter-revolutionary propaganda and agitation." In Quinchen prison, 20 miles outside Beijing, he was allowed no visitors and was kept for long periods in solitary confinement. Eventually he was moved to N°·2 Prison in Beijing where he was kept for several months in a small cell but was moved eventually to a larger cell and allowed one visit per month from his family.

Dissidents like Wang Dan are continuously harassed by the authorities—the Ministry of State Security and Public Security Bureau—once they are released from prison. They are followed everywhere by the secret police. If they talk to someone in the street the police stand close by to overhear what is being said and afterwards question the people they spoke to. The police stand outside the homes of the dissidents 24 hours per day. If an important foreign dignitary is in town or on the anniversary of the Tiananmen Square protest the authorities arrest and detain dissidents. It is a common practice to rearrest them regularly and hold them for a period of time or send them into the countryside to prevent them meeting foreigners or undertaking any activity. In some cases dissidents are released on the understanding that they go into exile eg. Wang Dan went to live in the USA in April 1998.

Dissidents like Wang Dang tried to put pressure on China's leaders by talking to the foreign media about the need for China to be more democratic.

(Adapted from an Amnesty International Report)

The events in Tiananmen Square taught an important lesson both to the government and to those who sought to criticise and change it. The government found that the level of repression it inflicted on the people had a high price in terms of international criticism. It hindered China's economic reforms and that is something the CPC does not wish to be repeated. The dissidents and the people learned that in an emergency the government will use extreme violence to protect itself. Both sides in China have thus come to realise that they must treat each other with some caution.

DISSIDENTS

In the mid-1990s there were a few active dissidents at liberty in China and they were closely watched by the authorities. Dissident organisations were infiltrated, their phones were bugged and they were continuously harassed and frequently arrested. The main dissident movement is the Labour Alliance. Its leader, Wei Jingsheng, was in prison until recently. He has spent most of his life in prison since calling for the 'fifth modernisation'—democracy. The Labour Alliance claims to have widespread support in the country. In November 1997, Wei Jingsheng was released after 18 years in the Laogai and banished into exile by the government.

An American-based human rights group, Asia Watch, claimed that political repression continued to increase in China throughout the 1990s. The group suggested that the Communist Party is feeling increasingly uneasy about the grip it has upon the country. The stresses created by economic change and the uncertainty caused by the death of Deng led the authorities to tighten their net around any dissent. Despite the peaceful transition of power subsequent to Deng's death, the CPC was unwilling to relax its grip on the dissidents.

Their treatment of those who criticise the policies of the CPC varies and depends on the level of tolerance in the CPC at the time and how secure the Party feels. It also depend on international pressure and the image which China wants to project to the world. The CPC continues to use its wide-ranging police powers to repress political dissent but events in Tiananmen Square have had a major effect on dissent in China over the past decade and on political opposition.

Dissidents are still persecuted but the government keeps an eye on international criticism, moderating some of its actions when it sees an advantage in this. The CPC has, at various times, ordered the release of dissidents when it is trying to court international support or goodwill. Dissidents will continue to argue against the system in China, but for the foreseeable future they will have to do so with considerable caution.

China's Economy

"We have only taken the first step in a march of ten thousand." Mao Zedong, 1949.

When Mao Zedong stood overlooking Tiananmen Square on 1 October 1949 and proclaimed the founding of the People's Republic of China, he was a strong leader who wanted not only to govern China but to increase the power and influence the country had in the modern world by eliminating its weaknesses. One of those weaknesses was its depressed economy.

The economic situation was grim. The urban economy was in a shambles. World War II and civil war had destroyed many of the industrial areas. The massive inflation of the late 1940s made running a business virtually impossible. Cities were cut off from their rural markets because of the disruption to the transportation system. Mao believed China had to undergo an industrial revolution to secure the economic power which would put industry and agriculture back on their feet again as well as gaining China international prestige. Mao's industrial revolution was modelled on the USSR because it had achieved the rapid growth of heavy industry in a poor rural country. This had been organised using a series of Five Year Plans.

Agricultural reform presented a difficult problem. Previous attempts at land reform had not helped to improve the country's poor agricultural production. Mao believed that China's system of private smallholdings had been a major factor hindering the growth of the economy and so he planned for the development of large-scale cooperative and collective farms to make the best use of labour and technology. This was called collectivisation.

In 1958 the Great Leap Forward was introduced. It was called the Great Leap Forward because it was designed to enable China to leap over the normal stages of economic development and create rapid growth in both industry and agriculture—'walking on two legs'.

THE COMMUNE SYSTEM

As part of the Great Leap Forward, the rural population was organised into *people's communes*. A commune was a unit which integrated government administration with economic production. Between 1958 and 1970, 50,000 communes were established throughout the country, each with between 10,000 and 40,000 people. Each commune had a management committee to oversee its political, economic and social development. It agreed production targets with the state planning organisation, although the committee decided which crops were to be grown. It oversaw the local factories and had responsibility for local health, education, road maintenance and political activities. The commune was the lowest level of state administration in the countryside.

The commune system produced a number of benefits for people in the countryside. *The infrastructure was improved*. Large-scale irrigation and soil reclamation projects improved farm yields and road construction made distribution and communication far more efficient. Projects like these were carried out especially in the winter months which meant that manpower was being used more efficiently.

Investment was also made in modern factory and farming equipment which benefited from the large economies of scale. This made the communes more self-sufficient and provided jobs. Welfare facilities were made available for everyone. The children were looked after which allowed the able-bodied women to work in the fields. These improvements and the increased use of fertilisers led to agricultural production increases of 2% per annum between 1958 and 1976. This increased output was just ahead of population growth enabling China to avoid serious famine—except in 1960–61. It also helped to improve the quality of the average diet and to increase life expectancy.

Unfortunately the Great Leap Forward failed in several ways. Firstly, it became impossible for the state bureaucracy to coordinate the new communes. Resources were wasted and factories were forced to close down because of shortages of raw materials. Secondly, the peasants resisted the shift from individual plots to communes. They did not like being told what to do by inexperienced party cadres. Eventually, the CPC criticised the commune system for crushing peasant initiative. Lastly, between 1959 and 1961 industrial and agricultural output slumped due to a combination of factors including floods, famine and the withdrawal of Soviet technical aid. Up to 30 million people died from starvation and ill health in 1960–61 as a result of The Great Leap Forward.

FOUR MODERNISATIONS

By 1975 Mao Zedong had accepted that there were 4 areas which needed to be modernised. These were agriculture, industry, science and technology and defence. The 'Four Modernisations' was the name given to the drive to achieve rapid economic growth in these areas. However there were two opposing proposals for achieving the Four Modernisations. Mao led one faction which wanted to retain the principles of tight Party control over communal methods of production. As he was the most powerful person in China it was this proposal which was adopted. A Ten Year Plan was devised which relied on mechanisation and moral exhortations to improve the economy rather than structural changes to improve efficiency. Before the plan was put into action Mao died.

Deng Xiaoping had huge support, especially from the state bureaucracy and the People's Liberation Army (PLA). When he won the power struggle which ensued after Mao's death, it was his view of how to achieve the Modernisations which was adopted by the CPC. He saw the way forward through introducing *competition* and *market forces* into the Chinese system.

The Thoughts of Deng

Deng believed that too much bureaucracy within the domestic economy stifled change and efficiency. Power had to be decentralised and at least part of the economy had to be opened up to private enterprise. This would force the state sector to become more efficient since it would face competition. Both the work force and the management should be selected on the basis of ability rather than political belief. Decision mak-

Cotton mill in Shijiazhuang— western investment was attracted by the plentiful supply of cheap labour

ing would be decentralised to the work force. Skill and initiative would be rewarded in order to encourage greater efficiency. China should also be opened up to foreign investment and markets.

INDUSTRY

Open Door Policy and Special Economic Zones

For its long-term national security China needed to catch up with international developments. However, China's economic structure was too weak to achieve this in isolation. It needed to improve its research and development capability and to develop production rapidly. This needed capital, technology and know-how which would only be available if China took part in the global economy.

To assist China in its goal of entering the global economy the 'open door' policy was introduced. Between 1949 and the late 1970s China had stressed the need to be self-sufficient. This had been possible because of the huge energy and mineral reserves which it enjoyed. However, this isolation hindered economic growth. Deng recognised that this was a stumbling block. He thought that China should attract capital and advanced technology from abroad. It could be paid for by exporting the production from new consumer goods industries. China could at-

tract these new industries because it could offer a supply of plentiful cheap labour as neighbouring countries such as South Korea, Taiwan and Singapore had done.

Diplomatic contacts were re-established with the West and government ministers were sent round the world to sign new agreements and to buy modern machinery. Japan and Germany became major trading partners. Thousands of Chinese students were sent abroad to study at foreign universities, especially in the USA.

The next stage was to attract foreign investment into China. To help with this, in 1979 several southeast coastal areas were designated Special Economic Zones (SEZs)— Shenzhen, Zhuhai, Shantou, Xiamen and Hainan. These areas became the focus for modern hi-tec export industries. Foreign investment was attracted by free land, local low cost labour and exemption from duties on imported raw materials. Today the economies of these SEZs are growing faster than those in any other areas of China. Special help is also given to other parts of China.

● *Pudong New Zone and the Open Areas along the Yangtse River*
This area has been established to enable Pudong to use Shanghai's advantages of geographical location, professional personnel and economic foundation to service the

China's Special Economic Zones

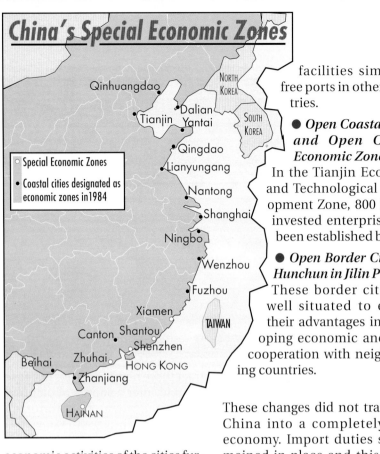

Special Economic Zones
Coastal cities designated as economic zones in 1984

Qinhuangdao
Tianjin · Dalian · Yantai
NORTH KOREA
SOUTH KOREA
Qingdao
Lianyungang
Nantong
Shanghai
Ningbo
Wenzhou
Fuzhou
Xiamen
TAIWAN
Canton · Shantou
Shenzhen
Beihai · Zhuhai
HONG KONG
Zhanjiang
HAINAN

facilities similar to free ports in other countries.

● *Open Coastal Cities and Open Coastal Economic Zones*

In the Tianjin Economic and Technological Development Zone, 800 foreign invested enterprises had been established by 1982.

● *Open Border Cities eg. Hunchun in Jilin Province*

These border cities are well situated to exploit their advantages in developing economic and trade cooperation with neighbouring countries.

These changes did not transform China into a completely open economy. Import duties still remained in place and this meant that external trade accounted for just 5–10% of GNP. Overseas firms were wary of setting up in China because they were unsure of the

permanence of the situation. Only Shenzhen SEZ (next to Hong Kong) attracted significant investment but this hardly covered the investment made by the Chinese government in order to establish the infrastructure. This led to a widening gap in imports and exports and a trade deficit grew. Technology imports from the West did improve the production of coal, steel and chemicals. Nevertheless, the boost the Chinese economy hoped to gain from its 'open door' policy was less substantial than anticipated.

However, SEZs have catapulted China into the 21st century. SEZs currently create 12% of China's total exports. More than 50% of their products are sold in foreign markets. Residents in the SEZs have higher incomes, better housing, more electricity and more cars than the national average. In Shenzhen, 'a socialist wonder', money is the main attraction for the workers whose average age is 25. They can earn as much as 1,500 yuan per

economic activities of the cities further up the Yangtse.

• *Free Trade Areas*

In China, a free trade area is a small special district with closed access

---

CASE STUDIES FROM SHENZHEN

JOINT VENTURES

CASE STUDY 1

Konka is a Chinese electronics company whose 2,300 workers assemble 500,000 TV sets a year. Some are sold in China but others are destined for the USA, Europe and Brazil. Like most companies in the SEZ, Konka is a joint venture with a Hong Kong firm which owns 36% of the stock.

In an assembly room the size of a football pitch, television cabinets, picture tubes and other parts are passed before blue-smocked workers who fit, tighten and solder. "Manpower costs are very high in Shenzhen," a manager said. Price competition in the Chinese TV market is fierce. Konka plans to move its factory farther into China, where workers can be hired for $60–$70 a month.

This is also part of China's national policy. China wants labour-intensive companies to create jobs in interior provinces, while the coastal areas seek to attract more sophisticated enterprises.

KONKA

CASE STUDY 2

The Schneider Group of France, an international leader in the electrical transmission and distribution, industrial control and automation sectors, recently announced the establishment of a new company in China. It is to be called the Schneider Electric (China) Investment Co. This is the company's first joint venture in China.

The list of cooperative partners in China include many famous Chinese enterprises—China National Aero-Technology Import and Export Corp., Shanghai Electrical Apparatus Co. Ltd. The group plans to have 10 joint ventures in China by the year 2000. China is currently strengthening its infrastructure facilities and Schneider's participation in the major power plants will contribute greatly to China's economic development.

month (about US $200)—not a great deal by British standards but more than a professor's pay at Beijing University. A middle level manager's pay might be US $400 per month as well a comfortable flat.

MODERNISING THE CHINESE ECONOMY

Another reason Deng had for moving ahead with the Four Modernisations was that the domestic economy was not operating successfully. Priority had to be given to internal economic development which would require the reorganisation of the state bureaucracy and the abolition of the commune system in agriculture. These were radical changes which might have been met by severe resistance. To make sure the Chinese people accepted these changes, Deng had to persuade them that China had fallen far behind other countries in economic wealth and living standards. For this reason, in the late 1970s he systematically sent leaders from the provinces on trips abroad to see and experience for themselves the wealth in developed countries. He used TV to present images of the outside world to China. Most people were shocked to see how backward China was.

Deng and his team of Hu and Zhao rejected the Ten Year Plan as the model to deliver the changes required because it relied too heavily on central control and bureaucracy which was one of the impediments to change they were trying to sweep away. Instead they introduced a number of reforms which resulted in a more decentralised system of market socialism.

In industry, there were two main aims. The first was to reduce the centralised state bureaucracy by devolving powers of decision making to the factories or state enterprises. The second aim was to introduce incentives and prices related more to the demands of the market.

Reduced Bureaucracy and Devolved Decision Making

The state bureaucracy was streamlined. Government departments were merged and a new one, the Ministry of Economic Restructuring, was set up. The idea was to cut red tape, speed up decision making and coordinate activities in the industrial economy far more efficiently.

Decision making was then devolved down to the state factory or enterprise level. Individual factories were given a production target set by the state, but once this was met they had the authority to adjust output according to the demands of the market. State enterprises could also keep part of their surplus profit. They were free to buy raw materials from any supplier including foreign companies.

Gradually more power was devolved to the state enterprises. They were given responsibility for planning, budgeting and wages and were directly responsible for their profits and losses. A new breed of market conscious managers emerged to run the factories. However, if the state enterprise did not prosper it was liable to be closed.

These changes were not introduced into the 'commanding heights of the economy,' the heavy industries of steel, engineering, energy and other basic industries. These industries remained firmly under central control.

Incentives

The second main thrust in the state enterprises was the introduction of incentives. One of the main problems in the state enterprises was low productivity and wasteful use of raw materials, especially energy.

Industrial workers were encouraged to work harder by being given a wage rise in 1977 which was the first since 1958. Bonuses and penalties were given to supplement their basic pay which the state still controlled. The higher wages led to higher standards of living which were further facilitated by the expansion of the consumer goods sector of the economy.

The state's guarantee of a job for life—the 'iron rice bowl'—was reduced. Factory managers could now employ the best people for the job and lazy, incompetent workers could be sacked. The price structure was reformed with prices for more than 50% of manufactured goods fixed at a level linked to the demands of the market.

The Collective Economy

The 'collective economy' employs 11 million people in the urban areas. In theory, these enterprises are supposed to be owned by the work force who must get 10% of the assets or part of the profit as a bonus. In practice, they are part of the state system because the state government still appoints the directors. The workers in the 'collective economy' do not get the 'iron rice bowl' benefits and this has acted as an incentive for several large enterprises to opt to become part of this sector.

Often there is little distinction between private and collectively owned enterprises. 20% of private enterprises register as collectively owned enterprises. This is called 'buying a red hat'. They do this in order to avoid high tax rates. For example, in Shanghai in 1988, 30% of big private enterprises were registered as being collectively run.

Conditions in these collectives are often poor. Quotes from the *China Daily* in 1993 said that wages were "most often decided by the will of their managers." "The working conditions of employees are currently quite low; their working hours are not regulated and there is no medical or retirement insurance for most of them." "The entrepreneurs are usually poorly educated and once the profits begin to roll in they often indulge themselves instead of further promoting their business."

A noodle restaurant in Shandong. By the end of 1997, China had 28.5 million registered self-employed workers.

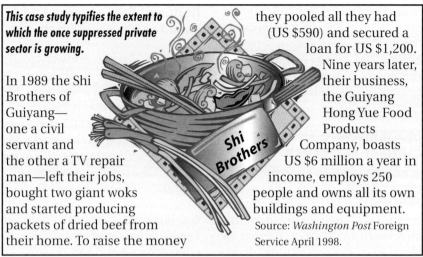

This case study typifies the extent to which the once suppressed private sector is growing.

In 1989 the Shi Brothers of Guiyang— one a civil servant and the other a TV repair man—left their jobs, bought two giant woks and started producing packets of dried beef from their home. To raise the money they pooled all they had (US $590) and secured a loan for US $1,200. Nine years later, their business, the Guiyang Hong Yue Food Products Company, boasts US $6 million a year in income, employs 250 people and owns all its own buildings and equipment.

Source: *Washington Post* Foreign Service April 1998.

Often sweatshop conditions exist. For example, the conditions in button factories in Qiaotou near Wenzhou are described as "dingy workshops in which female child labourers work a 12 hour day for a wage of 5 Remimbi. The employees work a seven day week with no breaks during the day and are forced to endure a primitive, noisy, dark and unhealthy environment."

In conclusion, central planning and one-Party control still remained and the prices of basic items were still subsidised. In the small factory and light industry sector a form of 'market socialism' was established. This was also known as 'socialism with Chinese characteristics' or 'Dengism.'

THE GROWTH OF PRIVATE ENTERPRISE.

The story of the Shi brothers above is typical of the business initiatives which are 'shaking the economic foundations of China.' The once suppressed private sector is growing fast. China's private businesses are now outpacing the state enterprises. They have gained 25% of the economy and seem set to move even further forward. Thirty years ago the Chinese government took a dim view of private businesses— now it fully supports them.

There are a number of reasons why the government has changed its mind. Included in these reasons is the fact that the private businesses pay lots of tax and so the govern-ment gets more revenue. Also, with more than 25 million people per year looking for work in the cities and 40% of the state enterprises losing money, the government cannot do without these private enterprises. According to the state-run *China Daily*, two-thirds of workers laid off by state owned enterprises who find new jobs do so in the private sector.

The officials in charge of the towns and cities want to maximise the speed of the growth of the private sector simply to meet the tremendous pressures for new jobs needed due to population growth. China's net population increase (births minus deaths) for the 1990s is about 14 million people per year—27 people per minute.

By the end of 1997, China had 28.5 million registered self-employed workers. The 960,000 private enterprises employed 39 million workers which is approximately one-third of the size of the work force of the state owned enterprises. Many work for huge multinationals such as General Motors, IBM, AT&T and Coca Cola. Motorola, the biggest private enterprise in China, has invested about US $2.5 billion and, in Tianjin alone, employs more than 10,000 workers.

The turn towards the private sector has political implications. Since the 1950s, the CPC has controlled the lives of people through the work place. The work unit would determine people's careers, housing etc. Now the private sector frees people from these controls and puts them in charge of their own lives. Hence the CPC is not such an important factor in people's lives. There are different opinions on this. Tony Saich, a China scholar, said "it is stunning; there is no other word for it." On the other hand, a report warned that "the drop in the proportion of the public sector and the shrinking of public ownership will inevitably weaken the Party's leading position."

IRON RICE BOWL

This is the term given to the job security, conditions and welfare system in China's state owned enterprises. The benefits of the 'iron rice bowl' for employees often exceed the total wages bill. These benefits are made up of access to company housing, ration coupons for clothes, coal and consumer durables, subsidised food, delivery of major social services and medical care. This is obviously an important range of benefits for the Chinese workers. Because pay levels are low these benefits help to maintain a reasonable standard of living.

In the USA, 45% of an average family budget is spent on housing, transport and medical care, but in China these constitute only 5% of the spending of urban families. As workers were paid off and state enterprises reduced their 'iron rice bowl' provision many workers saw their living standards reduced. As

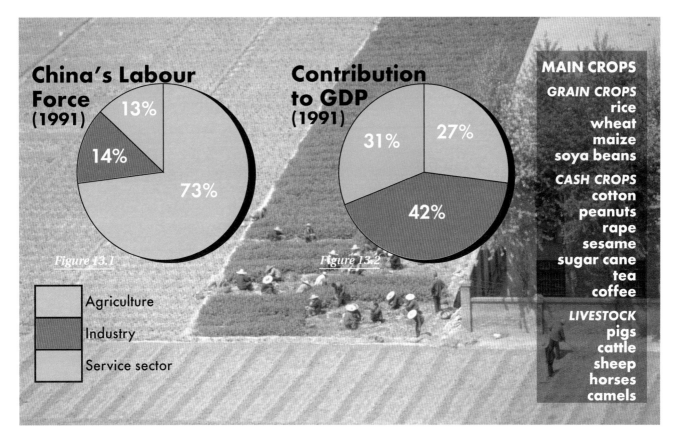

China's Labour Force (1991)

13%
14%
73%

Figure 13.1

- Agriculture
- Industry
- Service sector

Contribution to GDP (1991)

27%
31%
42%

Figure 13.2

MAIN CROPS

GRAIN CROPS
rice
wheat
maize
soya beans

CASH CROPS
cotton
peanuts
rape
sesame
sugar cane
tea
coffee

LIVESTOCK
pigs
cattle
sheep
horses
camels

more and more industries are run either by private enterprise or collectively, an increasing number of people face economic hardship and social problems as a result.

One of the consequences of the 'iron rice bowl' being 'smashed' is that many Chinese have lost their right to their own home and have to move in with relatives. According to the *Australian Journal of Chinese Affairs*, 40% of urban couples have to sleep in the same room as their children and more than 20% have to share a bed with their children. Over 7% have to share a bedroom with their parents or parents-in-law.

Although the price reforms of the 1980s made it difficult for many workers employed in the state system to buy consumer goods, the high prices meant that state subsidies were an important part of the 'iron rice bowl.'

AGRICULTURE

China's population is not spread evenly across the country. 85% of the people live on 35% of the land, mainly in the South and East. Only 11% of China is suitable for grow-

ing crops. China is faced with the problem of feeding 21% of the world's population on 7% of its arable land and with 8% of its water resources. Chinese agriculture therefore focuses on food for direct human consumption. Farming is also labour intensive.

Deng & Agricultural Reform

Agriculture was top of the list for the Four Modernisations. Agricultural performance was disappointing, so it was essential that a way was found to speed up agricultural production. Deng wanted to get rid of the commune system and totally restructure agriculture.

He believed that the way to stimulate growth was to give the peasant farmers incentives and to develop more intensive methods of production. If the peasants were given incentives, they would work harder and more efficiently than they would when directed by the commune management teams. Deng did not support a totally unrestricted free market, private enterprise system. He saw the plan as involving individual production but still within an overall strategic plan controlled by the CPC.

Deng's strategy was two pronged. Firstly, he dismantled the rigid, bureaucratic controls of the commune system by giving more decision making responsibility to production teams and family units. This was called the *responsibility system*. Secondly, he stimulated production by giving the farmers more money for what they produced. This was called *price reform*.

The Responsibility System

The earliest reforms took place in Sichuan in 1977. Political and economic power was transferred from the communes to the town and village authorities. Enterprises previously run by communes became joint stock companies which paid the communes an annual dividend.

From 1979–1984, most communes were progressively downgraded and dismantled, the land being allocated to families who wanted to farm it. A family usually meant an extended family rather than a nuclear family unit. The process took several years to sort out, but eventually the system began to deal with individual farmers.

Under the responsibility system farmers are allowed to sell excess produce on the open market.

Under the 'responsibility system' or the 'contract system' farmers took on a contract for the use of land on the basis of assuming some financial and production obligations. The contract required a 'production team' being contracted to supply to the government a fixed amount of produce at a fixed price and each farmer would have his share of the responsibility. The farmer could then consume or sell for a profit anything left after the contract had been fulfilled. Farmers had full control over what they could grow on the rest of their land. However, they did not own the land outright. The commune still retained the formal title to it.

Short-term contracts created incentives to use the land but not to maintain it. This could lead to farmers squeezing as much profit as possible from the soil in the short term, but failing to look after the land which would lead to its deterioration. In order to overcome this problem, many of the land contracts are now for up to 50 years. To further maximise output from the land, contracts can, within limits, be bought and sold and people with larger amounts of land can hire workers to help them to work the land. This means that efficient farmers can expand, while others can sell up and seek alternative employment. The trend has, therefore, been from communes to responsibility system to commercial farming of the land.

Another change was that about 15% of former commune workers were given permission to become 'specialised households' turning what had previously been sideline activities, such as craft work, into a full-time job organised on modern, professional lines.

Price Reform

Deng also introduced price reforms. He increased the prices paid to farmers for any crops they grew in an attempt to stimulate production. Between 1978 and 1984, the government also agreed to pay higher prices for any crops produced over and above the quota level. However, these price increases were not passed on to the urban consumers because it was felt that this would create hardship and social unrest. The government therefore put into place a system of subsidies. Deng also tried to stimulate agricultural production by an investment of capital. However, agriculture still received only about 14% of state investment capital compared to 46% for heavy industries.

RESPONSES TO THE RURAL REFORM PROGRAMME

Although the reforms have not created a totally free market system, farmers now have considerable choice combined with incentives to maximise their incomes. The reforms have had both positive and negative effects on agriculture.

Positive effects

China's agricultural output increased at a rate of 8% per annum between 1978 and 1985. Grain production rose by a third, the country becoming self-sufficient in grain as a result. Wheat and cash crop output increased by two-thirds. One reason for this dramatic improvement in output was the increased use of fertilisers but the main factor was the intensification of labour input by the peasants. The peasants quadrupled their earnings between 1978 and 1989. This led to an increase in house building as peasants used their new-found wealth to improve their living standards. Their increased demand for consumer goods led to an expansion of manufacturing industries with more jobs being created in the non-agricultural sector of the economy. It is estimated that by the year 2000 the number of non-agricultural workers in rural areas will be approximately 300 million.

Negative effects

Deng was delighted at the success of his reforms but some of the more conservative members of the CPC were not so happy about their side effects. They disliked the weakening of Party control and the lack of political education. The appearance of a new 'rich peasant' élite appalled them. They feared the re-appearance of rural class conflict.

The more moderate CPC members were worried by 3 other problems. Projects which once were carried out by the communes were being left untouched. For example, repairs to village irrigation schemes were no longer carried out. This had particularly serious effects on agricultural output in some of the drier areas in north-east China.

Secondly, there was a steady decline in the area sown with grain as peasants got more money from intensive cash crop cultivation and their sideline activities than from the grain subsidies given to them by the government. Also, with peo-ple becoming wealthier, demand increased for luxury foodstuffs. The proportion of land devoted to grain cultivation fell from 80% of the total in 1980 to 75% in 1985. Deng's critics predicted a serious food shortage unless policies were changed. The third problem was that the high cost of farming subsidies was causing serious financial problems for the government.

Some critics felt that the success of Deng's rural reforms would be short-lived. They felt that Deng's reforms had been introduced too rigidly with not enough consideration given to local agricultural conditions.

Rural Problems

Many rural problems resulted from the reforms. China's farmers now suffer from an economy geared to the demands of the urban population. In the late 1970s a considerable amount of money was pumped into agriculture both to dismantle the commune system and also via the price increases for agricultural produce. Consequently, agricultural output surged. Nevertheless, by 1984, to encourage further increases in farm production, substantial new investment was required.

However, the government turned its attention to the urban economy. It was relying on the farmers to spend their new-found income on their farms. Unfortunately this did not happen. The peasants put their money into new houses and consumer goods. Land was taken out of agricultural production for the new housing they built and also for the expansion of townships as large numbers of peasants moved to the towns to find work.

With less attention being paid to agriculture, the local CPC leaders began to manipulate the farmers. The prices farmers had to pay for fertilisers and machinery went up faster than the prices they received for their crops. The peasants were given IOUs instead of cash for their produce. Local officials diverted to investments in new urban enterprises money which had been allocated to help farmers. The farmers were effectively being exploited.

By 1994 these policies had led to widespread anger among farmers, especially those who did not live near large urban markets. Peasant revolts were reported in areas such as Sichuan in the South-West. Production of basic grain has not kept pace with the population growth. Rural/urban inequalities are growing and peasants are migrating to the urban areas in large numbers.

If the agricultural sector continues to be shortchanged, China faces both economic and political problems. The 'economic miracle' has reached the rural areas but in a form which has produced increasing frustration for the rural residents.

CONCLUSION

Deng's reform programme appeared to have been successful. According to the World Bank, industrial output and GNP grew by 10% per year in the 1980s. The standard of living for the majority of Chinese people rose. However there were some problems. Supply and demand for raw materials caused problems with bottlenecks developing and there was a significant waste of resources. A sizable minority of workers saw their position deteriorating as a result of unemployment or widening income differentials.

With the economy straddled between 'state socialism' and 'market capitalism,' social and economic problems appeared. Both unemployment and strikes were on the increase while significant inequalities developed between rural and urban areas. China also became aware of the damaging effects of corruption and inflation. Some of these problems are dealt with in Chapter 14.

Economic & Social Problems

14

THE PRESSURES OF CHANGE

China's economic reforms have improved the lives of millions of people but corruption, inflation, migration, unemployment and crime have also become part of the lives of an equal number. These economic and social problems are interlinked and must be resolved in order to produce the internationally competitive economy which China seeks as well as ensuring the stability and evolution of the political and social systems.

To produce an internationally competitive economy, certain issues of *efficiency* must be tackled. China has developed labour-intensive industries to make goods which are sold on the international market. The profits from these industries have paid for the technology which has helped to accelerate China's economic growth, but this situation may be difficult to sustain. China needs to find ways to preserve and increase its exports in the years to come. The reason for this is that China has become, for the first time, a net importer of food and energy such as oil. It has, in the past, relied on export earnings from oil, but now it will have to pay to import the oil it needs. This means that the import bill will be substantially increased just to maintain the basic resources of food and oil.

China may also face greater *trade barriers* in the US and European markets. For its economic wellbeing, it must continue to have access

to these—especially to the north American markets. China therefore must support the World Trade Organisation (WTO) in order to reduce barriers to international trade. It needs to allow greatly increased access to its home market which is highly protected. There are high tariff rates, secret quotas and licensing agreements as well as other administrative controls to restrict goods imported from abroad. The reason for this is to protect some of the less competitive state sector enterprises.

The government has accepted the idea that it must review the situation if it is to participate more freely in world trade. However, this may cause problems for the state enterprises. They have been coddled, are inefficient and have been protected from competition—both foreign and internal.

To encourage foreign trade, China must open up its domestic market which means *reorganising the state enterprises* and throwing large numbers of their employees out of work. The problem here is that the country is trying to create jobs for its new urban work force, not to make workers redundant. Ways have got to be found to make the situation easier to cope with.

Another broad economic problem is the need to produce a solid base of *skilled labour* and technical and scientific manpower. Since the 1980s, China has been a major centre for low-cost labour. Most component parts are imported and the

Chinese advantages of available land and low-skilled labour are used to assemble the final product at a low price. It is then exported. This has put pressure on areas like Hong Kong, Taiwan and South Korea. In these areas, land and labour have become expensive so they have had to develop new ways of competing.

For China, the problem is that although it currently occupies the niche of low-cost producer, in the long term this is not secure. Wage rates in the SEZs have increased since the 1980s and land prices are rising. It is not wholly satisfactory to shift production to the interior and China must therefore climb the technological ladder. To do this, people need to be encouraged to enter higher education and to undertake research. This should not be a problem given China's huge population, but the number of young people completing higher education is small and the country has difficulty in filling the 5,000 places in its post-graduate education structure. Even the number of children finishing primary and secondary school has gone down. This is because young people want to make money so they go into business instead of staying on at school. As a result, China is not producing its base of skilled labour and scientific manpower. Once these issues are faced and tackled, China may be able to produce the internationally competitive economy which it seeks.

CHINA'S ECONOMIC PROBLEMS

Corruption

The reforms, both urban and rural, seem to have increased corruption significantly.

The economic circumstances in China have created situations in which corruption is easy to achieve. This is because government officials, at all levels, can use their position to affect economic decisions. Granting licences and loans, forgiving debts and providing access to electricity, water, telephones and transportation are only a few of the types of decisions for which CPC officials now expect 'tea money' or bribes.

The problem was made worse by the fact that Deng Xiaoping ensured support among top officials for his economic reforms by allowing them to benefit disproportionately from them. They often became heads of trading firms or received other positions from which they could gain huge profits. Many have become very wealthy. Collectively, this group is called the 'princes' party' (taizidang). This creates social tension as workers feel that these wealthy individuals have earned their money through their position rather than through hard work.

Inflation

The economic reforms have also caused inflation. For example, the government's loss of tight control over the money supply means that nearly every year it ends up expanding the money supply far more quickly than had been planned. With decentralisation of the economy, local officials have used their power to turn local bank branches into money machines for the local economy. Money is lent to favoured personal projects such as residential complexes for local officials. When banks appear reluctant to oblige, the local Communist Party committee uses its powers to secure compliance. The committee determines who will head the bank and so its influence over lending decisions is enormous.

Beijing could put an end to this abuse by refusing to cover the financial losses of the banks and allowing them to close. However, local officials point out that the potential price to be paid is that of wage bills not being met and workers being paid off, followed by social unrest. Because of these considerations the centre has, for many years, had to print more money to meet the obligations rather than risk enterprises failing. This constant pumping of money into the system creates chronic inflation as too much money is available for too few goods.

The problems are exemplified in the construction industry. Much of the money is used to build new factories. Orders for cement, bricks and concrete outstrip production and the results are serious: bottlenecks occur which bring building to a halt midway; prices of materials soar; import bills for these scarce goods also soar as desperate firms buy in from Japan and elsewhere.

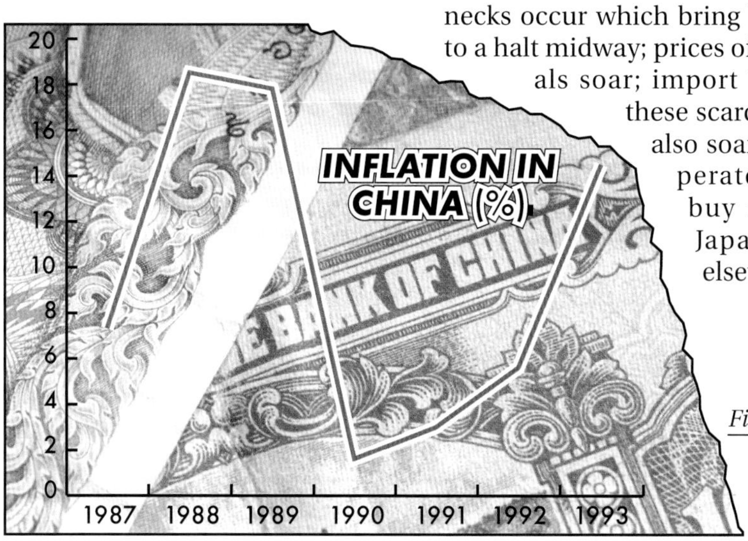

Inflation causes wages and benefits to increase which, in turn, creates demands for better housing and transport. The government has difficulty persuading people to put money into the banks as they feel that they should convert it into goods before inflation erodes its value. The government can, however, bring inflation down quickly by throwing the country into recession. It could do this by taking firm measures to control the economy. For example, after Tiananmen Square it demanded that banks call in bad loans and stop lending beyond their capacity. Furthermore, long-term savings were encouraged by the added incentive of higher interest rates. This 'boom and bust' inflation cycle is not good for China. The 'bust' part of the cycle, for example, reduces foreign confidence in the Chinese economy and risks large-scale social unrest. To break this cycle, the government must further limit the role of state planning, convert banks to profit and loss organisations and introduce a national taxation system.

Price Rises

In 1994, people in Beijing complained of price rises. The prices of grain, cooking oil, eggs, pork and vegetables—staples of the Beijing diet—were all at record levels. The root of the problem lay in the countryside where farmers complained that they were not being paid enough to make grain production worthwhile. In some provinces they were storing the grain in the belief that it would fetch higher prices after a few months when the cities began to feel the pinch of shortages. The resulting inflation might have been bearable had it been accompanied by wage rises but, for most, this was not the case.

In 1998, Chinese economists forecast a negative inflation. This led to lower prices which resulted from three main factors: the fight to bring down the high inflation early in the 1990s; a bumper series of harvests which brought down food prices and the fact that supply had

INFLATION IN CHINA (%)

Figure 14.1

been greater than demand. However, there has been concern that inflation had been brought down at the cost of higher unemployment.

Unemployment

Reforming the state sector has been one of the main reasons for the huge rise in unemployment in recent years.

Xiao Li was a mechanic in a state-owned factory in Beijing which made electronic spare parts. The factory cut his salary by 30%. Two months later it stopped paying him altogether and told him to stay at home. For 6 months, Xiao and his friends received no salary and no welfare or medical benefits although they still had state provided housing. For Xiao Li, this was a huge departure from the cradle to the grave 'iron rice bowl' package which Chinese workers once relied on. The factory had stopped production because, like many other inefficient state enterprises, the products could not compete with foreign imports and rival products from modern factories in the SEZs.

The total unemployment figures are hard to establish. Official urban unemployment is more than 5 million, but this does not take into account the 30 million who have little or nothing to do at their work unit. The rural situation is equally alarming. It is estimated that in the past 5 years between 60 million and 90 million people have moved from the countryside to find work in the urban areas. (See rural-urban migration on page 117.)

The government has tried out policies to solve the urban unemployment problem. For example, as early as 1980, Deng Xiaoping expanded the service and private sectors. He also made it easier for individuals to set up on their own in 'specialised households.' These measures did stabilise the employment situation in the 1980s.

However, nowadays different issues are emerging. One of these is the place of women in the employment market and the other is something known as 'stealth unemployment.'

Women in the employment market face greater pressures to accept jobs which conform to traditional 'women's roles'. Managers know that women who get married will have children and will require welfare benefits and labour protection. These managers complain that they are forced to take on too many women who are "high cost and low efficiency." In Shanghai, for example, birth costs are paid by the enterprise and average a minimum of 1,500 yuan and 2 years wages since paid leave is provided after birth. In Shanghai, women account for 70% of those recently made unemployed. They turn to illegal occupations to make ends meet. "A police officer said some bars sold food and drink by day and sex by night." (*China Daily* 20 July 1993)

'Stealth unemployment' is another term for underemployment. It is estimated that about 160 million (26%) of China's work force is 'stealthily unemployed' or underemployed. The Chinese government has predicted that, by 2005, they will still have about 150 million surplus workers or about 21.5% of the work force.

The government's research group on Employment Strategy for 1996–2005 has identified a number of issues. Firstly, 74% of the work force are in rural jobs, but of the 450 million rural workers only 150 million can be fully employed on the land. Other areas such as township enterprises can absorb about 190 million, but that still leaves 110 million surplus workers which is why rural workers pour steadily into the cities in search of jobs.

Secondly, in certain economically developed regions such as Chang Jiang Delta, economic growth will increase the demand for labour, leaving the local labour supply no longer able to meet the needs. Workers will then have to be attracted from other provinces. Since it is projected that the Chinese economy is going to remain in a high growth period for the next decade this is one way of solving the problem of surplus labour.

Thirdly, service (tertiary) sector jobs will increase in importance in the 21st century, becoming a jobs growth point. It is projected that the service sector will add over 10 million jobs a year accounting for, in the year 2000, about 30% of all jobs and 35% by 2005. This will need to be given strategic consideration.

Next, the government also has to invest more in regions which have employment problems. In the short term, workers from the central and western regions of China need to be sent to the developed eastern areas. In the long term, these areas need to encourage private investment.

Finally, to help deal with the unemployment issues the government has to look at its education policy, particularly with regard to vocational skills development. Priority has to be given to ensuring that the labour force is multi-skilled to a high level and is suited to the new types of jobs. The government also points out that it has to focus its family planning work on rural areas, especially economically backward areas where it needs to exercise tighter family planning controls.

Industrial Unrest

There are regular reports of clashes between police and demonstrators protesting at the lack of both work and pay. In 1996, in the worst-off industrial cities of Heilon province, up to 80% of the work force was laid off. Workers demanding unpaid wages staged sit-ins in factories or in front of local Party headquarters. This was not an unusual situation. A group of Chinese dissidents issued an open letter calling on China's millions of state workers to form trade unions and take to the streets to protect their rights. Each of China's state enterprises has a

A billboard advertising motorbikes—the most popular form of transport for the Chinese middle class

trade union branch, but all of them must register with the Beijing controlled All China Federation of Trade Unions (ACFTU). Workers' organisations not sponsored by the CPC are illegal. All foreign funded enterprises have to join ACFTU. Strikes in state enterprises tend to be hushed up.

RURAL–URBAN MIGRATION

One of the main reasons for the high unemployment rate is the fact that China has an internal migration problem. The internal migrant population is between 50 million and 100 million. Most are rural people who are attracted to the coastal cities, especially the SEZs, in search of a better life. This new mobility has resulted from many things including the increase in the surplus labour force in rural areas, a result of increased efficiency.

In theory, rural inhabitants have to get permission to move to urban areas, but many ignore the rules. Finding work and accommodation for these migrants is a massive problem and one which leads to social unrest. Most of the migrants living in the cities are still classified as rural residents regardless of how long they have been away from home and in that sense they are officially regarded as temporary migrants. This makes it difficult for them to be fully incorporated into city life and, in many cases, they are forced into the marginal spaces of the housing and labour markets.

This marginalisation, based on the fact that they are poor and from the countryside, has created a new underclass population in China's cities.

The migrants often congregate conspicuously in public places and outside railway stations. They can be found working on construction sites and in factories as well as selling things in the informal economy of the streets. They make their homes in a variety of makeshift and dilapidated spaces. They are easily identifiable: their dialects indicate they are outsiders; their appearance suggests they are peasants and the jobs they are doing signify they are poor and usually desperate for work.

During the Maoist era urban life was generally uneventful. The onset of rapid migration from the rural areas has brought with it fears of homelessness, poverty, crime, prostitution and drug abuse. Newspaper stories reinforce these fears by drawing attention to isolated events and blaming them on the migrants. The crime rate is rising in the cities but it is unjustifiable to attribute this solely to the rural migrants. They may look and behave differently—they are poor and uneducated—but the view that they are criminals and hooligans is actually only true of a small minority of them. There are more of the migrants working hard in the factories than there are causing a public nui-

sance, but it is the media image of squalor and disorder which is more likely to capture the imagination of the public and so influence their opinions about the migrants.

The quick pace of social and economic change in China has made urban life more chaotic than ever. The migrants are taking the blame for the increasing sense of disorder which happens in any society facing rapid economic transition.

INEQUALITIES

Economic reform has led to a widening gap between rich and poor in China. The rich enjoy an opulent lifestyle as exemplified below.

Guangzhou, part of an SEZ, has a population of 6.5 million, making it China's fourth largest city. The Pearl River divides the city. Along its banks are many open air restaurants. At night time couples arrive by motorbike, the popular form of transport for the middle class. The Cantonese, it is said, spend a third of their income on food. The in-places to go in Guangzhou are nightclubs or some place with karaoke music. The sauna is popular too. A reporter from *National Geographic* magazine described the nightlife in Guangzhou "I visited the Swan Club where I saw several men, rosy after a steaming, relaxing on cots. One was calling his girlfriend on a cellular phone. Others had come to the Swan Club for its restaurants, its bowling lanes or its pool tables. Some went to the nightclub to watch women prance about. To belong to the club an individual must pay a membership fee of more than $5,000. Family membership costs more than $7,500. This has not discouraged 1,500 traders, developers and bankers from joining."

"Free enterprise takes another guise as night brings crowds to restaurants and nightclubs. Touts hand out cards advertising 'massage parlours.' But prostitution is not the most serious offence. Several entrepreneurs have been kidnapped for ransom."

Most Chinese people do not make their fortune!

Two decades into Deng's 'economic miracle' and China's poorest 60 million peasants must still do without enough food, clothing and shelter to guarantee their survival. An additional 30 million farmers eke out livelihoods on less than US $1 per day—the World Bank's universal measure of poverty.

Xia Chunsheng is a businessman in Shenzen but he never goes out alone in the evening. He travels in an expensive German car with bulletproof glass and a chauffeur who doubles as a bodyguard. He enjoys tailored suits and expensive restaurants.

In contrast, despite years of economic growth, China still has some of the world's poorest people. Two decades into Deng's 'economic miracle' and China's poorest 60 million peasants must still do without enough food, clothing and shelter to guarantee their survival. An additional 30 million farmers eke out livelihoods on less than US $1 per day—the World Bank's universal measure of poverty. People in Sichuan earn only 15% of what their cousins in Guangdong take home. Beijing yuppies pay cash for cars but nine out of ten poor peasants cannot afford to see a doctor. The issue for the government is whether a mixture of poverty and resentment will explode into unrest.

Beijing leaders, in 1992, announced a plan called the '8–7 Poverty Reduction Programme.' It aimed to raise 80 million people above the poverty line in 7 years. It set aside US $2 billion per year for projects such as land reclamation, irrigation and new roads. Extra money went to basic education, health care, and family planning. By the year 2000, the government has guaranteed every Chinese person at least 2,100 calories a day, clothing and a modest home.

The UN has also been helping out. It set up 'demonstration projects.' The World Bank pledged US $250 million in help to the poor areas of the Southwest. For example, new rural schools and clinics have opened up. New food processing plants have created non-agricultural jobs. Poor farmers who are literate have been linked with factories in Guangdong. Each farmer gets a US $120 travel loan and a job which pays up to US $50 per month. However, often help sent from Beijing does not reach the rural poor. It is appropriated by local officials.

Still looking for better results, Beijing has tightened control over funds. In a circular the state council said that "no more new hotels, government office buildings, cellular phones or cars will be bought in poor areas before poverty problems are solved".

HEALTH
China has some important health problems which need to be dealt with. There are not enough health services, particularly in the countryside. There is shortage of health workers especially highly-trained and experienced ones. The population continues to increase, is growing older and is becoming susceptible to illnesses like cancer. Babies in rural areas are up to four times as likely to die as those in the towns.

The partial answer to these problems is to allow limited private practice to develop in the belief that newly rich peasants can afford to pay. Growth and modernisation of health services rather than redistribution is the aim. Hospitals have increased their fees to try to balance their budgets or even make a profit.

This is a far cry from the rural health policies of the 1960s and '70s. Then the government focused on the health needs of the countryside. This led to the introduction of the barefoot doctors, who were farm workers with basic medical skills. After a brief training, barefoot doctors could look after health needs ranging from snake bites to appendicitis. By the early 1970s, there were about 2 million barefoot doctors—about 1 for every 40 families in rural areas. The scheme was financed from the commune medical service into which each family paid a fixed amount.

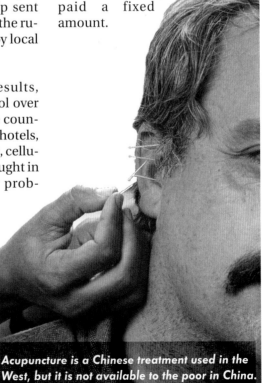

Acupuncture is a Chinese treatment used in the West, but it is not available to the poor in China.

More grey hairs for China's 1.236 billion people

China's population, the largest in the world, reached 1.236 billion at the end of 1997. It is a greying population which is moving to the cities. Targets for population size have been set: 1.3 billion by the year 2000 and 1.4 billion by 2010. Of the total population, 26% are aged between 1 and 14, 67.5% are between 15 and 64 and 6.5% are over 65. More Chinese are moving to cities from rural areas. 30% of the Chinese lived in towns and cities at the end of 1997. Urban migration has caused a headache for social planning and has led to an increased crime rate.

Why, then, did such a system have to change? There were several problems. The most obvious was the lack of skill of some barefoot doctors and the inability of some communes to pay to train them further. There were often disastrous results because of inappropriate prescribing of drugs, incompetent surgery and reluctance to refer cases to more experienced doctors. The amount of work was also a problem. The barefoot doctors were farm workers during the day and made visits to homes many miles away at night. When the responsibility system was introduced, many gave up being barefoot doctors to share in the prosperity. Communes were beginning to disappear and so there was insufficient money. The government was not prepared to finance the scheme adequately.

Some solutions have been proposed. One is the official encouragement of private practice. Barefoot doctors and traditional doctors were all encouraged to set up clinics which would be run as

The problem for centuries in China has been getting enough to eat. Now children of the new capitalists have grown so fat they have their own fat farm. The new rich indulge in western novelties such as hamburgers, chips and ice cream. "The Chinese have always liked to express their wealth through their food, especially in feeding their children," said Zhang Shuyu, a physician who founded the Tian Yu weight loss camp in 1990. These days children are spoiled all the more because of the government policy of one child per family.

Beijing Bunters fight the flab

private businesses. However, a system based on 'pay-for-your-service' discourages preventive health care. Why pay when you are not ill? Rather than producing more and better distributed health services, direct payment to a private doctor means that they move to areas where they will get more fees. On balance, the new health policies have not really increased the number of services although the quality may have improved. Paying for the service discriminates against the poor and makes medical care a response to demand rather than to need. It is possible that the move to a market economy will mean that families can spend more of their money on better food and housing which in turn may mean that health will improve.

15 Human Rights in China

China has been criticised many times for its record on human rights. While many non-governmental organisations such as Amnesty International and Asia Watch are openly critical, many foreign governments are more muted in their comments because they see opportunities in China to trade. Of course, we must be aware that the perception of human rights which we have is a western one and may be open to challenge from a Chinese viewpoint.

We will look at human rights in relation to:

● the process of law and punishment
● women
● the one child policy
● Tibet

LAW & PUNISHMENT IN CHINA

Aspects of law and punishment in China have been criticised by foreign governments, international organisations such as the UN and several non-governmental organisations who try to monitor events in the country. Imprisonment without trial, severe sentencing, public humiliation and execution, torture and degrading treatment while in custody have all been charges laid at the door of the Chinese system of justice.

Investigating Crime

The Chinese police use 'shelter and investigation' as a means of controlling the population. This policy allows anyone to be detained for up to 3 months. Detainees have few legal rights. Those held are often beaten to ob-

tain confessions and are at the mercy of the police for long periods. This frequently leads on to 're-education through labour' which allows those arrested to be detained for up to 3 years without trial. Human rights groups claim that, at any given time, at least 100,000 people are held under this system.

Human rights reports also highlight the extensive use of torture in prisons, widespread capital punishment and the practice of publicly parading those on their way to execution.

Trials

The Chinese criticise trials on the western model for favouring the criminal over the victim, for taking too long and for being too expensive. According to Amnesty International, trials in China "are frequently unfair, the process is heavily weighted in favour of the prosecution, defendants have little chance of adequate legal representation or the time to prepare their defence, guilt is often presumed in advance of the trial and the appeals process is severely limited."

Commonly, those accused are not allowed legal representation. They are normally forbidden to speak in their own defence and may only address the court to admit their guilt. They are on trial because the evidence of their guilt is "overwhelming" or they have "admitted their guilt." If they were not guilty they would not be brought to trial. Therefore trials are over quickly and sentencing is swift.

The Chinese Laogai—Labour Camps

THE LAOGAI is the name given to the network of prisons, labour camps and 'hospitals' which exist in China. The system works on two principles: hard labour and political thought reform. In China all prisoners are forced to work. The idea is that through forced labour prisoners will reform their ideas and will embrace communism and the socialist system. Human rights are ignored and torture, squalor and degradation are the norm.

There are five categories of prisoner in the laogai—detainees, convicts, those undergoing re-education, juvenile delinquents and people sent for forced labour. Some estimates suggest that there are as many as 1,000 forced labour camps and up to 10 million forced labourers in these camps.

The Chinese government uses the large prison population as a labour force. This huge network of millions of prisoners is forced to work on behalf of the state. The Chinese hold the view that society should not have to meet the costs of crime. For this reason they believe that convicted criminals must be productive to pay for the cost of keeping them in prison.

All the camps have two identities. They have a public face as an ordinary farm or factory. For example, the Shanghai Number Seven Labour Reform Prison is also known as the Shanghai Laodong Steel Pipe Factory.

Under Deng's guiding principle of "socialism with Chinese Characteristics", labour reform camps have been urged to become self-financing. Prisoners have always had to work, but now they are also required to meet strict production quotas and targets. Failure to meet them results in severe beatings. The reward for a full day's work is 2 cigarettes and failure to fulfil the high quotas is a dose of electrocution from the electric batons carried by all prison guards. Each meal is very basic—sour pickle soup with a little melon, pumpkin and seaweed thrown in.

The conditions which prisoners have to endure vary. In some detention centres the prisoner's family is able to visit and take food in. However, for many, particularly in the more primitive remote camps, conditions are exceedingly harsh. The work is often extremely dangerous with very little protective equipment. Prisoners may have to handle chemicals without breathing protection or go into mines without adequate safety equipment.

In Hanyang Prison in Hubei province, it was reported that prisoners made plastic products over a furnace which reached 180°C and that during the process they were forced to breathe in the poisonous fumes and the dust. They wore rubber gloves which were insufficient to protect them and they all had blisters on their hands. They worked eight hour shifts, often at night, seven days per week.

Various forms of torture are regularly practised on the prisoners. Electronic batons, whippings, beatings, the use of ankle and leg irons and various forms of water torture are used along with solitary confinement, the use of extremes of temperature, sensory deprivation and public and ritual humiliation. These are designed to break the spirit and bend people to the will of the authorities.

China is the world's largest tea exporter and a third of the tea crop is grown by prisoners. Products such as tea, coal, cotton, leather goods, tools, machine parts and light machinery are regularly exported although this is denied by the government. Some estimates suggest that the output from the Laogai constitutes as much as 10% of the Chinese Gross National Product (GNP) and is the mainstay of the economies of several provinces.

Normally, trials are not open to the public unless the authorities want a highly public trial to highlight some important point. For example, several trials of the Tiananmen students were held in public to frighten and warn the population and to create the image of the dissidents as criminals. Trials of corrupt officials may be made public to show that the authorities are being strong on crime and corruption. However, most of those accused are quickly and quietly dealt with, often without family and friends knowing anything about it. Sometimes even the accused themselves do not know until they are told in prison that they have been tried and found guilty.

The Death Penalty

Sixty five crimes carry the death penalty in China including embezzlement, corruption and hooliganism. The CPC campaign to root out economic corruption led to a rapid increase in the number of executions in some provinces for fairly petty crimes. In 1996, China executed more people than the rest

HUMAN RIGHTS OF WOMEN IN CHINA

The Chinese Constitution guarantees equality for women. Yet 50 years after Mao Zedong said that women "hold up half the sky," the majority of the country's 600 million women face discrimination and many have their human rights abused. Approximately one-third of women in China are illiterate. These are mainly older women and those who live in the more remote rural areas.

In the countryside the tradition for arranged marriages and the payment of a dowry has meant that many women are sold by their families as brides to pay off family debts. They are treated little better than any other commodity and are trapped in the marriage payment system. Women's organisations inside China estimate that up to one-third of rural women are unwilling brides and are forced by their families into arranged marriages in order to raise money.

In the cities women have other problems to contend with. Employment and housing is no longer guaranteed by the state and a disproportionately high number of females have lost their jobs as the loss-making state industries have closed. The economic changes have also affected the divorce rate. The divorce rate in Beijing doubled between 1990 and 1994 to reach nearly 25%. While many of these divorces are initiated by women, they have difficulty securing fair financial settlements for themselves and their children. Many women are, therefore, left to fend for themselves without any state help. Prostitution, which was all but stamped out by the old-style communists, is once more rife in the larger cities.

of the world's nations combined. Amnesty International recorded over 6,000 death sentences and confirmed that 4,367 executions had taken place although the organisation believes that the actual number is considerably higher. This was an increase from the 2,190 recorded executions in 1995. The increase is a consequence of the 'Strike Hard' campaign which was launched against crime and corruption. The Ukraine, having executed 167 people, is the second placed country.

Mass sentencing rallies commonly take place. Condemned prisoners are paraded through the streets carrying banners which detail their crimes or they are displayed in sports stadiums in front of tens of thousands of citizens. Afterwards they are shot in the back of the head. It has also been alleged that, following execution, their organs are removed for use in transplant operations.

Case Studies from Amnesty International

- Two men were executed in Shanghai for stealing pens and badminton racquets valued at US $7,000.
- Three other men were executed in Sichuan for attempting to steal tax receipts from a tax office.
- Lu Qigang was sentenced to death for sticking thorns and pointed sticks or needles into the buttocks of female cyclists. He was executed with six others, all charged with hooliganism.

POPULATION PROBLEMS IN CHINA—THE ONE CHILD POLICY

A major obstacle which may prevent China from raising its living standards and continuing to modernise is the country's population growth. The size and density of China's population have created problems for centuries, but the problem intensified between 1949 and 1976 as improvements in food supplies, sanitary conditions and medical practices led to a reduction in mortality rates and, hence, to an extra 390 million people.

A family planning programme was briefly introduced in 1962, but it was disrupted by the Cultural Revolution when Mao said that more babies would make China stronger. It was not until 1971 that the CPC began to consider seriously ways to curb population growth.

In 1979 in Sichuan province, a 'one child family scheme' was developed and it was subsequently adopted on a national level with the aim of keeping China's population under 1.3 billion by the year 2000 and reducing it to 700 million by the year 2050. It involved a mixture of *economic inducements* and *penalties*. One child families received preferential treatment in housing, education and employment as well as free medical care and a child benefit allowance. The penalties involved fines and loss of privileges.

The authorities used *social and administrative pressure* which sometimes included physical coercion. Couples required permission to be married and this was not given until men reached the age of 27 and women were 23 to 25. Permission to have a child was granted only if the quota for the area had not been reached.

Contraceptive devices were made widely available and couples, mainly the women, were pressured into undergoing sterilisation. Indeed, there are many documented cases of sterilisation operations being carried out without the permission or knowledge of the woman concerned. In the case of unauthorised pregnancies, forced abortions were also carried out.

The post-1971 population control campaigns were initially successful. Between 1965 and 1985 the demographic growth rate fell by more than 50% to 1.2% per annum while the birth rate fell by 53%.

They worked well for two main reasons. Firstly, the high standard of health services provided at the local level led to life expectancy rates reaching 71 for females and 68 for males, similar to life expectancy levels in developed countries. Secondly, the commune form of organisation, which remained in operation until 1980, provided old age security facilities for family elders. Large families therefore, were not necessary to ensure that at least some offspring would survive to look after elderly parents who could, instead, be cared for by the

The Chinese One Child Policy aims to control population growth to improve the prosperity of the nation.

commune system. Also there was direct social pressure from 'work team' colleagues who stood to be penalised if a family breached the one child norm.

Nevertheless, during the late 1980s and early 1990s concern began to mount as the population started to grow again. The new increase was concentrated in two main areas. The first of these was the minority communities of the West and South West who were exempt from the 'one child' family policy until 1989 and the other was among rural communities. The dismantling of the commune system and the switch to the 'household responsibility system' led to pressure to increase family size. Families hoped that more children would help the household to raise its production levels and secure larger land leases. More children would provide for

the future security of the parents as the commune welfare system began to disintegrate.

Since 1993 new measures have been introduced and the Chinese government has extended its one child policy. Currently, the government decides on the overall number of babies to be born. Each area is then given its quota. Before a woman can give birth she must obtain official permission. Marriage between people who have genetic diseases has been banned unless they agree to sterilisation or long-term contraception.

Birth Control and Human Rights

These birth control campaigns had an adverse effect on the human rights of families but, in particular, on the rights of tens of thousands

☛ Family planning officials from Fushan surrounded a village in the middle of the night. After a house to house search they rounded up all the pregnant women and forced them into trucks which were driven to hospital. One woman gave birth on the way to the hospital and a doctor killed the baby by giving it an injection. The other women were forced to have abortions.

☛ In Lingzhou county the unmarried sister of a couple who had fled and refused to pay fines for having too many children was detained in 1994. She was taken to a government office and locked in the basement with 12 other women. She was blindfolded, stripped naked and with her hands tied behind her back she was beaten with an electric baton. Others were suspended above the ground and beaten. Some were detained for several weeks.

Adapted from *Women in China*, Amnesty International, June 1995.

Chinese society has a long history of valuing males much more highly than females.

of women and children throughout China. Women's human rights are ignored as they are forced to endure abortion and sterilisation and may well be subjected to inhumane and degrading treatment, including detention and torture, before they succumb.

'Unauthorised' children should be aborted and if the parents refuse they face heavy fines. In rural areas, there are reports that houses have been demolished when people have refused to pay the fines, others have had their work bonuses withheld and state employees have been dismissed or demoted. In the city of Shenzen, over 900 families were given 15 days to leave the town because their families were over the authorised size. The government confiscated their residence permits, revoked their licences to work and ordered the housing department to stop renting them houses or premises to carry on their businesses.

The Human Rights of the Child

The 'unauthorised' children face a life of discrimination in education, medical care and other social benefits. Several million children have been the victims of abortion under the one child policy and countless others have been killed by doctors after birth. In some areas infanticide is not unknown. Usually the victims are either children with mental or physical birth defects or girls.

Chinese society has a long history of valuing males much more highly than females. If only one child is allowed then many parents wish it to be a healthy boy. Consequently, girls are abandoned so that the parents can try again for a boy. In the mid-1990s, the *Dying Rooms*, a TV documentary, showed several orphanages in China in which infants were being left to die from neglect—the majority of them were girls or deformed boys.

This video evidence supported a Human Rights Watch document which claimed that up to 90% of children admitted to one of China's largest orphanages died within a year of admission. Unofficial figures suggest that, nationally, 50% of all admissions die within the year.

The report catalogued the abuse and neglect of the children in the orphanages and suggested that there was "a pattern of cruelty, abuse and malign neglect" which "now constitutes one of the country's gravest human rights problems." The abuse was kept secret because the department which ran the orphanages was also in charge of the crematoria and could falsify the records which identified cause of death. Human Rights Watch based much of its evidence on the testimony and records of Dr Zhang Shyun who had been a doctor at the orphanage and who escaped from China to the West in 1995. The Chinese authorities claimed that the reports were lies and that Dr Zhang was 'crazy' but they arrested her brother two days after the publication of the report. Despite his release over a week later, the Chinese authorities could give no clear reason for his detention.

The one child policy is causing another problem for the authorities in China. Currently there are 115 males being born for every 100 females. By 2020 there will be up to 50 million more males than females. The problem for the government is that there will be many young males who will have no opportunity to find a female partner and major social problems may well result.

The Potato Palace in Lhasa with prayer flags left by the faithful even although the Chinese authorities discourage such traditions.

TIBET

Tibet has been occupied by China since 1949. The Chinese consider it to be part of the People's Republic of China while most Tibetans see themselves as an independent country under occupation. China argues that it did not "invade" Tibet, but "liberated" it. In 1992, China said that its intent had always been to bring "democratic reform" to Tibet.

The Chinese initiated a number of campaigns designed to stamp out Tibet's Buddhist faith, nationality and culture. Firstly, China radically reduced Tibet's borders. Much of (pre-1949) Tibet was redefined as "Chinese provinces" on modern Chinese maps. China created the Tibet Autonomous Region (TAR) in 1965, with an area approximately half the size of historic Tibet.

Secondly, China effectively outlawed freedom of speech, assembly and religion. The Chinese authorities continue to crack down on Tibetans who question Chinese rule.

Finally, the Chinese authorities systematically tried to eradicate the monks and nuns who were effectively Tibet's ruling élite. Nearly all of Tibet's 6,000 monasteries were destroyed and fewer than 10 remain standing today.

The Tibetan government, in exile, claims that 1.2 million Tibetans died between 1949 and 1979 as a result of the Chinese occupation including:

- 173,221 Tibetans who died after being tortured in prison.
- 156,758 Tibetans executed by the Chinese.
- 432,705 Tibetans killed while fighting Chinese soldiers.
- 342,970 Tibetans who have starved to death.
- 92,731 Tibetans who were publicly tortured to death.
- 9,002 Tibetans who committed suicide.

Since 1990, Amnesty International says it has documented the deaths of 24 Tibetans as a result of torture.

"The Chinese are practising cultural genocide in Tibet," the Dalai Lama, Tibet's spiritual and political leader, said in an interview. Organisations like Asia Watch and Amnesty International suggest that Chinese oppression has intensified in recent years partly through "re-education."

Part of this re-education is aimed at wiping out the Tibetan language and culture through re-educating the next generation. The Chinese replaced the Tibetan school system with 'People's Schools,' where teachers teach Communist Party ideology—in Chinese. Children are taught about Chinese history and about the superiority of Chinese culture but are told nothing about Tibet's culture and history. The Tibetan language is the only subject students may study in their native language. Everything else in school must be taught in Chinese. Teaching methods must include Chinese Communist Party propaganda. In classrooms, monasteries, nunneries, jails and public meetings, Chinese officials preach that Tibet was never an independent country and that Tibetans are better off under Chinese rule.

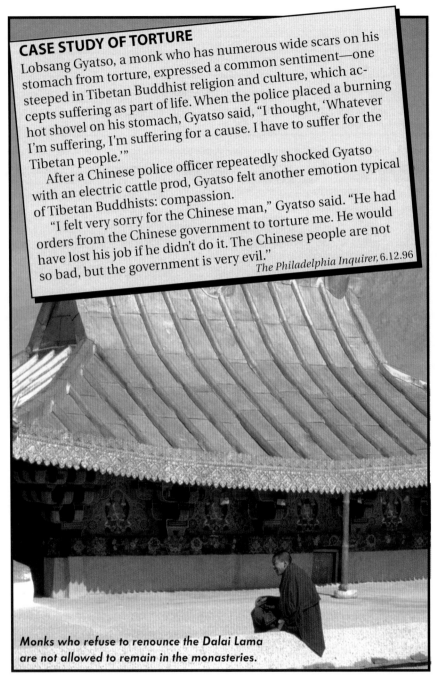

Monks who refuse to renounce the Dalai Lama are not allowed to remain in the monasteries.

had been successful. Chinese government policy relocated 7.5 million Chinese to Tibet so that the Chinese now outnumber the 4.6 million Tibetans. China offers economic incentives for working-class Chinese to emigrate to Tibet, while making it more difficult for ordinary Tibetans to earn a living.

Tibetans only own approximately 25% of the businesses in Lhasa whereas 40 years ago they owned nearly all of them. Tibetan shopkeepers were forced out of their shops by the authorities and their businesses were turned over to Chinese merchants.

Lastly, the Chinese police routinely arrest, jail and torture Tibetans who question Chinese authority. Estimates suggest that there are currently over 2,000 political prisoners in Tibet, nearly all of whom have been tortured. Torture and intimidation have become a daily fact of life for many. Chinese police and prison guards beat prisoners with chains, metal rods and wooden sticks spiked with nails, usually while the victims are shackled or hanging from a ceiling. The most common instrument of torture is the electric cattle prod.

China's official response to such reports is that it "... is not government policy. Chinese law forbids torture in jail" but officials could not "... say this never happens. It depends on certain people."

Few political prisoners have trials or appear in courtrooms before judges. Most say they were simply handed a document in prison stating their sentence and crime. Frequently this is merely "saying counterrevolutionary words." Many are released after being tortured for months, without any charges being brought.

Another part of 're-education' involves sending units of Chinese soldiers into monasteries to interrogate every monk about his allegiance to the Dalai Lama. The interrogations are called 'examinations.' Those who refuse to renounce the Dalai Lama are not allowed to remain in the monasteries. Some are jailed and tortured. Photos of the Dalai Lama have been forcibly removed from mon-

asteries. When monks at Ganden Monastery resisted, police opened fire, wounding several and arresting dozens. Children in middle schools in Lhasa were told that they must not carry photos of the Dalai Lama or wear red cords which are blessed by a lama.

In 1993, Chinese officials claimed that "the final solution", the mass migration of Chinese into Tibet,

Background to the Politics of Food

Everyone is born with a number of basic rights and one of the most important of these is the right to have food. However, there is a big difference between having a right on paper and having one in practice. Although everyone has the right to food, there are about 730 million people in the world who are hungry.

Where, then, does the politics come in—politics of food? In many ways, providing for a person's basic needs would be easy if there was no limit to the resources available. However, the amount of money available to many governments is limited. Most governments want to provide the basics, but they have to choose their priorities and often food is not one of them.

The government in a country can also exercise great power over what happens to aid that comes into the country. In many ways, whether people in a country receive enough food depends on the power of the government of that country. This, then, is where the politics comes in.

Did you hear about the famine in North Wayshire? People are dying of hunger every minute. No food is getting into the area. It is a disaster! No? You've never heard about that famine? Not surprising! We only hear about disasters like famine when they hit the media. The people in the affected country may have been aware that famine has been approaching but often no one takes any notice until it is too late.

The causes of food shortages and the solutions to these problems are very complex. In the following chapters we attempt to explain them. Examples will be taken from the countries of Northeast Africa (excluding Egypt) and Southern Africa. Tables 16.1 and 16.2 give some of the main development statistics of some of these countries. Study them carefully to help you to understand more about the countries.

	Area (000 sq. km.)	Population (000)	Demographic growth (%)	Children per woman 1992	Under-five mortality 1994	Calorie consumption % of required 1995	Primary school students/teacher 1992
Angola	1,246,700	10,442	2.3	6.6	292	85	32
Burundi	27,830	6,183	3.5	6.8	176	88	63
Central African Republic	622,980	3,234	1.0	5.8	175	86	90
Congo	342,000	2,577	1.6	6.6	109	98	66
Djibouti	23,200	603	0.5	5.8	158		43
Mozambique	801,590	15,463	3.9	6.5	277	80	53
Namibia	824,290	1,508	2.8	5.4	78	85	32
Rwanda	26,340	7,755	1.9	6.2	139	85	58
Eritrea	125,000	3,482			200		
Ethiopia	1,097,000	54,890	1.9	7.5	200	81	27
Kenya	580,370	26,017	2.8	5.1	97	89	31
Somalia	637,660	8,775	1.4	6.8	211	86	
Tanzania	945,090	28,817	2.9	6.3	159	92	36
Uganda	235,880	18,592	2.4	7.1	185	91	35
UK	244,880	58,395	0.3	1.8	7	110	20
USA	9,363,500	260,650	0.9	2.1	10	117	
Democratic Republic of Congo (Zaire)	2,344,860	42,540	1.0	6.2	186	89	
Zambia	752,610	9,203	0.6	6.5	203	89	44
Zimbabwe	390,760	10,778	2.3	4.6	81	92	38

Table 16.1

Angola

Population: 10,442,000. Population density is low due to centuries of slave trade. To keep control over the country, Portuguese fostered local divisions among the various ethnic groups – Bakondo, Kimbundu, Ovimbundu etc.

Capital: Luanda

Environment: Tropical in the North and sub tropical in the South. Coffee is main export crop. Abundant mineral reserves – diamonds, petroleum, iron ore. Number of problems aggravated by civil war – lack of drinking water, soil erosion and deforestation due to export of valuable timber.

Religions: Catholic (51%), Protestant (17%), non-Christian (32%).

Political parties: The People's Movement for the Liberation of Angola (MPLA); National Front for the Liberation of Angola (FNLA); National Union for the Total Independence of Angola (UNITA).

Government: Jose Eduardo dos Santos, President: Single chamber assembly: National assembly elected by direct popular vote.

Wars/History: Angola became independent from Portugal in 1975 and since then there has been continual civil war.

Zambia

Population: 9,203,000. 73 ethnic groups mainly descended from Bantu.

Capital: Lusaka:

Environment: Tropical high plateau. Copper mining.

Religions: Christian (80%) also Muslim and Hindu minorities.

Political Parties: Movement for a Multi-Party Democracy: United National Independence Party. (UNIP)

Government: Republic led by a President. President appoints 10 of the 150 members to the National Assembly and the other 140 are elected.

Wars / History: Mainly peaceful. Zambia supported: independence movements in Angola and Mozambique and helped the ANC in their struggles against Apartheid in South Africa. On several occasions the South African government invaded Zambia to attack camps and bases in the country. In 1980, South Africa also backed an attempted coup against President Kaunda. Kaunda resigned after losing the 1991 election to the Movement for a Multi-Party Democracy which was led by Frederick Chiluba.

Zimbabwe

Population: 10,778,000. Bantu (Shona) and Ndebele (Zulu)

Capital: Harare

Environment: Tropical high plateau. Severe soil loss. Mineral wealth.

Religions: Christian (45%) African traditional beliefs.

Political Parties: Zimbabwe African National Union-Patriotic Front (ZANU-PF):

Government: Republic with an elected President and two chamber assembly.

Wars/History: In 1965 the UK intended to give Rhodesia independence with black majority rule. The white leaders of Rhodesia declared Independence. A guerrilla campaign was launched by ZANU and ZAPU against the white Rhodesian government. The armed struggle continued until 1980 when Robert Mugabe's ZANU Party came to power. Between 1980 and 1987 there were tensions throughout the country between ZAPU and ZANU. In 1987 the two parties agreed to form one party – ZANU-PF. The overwhelming power of ZANU-PF enables the government to operate as a one-party state. There are other political parties but they are completely ineffective.

Tanzania

Population: 28,817,000 (1994). 120 ethnic groups.

Capital: Dodoma

Environment: Tropical coastal plain, mountainous North, irrigated farmlands around Lake Victoria. Soil erosion due to intensive farming in semi-arid areas. Deforestation

Political Parties: Revolutionary Party of Tanzania (CCM): The Civil United Front (CUF)

Government: Democratic Republic led by a President with a single chamber assembly elected by the people.

Wars/History: Largely peaceful since independence in 1961.

Ethiopia

Population: 54,890,000 (1994). Amhara and Oromo (67%), several small ethnic groups including Tigre and Somali.

Capital: Addis-Ababa

Environment: Mountainous, desert, deforestation, erosion and drought. Grows coffee and cotton.

Religions: Mostly Christian but large number practice traditional African religions.

Political Parties: Ethiopian People's Revolutionary Democratic Front; All Amhara People's. Organisation; Oromo Liberation Front; Ogaden National Liberation Front .

Government: Federal republic with parliamentary elections.

Wars/History: Haile Selassie, Emperor of Ethiopia, deposed in 1974. Military government under Colonel Mengistu came to power in 1977. Civil war ongoing on 4 fronts including Eritrea, Ogaden and Tigray. Mengistu fled the country in 1991. Parliamentary elections were held in 1995 and the new federal republic was established.

	Newspapers	TV sets	Radio sets (per 100,000 households, 1995)	GNP per capita (US dollars) 1993	Energy consumption per capita (kg) 1994
Angola	85	83	81	700	7
Burundi	82	82	81	180	23
Central African Republic	81	82	81	400	29
Congo	87	83	86	950	147
Djibouti	87	95	85	–	–
Mozambique	83	82	79	90	40
Namibia	98	85	89	1,820	–
Rwanda	84	81	82	210	27
Eritrea	–	–	–	100	–
Ethiopia	81	82	93	100	21
Kenya	88	84	90	270	107
Somalia	81	84	80	120	–
Tanzania	85	82	78	90	34
Uganda	82	83	85	180	23
UK	108	105	110	18,060	3,754
USA	104	111	123	28,740	7,905
Democratic Republic of Congo (Zaire)	82	82	88	220	–
Zambia	86	87	83	380	140
Zimbabwe	95	89	86	520	432

Table 16.3

AFRICAN COUNTRIES

Population: 15,463,000 (1994), Tsonga and Sera

Capital: Maputo:

Mozambique

Environment: Coastal plain rising to inland plateau. Hot and dry with great agricultural potential.

Religions: Traditional religions in rural areas. Christian and Muslim in towns.

Political Parties: Mozambique Liberation front (Frelimo), National Resistance of Mozambique (Renamo).

Government: Democratic Republic

Wars/History: War of independence plus South African backed civil war has destroyed the entire economy, agricultural base and infrastructure over the past 30 years. Country heavily landmined.

Population: 18,598,000 (1994). Integration of a series of African ethnic groups

Uganda

Environment: Tropical and largely fertile. Rainforest provides timber for export. In addition to subsistence farming of rice and corn there is extensive cash crop cultivation - coffee, cotton, tea and tobacco. Fish from Lake Victoria is also important.

Religions: Christian (48%) Traditional Religions (33%).

Political Parties: National Resistance Movement (NRM). All other parties have been disenfranchised by the government.

Government: One-Party State led by a President.

Wars/History: In 1971 Idi Amin came to power in a military coup. He was an authoritarian ruler who ordered the expulsion of all Asians in 1972. He declared himself President for life and presided over a reign of terror and bloodshed. In 1979 he was forced to flee when he was opposed by the Ugandan National Liberation Front aided by troops from Tanzania. Political violence continued despite elections. Between 1981 and 1985 there were 16 major military offensives against opposition guerrilla bases. The country experienced continued civil war and a series of attempted coups. In the 1990s the ruling group refused to allow political parties and banned them in 1995. Tribal divisions are increasing tensions throughout the country.

Population: 26,017,000 (1994). Kikuyu, Luhya, Luo

Capital: Nairobi

Kenya

Environment: Coast tropical. Mountainous interior. Deforestation, soil erosion and desertification.

Religions: Christian (73%) Muslim (6%) Traditional African (20%)

Political Parties: Kenya Africa National Union (KANU), Democratic Party, Kenya National Congress.

Government: Democratic Republic with President and elected single chamber assembly. Effectively a one-party state.

Wars/History: Late1940s to 1964 – struggle for independence. Bloody terrorist campaign and concentration camps. After 1964, ethnic conflict followed independence. In 1978, KANU was the only party authorised to run candidates and its leader, Daniel Arap Moi became President. He has continued in power for the past 20 years. The Democratic Party was formed in 1992 to provide opposition and to demand a democratic multi-party system. Amnesty International constantly accuses Moi of human rights violations.

Population: 44,540,000. Over 200 ethnic groups.

Capital: Kinshasa:

Zaire Democratic Republic of the Congo

Environment: Mostly in Congo river basin. North and Centre covered in equatorial rainforest. Rubber and mining (copper and gold) are important industries.

Religions: Traditional African (60%) Christian (40%)

Political Parties: People's Revolutionary Movement, Sacred Union of the Radical Opposition and Allies (USORAS)

Government: Republic with a powerful President

Wars/History: From the 1960s the country was controlled by President Mobutu through a kleptocracy. After elections were not held in 1991, opposition grew and in 1997 Mobutu and his government were ousted by General Laurent-Desire Kabila and his rebel army which swept through Zaire from the eastern border with Rwanda.

Population: 7,755,000. Hutu(84%) Tutsi (15%)

Capital: Kigali

Rwanda

Environment: Mountainous, well irrigated with lakes and rivers. Subsistence agriculture. Deforestation and erosion due to demands for energy.

Religions: Traditional African Religions (70%) Catholics (20%).

Political Parties: Rwandan Patriotic Front, Republican Democratic Movement.

Government: Republic – currently government of national unity.

Wars/History: Long history of tribal wars between the Hutu and the Tutsi. In 1994, genocide (Hutu majority slaughtered the Tutsi minority) and civil war led to the deaths of over 1 million Rwandans and over 2 million fled to neighbouring countries.

Population: 8,775,000. Hamitic

Capital: Mogadishu

Somalia

Environment: Semi-desert. North mountainous, South desert. Increase in livestock has led to desertification.

Religions: Islamic

Political Parties: United Somali Congress (divided into several factions).

Government: Dictatorship

Wars/History: Following a coup d'état in 1991, the Revolutionary Socialist Party of Somalia (RSSP) is the only legal political group in the country. Since then a civil war between various factions led by local clan leaders eg. General Aidid has meant that the government is very unstable. Under pressure from the US, the UN sent troops into Somalia in 1992. They were mainly US troops. They were unable to bring peace and were forced to withdraw after sustaining casualties and criticism from other countries.

Population: 3,482,000 (1994). 9 ethnic groups eg. Afar, Tigre,

Capital: Asmara

Eritrea

Environment: Dry plains and hot desert. Deforestation and erosion are responsible for frequent drought.

Religions: Half Christian and half Muslim

Political parties: People's Front for Democracy and Justice.

Government: Since independence in 1993 multi-party elections have been promised. Country run by provisional National Assembly and President.

War/History: 30 year war of independence against Ethiopia. Continued fighting within country after independence. Renewed hostilities with Ethiopia over Border dispute (1998).

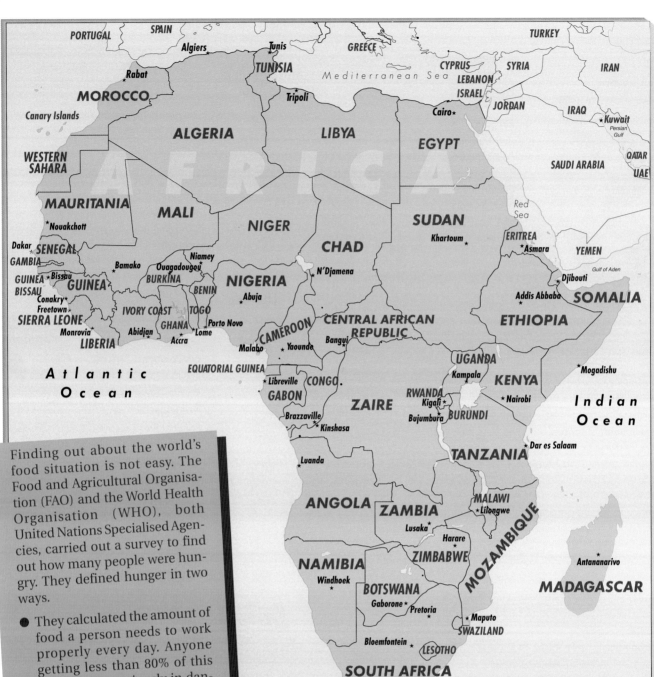

Finding out about the world's food situation is not easy. The Food and Agricultural Organisation (FAO) and the World Health Organisation (WHO), both United Nations Specialised Agencies, carried out a survey to find out how many people were hungry. They defined hunger in two ways.

● They calculated the amount of food a person needs to work properly every day. Anyone getting less than 80% of this amount was seriously in danger of disease. They found that some 350 million people were in this group.

● Anyone getting less than 90% could not live a full and productive life. They found that this group consisted of around 730 million people.

In human terms this means that:

✚ between 20 and 30 million of us die every year of hunger related causes

✚ one in five of us suffers from undernutrition

✚ the number of people affected increases daily

THE LEVEL OF HUNGER IN THE WORLD

Region	Number of people affected (millions)	% of total
All developing countries	730	34
Sub-Saharan Africa	150	44
Asia	510	32
Latin America & Caribbean	50	13
Middle East & North Africa	20	10

Table 16.3

Food Insecurity In Africa

"Food security exists when all people at all times have access to enough safe and nutritious food to maintain a healthy and active life."

(FAO, Food Security Assessment, Rome, January 1996)

Food security is recognised as a basic human right in a number of international declarations.

Since the World Food Conference was convened in 1974, progress has been made towards reducing undernourishment. By 1998, the world's 5.8 billion people had, on average, 15% more food per capita than twenty years before when the population was 4 billion. In 1969-70, the average person in the developing world received 2,120 calories per day. By 1990 this figure had risen to 2,470 calories. During 1969-71, an estimated 35% of the population of developing countries was undernourished, but by 1990-92, that figure had fallen to 20%.

However, in the 1990s one person in every seven, 800 million people, is still chronically undernourished, while millions more suffer from diseases linked to nutritional deficiencies and one-third of the world's children are malnourished. Even in the developing world these problems do not affect all countries equally. While countries in Asia and Latin America have nearly caught up with developed countries in terms of average calorie availability, sub-Saharan Africa has fallen further behind. In 1969-71, the average daily consumption in sub-Saharan Africa was 1,000 calories below that of developed countries.

By 1992-94, that gap had widened to 1,100 calories. Figures show that per capita food production in sub-Saharan Africa has fallen for three successive decades.

The world's demand for food is projected to rise by up to 50% over the next 15-25 years as a result of population growth and rising incomes. Although agricultural production is also predicted to grow, at a rate of 1.8% a year, the number of chronically undernourished people might still be about 680 million in the year 2010, with over 300 million of them in sub-Saharan Africa. While food insecurity is a problem for many people around the world it is a major problem for the people of Africa.

Food insecurity and famine appears to be a fact of life faced by the populations of many African countries. Images of pot-bellied, skin-taut skeletons attended by swarms of flies are shown in the media with mind-numbing regularity. If the question 'what causes these famines?' is asked, the reply is often 'too many people' or 'bad weather.' Nature does affect food supplies to a certain extent, but the main causes of food insecurity are complex and varied and usually relate to the failure of people to work with nature and to make the best use of the land and the climate. Political, economic and social reform could eliminate food insecurity throughout the African continent.

Gerhard Heilig wrote a book about food production called *How many People can be fed on Earth?* After a lengthy and complex analysis he

concluded that, with the current level of technology, the Earth could support and sustain between 10 and 15 billion people. Currently the world's population is 5.8 billion. The question is, therefore, why are we unable to prevent the frequent images of famine?

Heilig suggests that the factors which limit food production are political, social and economic, not natural. Right now Africa could produce more than enough food for its population even with its traditional forms of low level agricultural input. One estimate suggests that a nation such as Sudan could, by itself, feed the entire population of Africa if it adopted modern techniques. Yet Sudan regularly suffers from famine.

Unfortunately the political will is not there to ensure that this can happen. Individual African countries and the international community have engaged in policies which actively discourage farmers from producing food. As Heilig states, "...if we can prevent (civil) wars with soldiers plundering harvests or devastating crop fields with land mines; if we can stop the stupidity of collectivisation and central planning in agriculture; if we can agree on free trade for agricultural products; if we redistribute agricultural land to those that actually use it for production; if we ... avoid environmental destruction; if we implement optimal water management and conservation practices. If we do all this during the next few decades, we could certainly be able to feed a doubled or tripled world population." (Heilig, pages 253-4.)

Heilig's analysis is supported by a Food and Agricultural Organisation (FAO) survey in 1984. It projected that the population of Africa would be 780 million by the year 2000. Their analysis suggested that if African farmers used "no fertilisers, pesticides or improved seeds and no long-term conservation measures," the continent could feed 1.2 billion people. If farmers could develop their methods and use "some fertilisers, pesticides and improved seeds, conservation measures and improved cropping patterns on half the land," the continent could produce enough food to feed 4.5 billion people.

A study of estimated grain production by Bender and Smith in 1997 concluded that Africa could produce 10,845 million metric tons of grain whereas it only produced 88 million metric tons. From these figures, Africa is currently producing less than 1% of its potential output.

THE EFFECTS OF POPULATION AND CLIMATE ON FOOD SECURITY

Nature has a major impact on food security. Population growth creates increased demand for food while, at the same time, often reducing the area which can be used to grow it. A change in climate may cause prolonged drought or excessive rainfall or it may lead to long-term temperature change. Unless the change is cataclysmic, it is how people adapt to these changes which determines whether they will face food shortages. Famine is a consequence of the failure of people to interact appropriately with their environment and its changing nature.

Records show that through recorded history African peoples faced food shortages caused by climate changes and that they developed effective ways of dealing with these problems. However, at the end of the 20th century a variety of factors are interacting to intensify the problems.

Population growth is far more rapid than at any time in Africa's history

KEY FACTS

The world's 5.8 billion people have, on average, 15% more food per capita than 20 years ago when the global population was 4 billion.

In 1969–71, an estimated 35% of the population in developing countries was undernourished. By 1990–92, it had fallen to 20%.

One in seven of the world's inhabitants, or 800 million people, are still chronically undernourished. One-third of the world's children are malnourished.

Most of the hungry are in developing countries: 37% of the population in Africa, 32% in Asia and 13% in Latin America and the Caribbean still have inadequate food. Sub-Saharan Africa is the one region where the situation is worsening.

Global demand for food is projected to rise by up to 50% in the next 15–25 years as a result of population growth and rising incomes.

World food production grew 3% annually in the 1960s, 2.4% in the 1970s, 2.2% in the 1980s, and 1.6% in the ten years between 1985 and 1995. The FAO predicts the figure will be 1.8% up to 2010.

Stocks of wheat are at a 20-year low, while those of maize are at a 50-year low. The shortages have pushed up world market prices by 30–50%, adding an estimated US $3 billion to the food bills of 'low income food-deficit countries'.

Some 60% of global food stocks are in the hands of private companies, while 70% of world grain trade is carried out by six companies.

Aid to agriculture in developing countries has fallen from $10 billion in 1982 to $7.2 billion in 1992 (in constant 1985 US$), indicating, in the FAO's words, a "decreasing political will to address the problem" of world hunger.

Since 1974, world agricultural trade (including fisheries and forestry) has grown from $148 billion to $485 billion. However, developing countries' share of world agricultural exports (excluding fisheries and forestry) fell from 40% in the early 1960s to 27% in 1993.

For the least developed countries, food imports currently absorb more than one-third of export earnings. The FAO estimates that the food import bills for low income food-deficit countries will be 55% higher in 2000 than in 1987–89, with 14% of the increase ($3.6 billion) due to GATT (General Agreement on Trade and Tariffs now WTO–World Trade Organisation).

Source: *Panos Media Briefing* October 1996

and this amplifies the pressure on the resources caused by climatic change. Added to this are the man-made problems of modern technological warfare which can affect far more people far more quickly than in the past. Globalisation of economic dependency also means that poor people today are at the mercy of many more forces over which they have little or no control than they ever were in the past.

Population Growth

Population growth in the past 40 years has put considerable pressure on resources and has helped to promote food insecurity in various parts of Africa. In Northeast Africa—Ethiopia, Eritrea, Sudan, Somalia, Kenya, Burundi—population growth rates were very low before 1950. However, between 1954 and 1994 the population trebled from 61 million to 186 million.

In many areas, such rapid increases in the population are more than the environment can sustain. The increased demand for food means that farmers upset the traditional patterns of farming which have enabled the soil to recover. Farmers no longer leave the ground fallow long enough between cropping seasons to allow it to renew itself. Subsequent crop yields are significantly reduced until eventually they dwindle away to nothing as the soil becomes exhausted.

Desertification even encroaches on towns in Ethiopia

Marginal land is forced into production and its cultivation may exhaust the soil within one or two seasons. Alongside increases in livestock, this can lead to overgrazing and to further soil exhaustion. Inappropriate aid can worsen the situation. In one project in Ethiopia, wells were dug to improve the water supplies and sustain the livestock. The extra water enabled the farmers to enlarge their herds, but unfortunately the increased number of animals soon exceeded the ability of the land to sustain them. Consequently, the grazing land could not renew itself and the process of desertification began.

As the land becomes exhausted, it cannot sustain the plants and bushes that cover and bind the soil. Wind and rain rapidly erode the soil and very quickly the area can turn into a desert. Desertification of large tracts of Africa, particularly in the Horn region, is partly a consequence of population growth but has also been caused by changes in climate.

Population growth also creates deforestation. The demand for marginal land to cultivate may lead to the widespread removal of trees. Trees are in high demand for use as fuel and shelter. Deforestation often leads to soil erosion. For example, on hillsides after heavy rains the soil is washed away because there are no roots to bind it together nor trees to slow down the speed of the water flow.

As the forests are used up, the people use dried dung and unused plant material as fuel instead of as fertilisers. Wind and water erosion increase. Estimates suggest that about 130 million people throughout Africa live in areas where fuel wood consumption is greater than the capacity of the tree cover to regenerate itself. Around 1900, over 40% of Ethiopia was covered in forests. By 2000, the figure is projected at 4% and falling.

The UN has estimated that Ethiopia loses over 1.6 million tons of topsoil each year. In places where at one time the soil cover was to a depth of over 5 metres it has now fallen to less than 10 centimetres, where it can only be used for grazing. The pressure of overgrazing then reduces large areas to bare rock.

Climate Changes

Climatic change can intensify the pressures placed on the environment by population growth. In the last few years there have been significant changes in climate affecting several countries in Africa. In those areas of the Horn of Africa that are prone to drought, the number of droughts have doubled. The chances of a drought occurring have increased from one year in six to one year in three.

The long-term weather pattern has also changed. In southern Sudan the annual average level of rainfall has been reduced, making farming less viable in many areas. In a crescent-shaped zone through Tanzania, Kenya, Ethiopia and Sudan the timing and the amount of rainfall is varying significantly from year to year, making farming less viable.

War destroys local villages and creates refugees

EFFECTS OF ARMED CONFLICT ON FOOD SECURITY

Armed conflict creates food insecurity by disrupting and destroying both the production and distribution of food supplies. In some cases, the damage done by war is incidental but, on many occasions, depriving the enemy of food is part of the strategy of war.

In Ethiopia, in the 1980s, government forces employed a 'scorched earth policy' which destroyed hundreds of thousands of acres of food-producing land in Tigray province. It is a strategy common to many wars in Africa. Troops enter an area, destroy the crops in the fields by setting them on fire, either destroy or remove any grain held in storage and kill or remove all livestock. Water may be contaminated by shooting livestock or villagers and dumping the bodies into the wells.

A 'scorched earth policy' denies food sources to the enemy but also, by intimidating the people, it creates large-scale migrations of refu-

gees to feeding centres and towns. This ties down large numbers of enemy troops who have to be used as security to prevent food riots in the larger towns instead of being deployed at the front.

The massacres of people and livestock in the Kongor area of Sudan reduced the number of cattle from around 1.5 million to less than 50,000. In many African countries, cattle are used as a standard measurement of wealth and are the main means by which people hold their savings. Rents, dowries etc. are calculated in cattle. The destruction of livestock totally undermines the rural economy and can wipe out all of a family's savings and wealth. It also creates particular problems for the nutrition of young children who rely on milk as part of their basic diet.

Conflict in a region creates fear. Farmers, who are often women and older children, become frightened to work on farmland at any great distance from their homes, so the area under cultivation is reduced.

If their fear intensifies as the conflict draws near or if they fear attack from bands of militia, the people will abandon their fields and become refugees to escape from the fighting. They flee because they fear being massacred. They flee to protect their children from being abducted and forced to serve in the army of one side or the other. They flee to stop their children being abducted and sold into slavery as they currently are in Sudan.

Once they become refugees they become non-productive and aid dependent. They may lose the occupancy of their land forever, even if they eventually return to the area in the future.

Conflict also adversely affects the economic routine of the country. Even in developing countries most households, including rural households, rely on purchases at the local market to meet their food needs. However, war disrupts the economy and the quantity, quality and variety of the food supply is reduced. Food becomes scarce in

Rebels and government troops disrupt the normal pattern of life and survival becomes impossible

the countryside and those who are landless and who usually find work on the farms of the wealthy become unemployed and cannot afford food because its price soars.

The position in the urban areas can become more acute. Large numbers of unemployed, starving people develop into a major problem for the authorities. People often resort to looting to feed themselves and this leads to lawlessness and the escalation of violence. To avoid this the authorities direct the available food to the main population centres, thus heightening the problem in the rural areas. People from the rural areas then become refugees and head to the cities swelling the size of the problem.

Conflict also disrupts the distribution of aid. There are the physical problems of inadequate road and rail communications to remote areas. The dangers of medical and feeding centres coming under enemy attack and of aid convoys being hijacked are also present. It is also difficult to assess where to send the available aid in a rapidly changing situation with thousands of refugees travelling in all different directions to escape the fighting. Finally, warring factions could block relief supplies or divert them for their own use.

Children, in particular, are at high risk as the result of armed conflict. Armed conflict places major stress on the care system. Mothers and other family members are forced to spend much more time foraging for food, water and work and therefore have less time to care for their children. When the family become refugees, the children face a high risk of malnutrition and infection.

Children suffer when they are in areas that do not have adequate supplies of food. They suffer because they are last in order of importance for food. The military and the rich and influential are first in line, then come the men and lastly come the women and children. If a refugee family loses its male head then its chances of survival are very much reduced. If both parents perish or become separated from the children, then the children are at even greater risk unless they can get help from other adults.

Hygiene suffers during conflict and this raises the chances of infection. Unsatisfactory waste disposal, dead and decomposing bodies, untreated wounds and inadequate or contaminated water supplies add to the cycle of malnutrition and infection. Children are seriously affected because of the way they are fed. Food that is not prepared properly or rapid changes to their diet harm young children. The quality of their diet is also important. Young children can only eat small quantities of food at one time, so they need a frequent intake of food. Conflict creates long periods when food is not available and when it does appear the quality may be poor. Children suffer because they cannot do without food for as long a period as adults.

Another problem is that the family may not have the means or the knowledge required to adapt to the conditions to ensure that their children have an adequate diet. Mothers experience hunger, exhaustion and stress which can affect their ability to breast-feed their babies. Also, the conflict can separate nursing mothers from their babies

Effects of Population Pressures, Climate Variations and War on Food Security in Rwanda

More than 200,000 Rwandans, mainly from southern Rwanda, expect poor harvests this season.

"Erratic rainfall and flooding over the past several months have meant that many people in these areas didn't harvest a good crop earlier this year and the meagre reserves people have been drawing upon up to now are finally running out," a representative of the World Food Programme said.

"Many of these areas are traditionally food-insecure," pointed out the WFP representative.

"Some people in these areas are forced to cultivate on poor soils or steep slopes as a result of land pressure. Others are living in villages where there are too many people trying to survive off too little land," he added. "As a result, small setbacks in a harvest can be devastating for these people."

The war situation prevailing in northwestern Rwanda, normally considered the breadbasket of the country, has also aggravated food insecurity in the area. People living in these areas are continually on the move, fleeing from the fighting.

This situation has prevented the people from cultivating their fields, and the little that is produced in the fields is looted or taken by force by the Hutu militia.

"Continued insecurity and banditry in these areas have wreaked havoc in many communities. Thousands of families live in constant fear and have seen their crops destroyed, food reserves stolen and cattle slaughtered by armed militias," the WFP said.

Although a slight improvement in food security was expected in July, a damper has been put on this forecast by the ongoing flooding attributed to El Nino.

In some areas, crops have been washed away, roads cut off, and rivers have flooded.

In its March 1998 assessment of the food situation in Rwanda, the Famine Early Warning System (FEWS), financed by the United States Agency for International Development (USAID), noted that "many rural roads are nearly impassable due to damage caused by rainfall, flooding and landslides". Rwanda's Meteorological Office believes that the heavy rains, which are above normal, will go on for quite some time.

Adapted from WFP *To Bring Food to Thousands Threatened by Famine* by Jean Baptiste Kayigamba, 28 April 1998

---

which places the babies in grave danger.

War also breaks down the normal social structures which enable knowledge and support to be passed between the generations. Young mothers with limited maternal skills may not be able to feed their children because they become traumatised by their situation or they may not be able to adapt to changed circumstances. They may become dependent on the handouts of powdered milk at the feeding stations and stop feeding their children themselves. This leaves the children wide open to infections and at risk of starvation if the aid is discontinued.

Even after the conflict is over it may take time for feeding patterns to return to normal. The FAO reported that "in Mozambique, for example, some young couples returning to the country from refugee camps did not know how to prepare any foods other than the maize, beans and oil that had been distributed to them as rations. They were not familiar with traditional foods or feeding practices and did not know which local foods to use during weaning. Where parents or grandparents had been lost, there was no one available to teach them."

THE EFFECTS OF TYPE OF GOVERNMENT ON FOOD SECURITY

The type of government which a country has can affect food security. Most countries in Africa have authoritarian governments and many of them are military dictatorships.

In the absence of democracy people are unable to express their opposition through elections and elected representatives. They may feel forced to resort to armed conflict in an attempt to gain their objectives. Consequently, many governments throughout Africa depend on the military to maintain them in power.

As Figure 17.1 shows, in a number of African countries spending is diverted to the military from projects which might improve the development of the countries and increase the food supply. Another problem is that although the majority of the population is rural, much of the available funding goes to the cities. Development programmes often ensure that people in the main cities get the best treatment because it is unrest in the cities which often poses the greatest threat to the ruling élite.

This high priority for the military means that areas like education are starved of adequate funding. In the countries of the Horn of Africa, for example, illiteracy rates are above 50%, with those for women in some countries being above 85%.

In order to improve food security, a country needs to improve its farming techniques. Development programmes need to be put in place to teach farmers how to in-

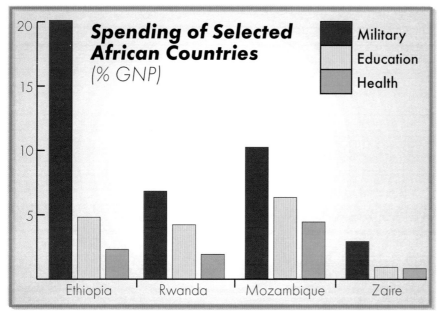

Figure 17.1

crease their output of food. This would be made much easier if the majority of farmers were literate. If education is a low priority, as it is in so many countries, then the prospects for improving agriculture throughout Africa are bleak.

Government Kleptocracy

Another consequence of an authoritarian society is mismanagement and the freedom it gives the ruling élite to indulge in corruption. Dictators and ruling cliques have to ensure that they have enough support to keep themselves in power. To maintain sup-

port they may divert funds to equip and pay for the military. However, they also have to allow senior officers and senior government officials to steal funds in order to give them a stake in the current system of government.

Influential people who do not have a stake in the corruption might become the centre of opposition. On the other hand, those with a significant share will continue to support the system which supplies them. Many African countries have inadequate infrastructures because development money has been diverted to the private accounts of

the country's leadership. This is called a kleptocracy.

Inadequate road and rail links exist throughout Africa because the money to improve them has been siphoned off. Roads go nowhere because one section of society or a particular tribal group has to be given a handout for some reason, so a road is built in their area although it serves little purpose. Contracts are padded out for extravagant airport projects, government buildings, palaces and other such schemes in the capital cities because jobs have to be found to pacify or impress the population or to ensure that enough wealth trickles down to the middle classes.

The structure and type of government, leading as it often does to armed conflict and to the diversion of development funds, has become one of the main causes of food insecurity and famine in Africa over the past 40 years.

THE EFFECTS OF LAND TENURE & USE ON FOOD SECURITY

Land tenure concerns the rights that a person holds in relation to land. Security of tenure is extremely important to the development of food security. If tenure is secure, the holder is more likely to improve the land and see it as a

---

CASE STUDY OF A KLEPTOCRACY

ZAIRE
(DEMOCRATIC REPUBLIC OF THE CONGO)

★ Kinshasa

On arrival in Kinshasa, we are included in a select group taken off the plane before the other passengers, put into a holding pit with velveteen couches and free alcohol.

The pit is full of men in bullet-proof vests with walkie-talkies. Everyone else carries cellular telephones. (We find out later that this is a necessary luxury. The phone system has been deliberately neglected for years, as Mobutu does not want his opposition conspiring with the outside world.)

The guns, the vests, the walkie-talkies and even the phones are used to protect

Zaire's rich from Zaire's poor. Almost everyone in Zaire is a thief of some kind. In fact, stealing is government policy. Zaire is one of Africa's most naturally endowed countries with billions of dollars in gold, diamonds and precious minerals. But the average Zairean's annual income is $160. Perhaps that is why the President once told his citizens at a public rally: 'Go ahead and steal, but don't steal too much, or you will get caught.' As a result, Zaire is a kleptocracy: soldiers loot, policemen mug, and hospital nurses won't admit

patients without a bribe.

From the moment Mobutu seized power in 1961 ... he never looked back. He spent the next three decades building two things: a pirate's fortune of almost unparalleled size (estimated at between $5 billion and $8 billion—with a single personal cheque he could wipe out his country's crippling foreign debt), and a personal mythology ... the President and his retinue were free to indulge themselves with French champagne, preferably pink Laurent Perrier and Mercedes Benz sedans.

(continued on page 138)

Inadequate road and rail links exist throughout Africa because the money to improve them has been siphoned off.

long-term investment rather than as something to be exploited in the short term. Secure tenure allows the holder to make management decisions about the best way to use resources in order to meet both immediate household needs and long-term sustainable investment.

One of the most serious obstacles to increasing the agricultural productivity and income of rural women is their insecurity of land tenure. Less than 2% of land is owned by women although women do most of the agricultural work. In Africa, custom excludes women from ownership. Property is held in a man's name and is passed through the male line. A widow's right to remain on the land is not secure. If a woman loses her husband, it is not unusual for the family of her late husband to pass the ownership of the holding to his brothers and in some cases the wife may be forced off the land.

If the tenure of the land is in doubt, then women do not have access to credit to purchase the equipment that might improve the land they are farming—improved seeds, fertilisers and pesticides. They are also often excluded from membership and decision making in farming associations designed to improve agriculture. The Women in Development Service of the FAO stated in a 1998 Report, "Without land and secure tenure a woman cannot access credit and membership in agricultural associations, particularly those responsible for processing and marketing. If tenure is secure,

---

(continued from page 137)

Some of Mobutu's fortune is 'above board'. In 1981 his presidential salary amounted to more than 17% of his country's annual budget. But most of the money is simply plundered from World Bank loans and illegal business deals with foreign governments and contractors. Mobutu has got away with stealing because he let his friends get away with it too. In 1975, a regional commissioner made up to $100,000 a year—and only 2% of it was his annual salary.

...We are flying to Mobutu's palace hideaway,

the 'Versailles in the Jungle', his home village of Gbadolite. It is no longer appropriate to call Gbadolite a village though. Where there had been a scattering of shacks and skeletal cows, now there is a mock-industrial city, with its own international airstrip and waiting Concorde for presidential shopping sprees and fast getaways.

While Kinshasa is plagued by blackouts and poisoned water, Gbadolite has its own billion-dollar hydroelectric dam. While the roads in Kinshasa and everywhere else turn to mud,

the roads in Gbadolite are maintained in the manner of an orderly American suburb. But since the improved Gbadolite has no other function than to serve the President and his entourage, the place turns into a ghost town when he is away. The presidential palace eclipses everything else. The pink marble monolith boast football stadium-sized gardens, computer operated fountains, artificial lakes and flowers imported exclusively from South Africa.

Extracts from *Zaire in crisis. Blame Mobutu's PE teacher* by Heidi Kriz in *The Observer Review* 11 May 1997

Postscript
In 1997, President Mobutu was overthrown by a rebel army from the eastern provinces led by Laurent Kabila. Mobutu fled the country to continue his fight against cancer in Switzerland and France and to enjoy his personal fortune. The new leaders changed the name of Zaire to the Democratic Republic of the Congo. Democratic reforms were promised but two years later the new regime was carrying on business much as before. Mobutu died in 1998.

The Politics of Food

Drought in Sudan

A dried up river bed in the Sudan is a problem which local people are adept at coping with. When this is combined with war, survival becomes impossible.

In 1998, chronic food shortages affected the entire region of South Sudan, with Bahr el Ghazal, Western Upper Nile, and parts of Eastern Equatoria being particularly affected. The situation in South Sudan has deteriorated over the years. The longstanding conflict in the region, the difficulties of access and adverse environmental conditions, (including a very poor harvest in 1997) stripped people of their assets leaving them with nothing to fall back on.

While aid agencies had expected 1998 to be a bad year in terms of food security, the situation became critical more rapidly than first anticipated and continued to worsen. The number of malnourished children is rising daily and the risk of both epidemic and diarrhoeal diseases is high.

Save the Children (UK) field staff in South Sudan have recently carried out an assessment in Bahr el Ghazal where they report the situation is the most acute. The recent fighting has forced thousands of people from their homes. An estimated 350,000 people in Bahr el Ghazal have no food whatsoever and will be unable to sustain themselves or their children through the dry season until the next harvest which is due in six months.

The southern Sudanese are traditionally very adept at surviving in a difficult environment. However the war and current drought in the region have reduced other opportunities for finding food. There is limited potential for fishing and pastures are poor for grazing livestock which, in turn, has depleted milk and meat supplies. Some have resorted to drastic survival mechanisms such as excavating ant hills to find grain; the large-scale slaughter of livestock; consuming seed supplies, and eating wild foods. Save the Children staff report that some food aid has been made available in government towns and some of the recently displaced are attempting the long trek of between 50 and 150 miles into these areas. Although already weakened by hunger, they are walking in temperatures of up to 120 degrees Fahrenheit.

Save the Children is concerned that an anticipated huge shortfall in the harvest this year will compound this crisis. People in the region have been unable to maximise planting opportunities either because they have eaten their seed out of desperation, have no seeds or have lost their seeds due to their displacement by the conflict. With nothing to fall back on communities will eat whatever grain they have left, exposing themselves to even further hardship.

Seed supplies are urgently required to capitalise on the current planting season. Seeds will have to be planted by the end of May to be in time for the September harvest. Apart from food and seeds, there is also an urgent need for non-food items. Many people have no tools with which to prepare the ground for planting seeds. Blankets, mosquito nets and relief nets are also required.

Extracts from BRIEFING: SUDAN EMERGENCY Save the Children (UK) press office 24 April 1998

a woman can invest in, rather than exploit, the land's productive potential and is more likely to adopt environmentally sustainable farming practices. She can plan and adjust resource allocation decisions under changing climate or economic conditions and rely on the productive results of her labour."

"Security of tenure is often the key to having control over major decisions such as what crops to grow, what techniques to use, what to consume and what to sell. Given women's tendency to grow food as opposed to cash crops and to spend income on family food, security of tenure for women must be viewed as a key link in the chain from household food production to national food security."

Women, Education and Food Security

Education plays an important role in the development of food security. Several studies have shown that farmer training improves agricultural production. In 1992, researchers examined the effects of education in small-scale agriculture. It found that if the educational level of a farmer was increased by one year, the average addition to agricultural output was 24%. The study concluded that "investment in farmers' education or a successful policy of bringing educated persons into agriculture can accelerate agricultural production."

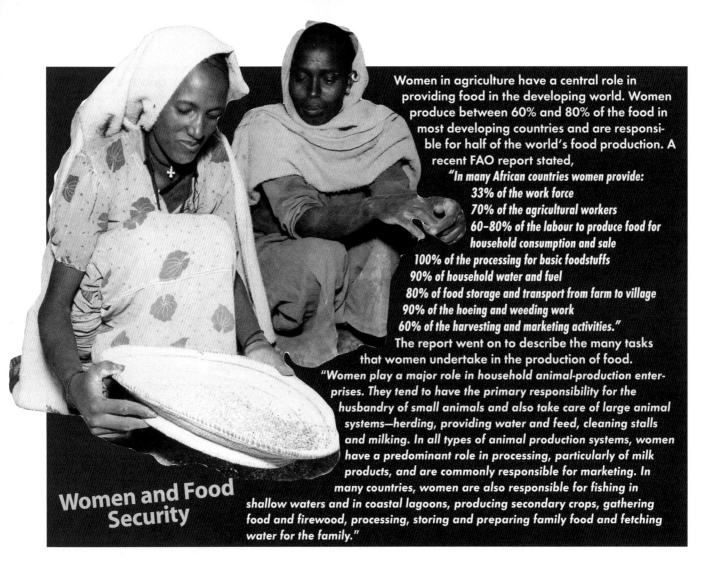

Women in agriculture have a central role in providing food in the developing world. Women produce between 60% and 80% of the food in most developing countries and are responsible for half of the world's food production. A recent FAO report stated,

"In many African countries women provide:
33% of the work force
70% of the agricultural workers
60–80% of the labour to produce food for household consumption and sale
100% of the processing for basic foodstuffs
90% of household water and fuel
80% of food storage and transport from farm to village
90% of the hoeing and weeding work
60% of the harvesting and marketing activities."

The report went on to describe the many tasks that women undertake in the production of food.

"Women play a major role in household animal-production enterprises. They tend to have the primary responsibility for the husbandry of small animals and also take care of large animal systems—herding, providing water and feed, cleaning stalls and milking. In all types of animal production systems, women have a predominant role in processing, particularly of milk products, and are commonly responsible for marketing. In many countries, women are also responsible for fishing in shallow waters and in coastal lagoons, producing secondary crops, gathering food and firewood, processing, storing and preparing family food and fetching water for the family."

Women and Food Security

Women are the major contributors to agricultural production. However, through custom and economic pressures, few women receive the basic literacy and numeracy skills. At present, in sub-Saharan Africa, fewer than half of the girls aged 6–11 are estimated to be in school which means that more than half of the girls in the region will never receive any formal education. This has prevented women from becoming involved in farmer training. It is now being recognised that the failure of many agricultural development efforts can be attributed to the fact that women farmers have been excluded due to illiteracy and custom from agricultural training and information.

THE EFFECT OF FREE TRADE ON FOOD SECURITY

Until the 1960s most experts believed that national self-sufficiency was the best guarantee of food security. Every country should aim, as far as possible, to produce all the basic food it needed. This was the philosophy that led to the creation of the European Union.

However, by the 1980s, this viewpoint had completely changed. The new idea was that there should be a free market for food throughout the world. Countries would buy the food they needed at the best price on the international market, earning the foreign exchange to do so by exporting whatever they could produce most efficiently.

Since 1974, world agricultural trade has grown from $148 billion to $485 billion. It appears that there is a great deal more food available and therefore more people should be able to be fed. Nevertheless, most of this food is consumed in the developed world and those parts of the developing world which are improving their incomes. For example, in the Far East and China diets are changing because the people are becoming wealthier and are consuming both more food and more expensive food. The total value of the food produced has in-

creased, but the poor in Africa do not get more because it is too expensive. In 93 developing countries studied by the FAO, consumption of agricultural products grew 10% faster than production between 1970 and 1990.

Critics of free trade also argue that it favours rich countries and large corporations and producers. It creates dependency and impoverishment for poor countries and households. They argue that free trade will quickly exhaust natural resources in African countries and will use high cost production methods which cannot be maintained. Many crops grown for export use large amounts of chemicals and water which the environment cannot sustain and they divert much of the best land from family food production.

A local farmer's production can be undercut by cheap imports and dumping. A producer like the EU, with a surplus to dispose of, can offer it with a large subsidy to an

Look at the label of those delicious little mangetout peas in the supermarket. Where do they come from? Probably not France. More likely Kenya, Zaire, Zimbabwe or Mozambique, flown in fresh for the convenience of the British consumer. Meanwhile the malnourished poor in those countries—which used to be able to grow enough food for their populations—are relying heavily on cheap grain imports from North America for their survival.

Adapted from *Food grown for the white man's table* Paul Brown, *Guardian Weekly*

African country which is desperate to buy food as cheaply as possible. However, this will force the local farmers out of business and the following year there will be no food for the people to buy because the farmers were undercut and driven out of production.

Cheap grain aid distorts local markets. Mari Marcel Thekae-kara, a worker for Accord, which encourages self-help, describes a "deep burning anger" caused by aid which undercuts the price of local foods and cripples their efforts.

In the name of free trade and to make money to pay off national debts or for 'development', food is no longer something grown locally to be eaten locally. It is a cash crop for consumers in a rich foreign country. Farm land anywhere is now a resource to be used by the industrialised world. Much of the most productive land in Africa and other poorer regions is now turned over to growing cocoa, coffee, tea and cut flowers for Western markets. The old subsistence crops have been swept away to more marginal lands where farming is more difficult because all available water for irrigation is poured into keeping up the quality of the cash crops.

Take one ancient source of food. World Watch president Lester Brown says that from 1950 to 1990 world fish catches increased dra-

matically, but since then have remained static, because the 17 major world fisheries are at maximum capacity and some have been overfished. Catches have declined 9% since 1990, and fish is more expensive than meat in many countries. Western purchasing power and catching technology are depriving poorer countries of their most important source of protein.

Professor David Hall, a plant biologist from King's College, London, says there are scientists who believe it is possible to feed 8 billion people. If grain were used to feed chicken rather than beef it would free millions of acres of land to grow more grain—and technology to improve grain harvests 30-fold already exists. All we need are the correct political and economic policies.

DEBT AND FOOD SECURITY

The origin of the debt

For a variety of reasons, between the 1960s and the 1980s the governments and banks in the developed world lent enormous amounts of money to countries in Africa.

Many of the newly independent African countries were led by inexperienced governments and therefore the projects financed by donors were poorly designed and unproductive—for example, roads which went nowhere, factories which never made anything and

power plants which remained incomplete. These countries were left with massive debts but with little productive industry to earn money to pay them off. In addition, some leaders wasted the loans on military expenditure and personal corruption.

This debt caused many African countries to move away from self-sufficiency in agriculture. A large amount of the borrowed money went on projects which transferred the most arable land from subsistence farming to cash-crop farming. It was thought that a country could develop its production of cash crops to pay off the debt and also have enough surplus to import food. However, many of the rich areas like the EU and the USA had protected their markets which made it difficult for African countries to sell their crops. Also, throughout the period the world price of many cash crops fell because of over-production or because of the activities of the large multinational corporations which controlled the price of many world commodities.

African countries thus had inadequate resources to reduce their debts. Governments built up huge arrears. They struggled to repay part of their debts, especially to the International Monetary Fund and other institutions. Interest payments which were not met were added to the original amount that was borrowed. Their debts simply mushroomed.

Between 1980 and 1995, sub-Saharan Africa's external debt rose from 91.7% to 241.7% of annual exports of goods and services. To add to the problem, international financial institutions and donor governments gave African governments poor advice on how to reform and improve their economies. Land which might have fed millions of people was now being used unsuccessfully to try to pay off these enormous debts. Countries which had intended to import food to feed their populations could not afford to buy enough. These coun-

"My deepest wish is to go back to school. I haven't been for many years, but I remember it was a good time. It will be a beautiful day for me when I can learn to read and write. Then I will be happy."

Anna Asiimwe is a nine-year-old girl living in the Kabale district of southern Uganda, one of the poorest regions in one of the world's poorest countries. She has something in common with over two million other children in her country, and many millions more across Africa and other developing regions: Anna Asiimwe is not in primary school. From Uganda to Ethiopia and Mozambique, a crushing burden of foreign debt results in governments spending more repaying creditors than they spend on the health and education of their citizens. Inadequate public spending on social provision means that families must meet the costs of education out of their own pockets, and Anna's parents are too poor to pay. Until last year prospects for change appeared bleak. Then the government of Uganda announced an ambitious plan to provide free primary school places for up to four children in each family.

The plan, an element in the Ugandan government's strategy for eradicating poverty, was to be financed partly through domestic revenues and partly by transferring savings from debt reduction provided under the Highly Indebted Poor Countries (HIPC) initiative, which was adopted by the Boards of the International Monetary Fund (IMF) and the World Bank in September, 1996. Along with around 30 other children in her village, Anna Asiimwe was registered for a place in primary school. Her hopes for an education and a better future soared. Now they have plummeted.

Having promised early debt relief for Uganda, some of the world's most powerful countries have used their influence to delay action for at least one year. The Ugandan government is sticking to its plan for providing free education.

But, faced with a higher than expected debt repayments bill, the timetable for implementation has been delayed. For Anna Asiimwe and other children in her village, it means another year without school, another lost opportunity.

Extracted from Poor Country Debt Relief: False Dawn or New Hope for Poverty Reduction?, Oxfam

tries could not raise adequate funds to invest in the development of education, the infrastructure or agricultural projects all of which might have given their people greater food security. For these reasons the debt acquired by many African nations since the 1960s has helped to create the food insecurity across the continent.

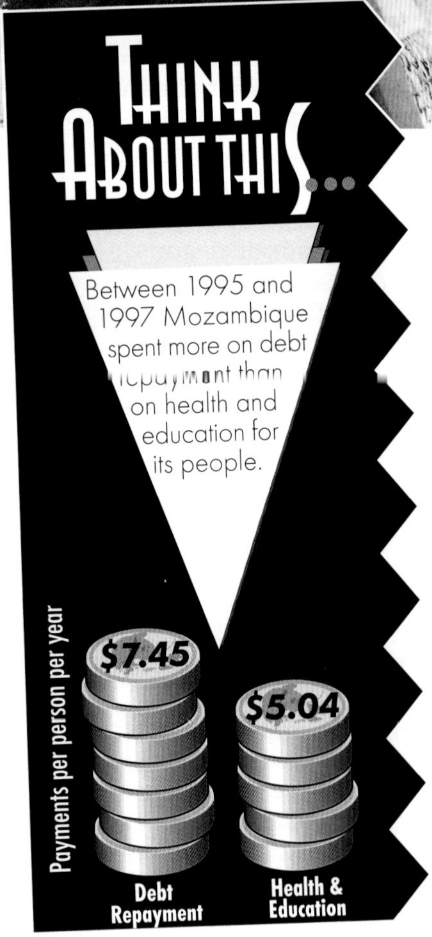

The Effects of debt

Of the 32 countries classified as severely indebted low-income countries, 25 are in sub-Saharan Africa. Sub-Saharan Africa continues to pay out large amounts to repay its debts. In 1996 it received US $15 billion in loans but it paid out US $12 billion on its debts.

High levels of unemployment make the situation worse. People cannot afford to buy food. The fact that there are fewer taxpayers means that governments are able to raise less through taxation which, in turn, means that they cannot invest in agricultural development.

Repaying debt means that countries must increase their export crops. However, as many poorer countries are encouraged to grow the same crops, they cause a glut on the international market and prices fall. Consequently, the farm workers get even lower wages or they become unemployed. This increases food insecurity.

THINK ABOUT THIS...

Between 1995 and 1997 Mozambique spent more on debt repayment than on health and education for its people.

Payments per person per year

$7.45

$5.04

Debt Repayment

Health & Education

Figure 17.2

Debt and the Rwandan Genocide

The events which led up to the genocide in Rwanda had been set in motion long before. During colonial times, communal lands in Rwanda were converted into individual plots to grow cash crops—the most important of which was coffee. After independence this cash crop economy continued, with coffee alone bringing in more than 80 per cent of Rwanda's foreign exchange earnings.

1970s and early '80s

The economy grew at about 4.9% per year (1965–89). School enrolment increased. The recorded inflation rate was one of the lowest in sub-Saharan Africa at less than 4% per year. In most areas people had enough food from their own plots and farms, so imports of cereals, including food aid, were minimal until the late 1980s.

1989

Coffee prices plummeted by more than 50% in the space of a few months. Famine swept across the country. Meanwhile, shops in the West were selling coffee at more than twenty times the price paid to the Rwandan farmer. Government income fell drastically and the country found itself in deep

A cash crop—when world prices crashed, developing countries' incomes fell and debts could not be repaid.

debt. It was forced to turn to the IMF.

A plan recommended by the World Bank in 1988 was finally adopted. Under this plan, trade was liberalised; the currency devalued; subsidies to agriculture were lifted; state enterprises were privatised and civil servants were dismissed.

1990

In September 1990 the Rwandan Patriotic Front (RPF)—a rebel army of exiles—entered Rwanda from Uganda. In the same month the government decided to devalue the Rwandan franc, but waited. In early October, while government troops began fighting with the RPF, the IMF agreed to deposit millions of dollars of 'aid' into the Central Bank. Much of this money was probably used to buy arms. In the same month the government devalued the Rwandan franc by 50%. The armed forces increased overnight from 5,000 to 40,000 men— mostly recruited from the newly unemployed.

1991-94

The fall of the Rwandan franc triggered inflation and the collapse of real earnings. Inflation increased from 10% in 1989 to 19.2% in 1991. Export earnings dropped by 50% between 1987 and 1991. The number of recorded malaria cases increased by 21% because of shortages of antimalarial drugs. Imposition of school fees led to a massive decline in school enrolment. Outstanding external debt, which had already doubled since 1985, increased by 34% between 1989 and 1992. The economic crisis reached

its peak in 1992 when the Rwandan farmers uprooted 300,000 coffee trees because they could no longer make enough money from coffee sales. In June 1992, a second currency devaluation was ordered and fuel prices rose. Coffee production fell by another 25% in a single year. Meanwhile, inappropriate food aid from the West was dumped on the local markets. The entire agricultural system was pushed into crisis. Neither cash crops nor food crops were economically viable. In 1992 the World Bank's International Development Association ordered the privatisation first of Rwanda's state enterprise Electorogaz, and then of the state telecommunications company. The money from the privatisation was to go towards debt servicing.

Ethnic tensions were rising. Electricity workers were dismissed and the price of electricity rose at once, paralysing services in the cities. The economic shock therapy was disastrous. In 1994 hundreds of thousands of Rwandans died in a brutal and catastrophic civil war.

Adapted from an article in *Debt, the Most Potent Form of Slavery* by Ann Pettifor, Debt Crisis Network Z

Responses to Food Insecurity

18

WHAT IS AID?

Aid is the formal word used for particular sorts of help—money, goods or services given by countries and institutions. It is given within countries to a range of schemes and projects and to other countries which are poor or which have been hit by disaster.

Aid money can either be given or loaned, to be repaid later. Some aid is given with nothing expected in return but a lot of aid has strings attached. Recipients (countries receiving aid) may be expected to behave in a certain way, to change their policies or to buy goods from the donor country. Even food aid, which in emergencies can be a life saver, is often used as a way of dumping crop surpluses and can affect local farmers who find that they cannot sell their crops when people are given free food.

The recipient countries sometimes use the aid they get unwisely so it never reaches the people who need it. Some governments have spent aid money on expensive and wasteful prestige projects. Aid is big business and a big temptation. Companies can offer 'sweeteners' to get lucrative contracts and officials from governments receiving aid are sometimes accused of using the money for their personal benefit.

TYPES OF AID

Aid can be given in many ways.

Bilateral aid

This is government to government aid which goes directly from a developed country to a developing country. This type of aid can be distributed in three main ways:

£ direct payments to the government of the recipient country, paid into the treasury and used to balance the budget. In practice, this often takes the form of debt cancellation.

£ payment for individual, nationwide projects such as a literacy programme or mass inoculation.

£ localised projects in defined geographic areas such as a slum i m p r o v e m e n t scheme or a water project.

Most bilateral aid is *tied*. This means that it is given in the form of, say, British goods or services, such as a contract to a UK construction company to build a road in Ethiopia. Although bilateral aid is quick to implement and credit rates may be low, it has disadvantages in that the technology given is often unsuitable and linked to a particular project. Also, the recipient country has to buy goods from its donor country. Developing countries often refer to this as 'economic colonisation'.

Multilateral aid

Government contributions to international agencies like the United Nations to allow them to support developing countries is known as multilateral aid. For example, the

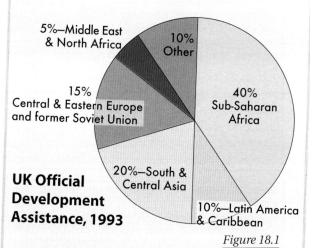

OFFICIAL DEVELOPMENT ASSISTANCE

The sum of all government aid is known as Official Development Assistance. For example, in 1993, the UK government gave £1,948 million in Official Development Assistance. The pie chart shows which areas of the world benefited from the UK government's Official Development Assistance in 1993.

- 5%—Middle East & North Africa
- 10% Other
- 15% Central & Eastern Europe and former Soviet Union
- 40% Sub-Saharan Africa
- 20%—South & Central Asia
- 10%—Latin America & Caribbean

UK Official Development Assistance, 1993

Figure 18.1

Advantages of government aid

✔ Its large size means that it can bring benefits to hundreds of thousands of people.

✔ Developing a poor country's industry and infrastructure can help to boost economic growth.

✔ Aid can help to create a more prosperous and less dangerous world.

Criticisms of government aid

✘ Quantity is not everything—not enough aid is targeted at the poorest sectors of the population.

✘ Wealth rarely trickles down to the rural poor so those who benefit are mainly urban dwellers, particularly those who are already well off.

✘ Some people argue that charity begins at home and that we should sort out our own problems before spending money on helping others.

WHAT FACTORS MAY BE TAKEN INTO ACCOUNT BEFORE GIVING AID?

Social factors

- Education levels in the recipient country eg. how many people can read/write
- Unemployment levels in both donor and recipient countries eg. could giving aid have an effect on unemployment at home or could it create jobs?
- Birth rates/death rates and health factors in the recipient country
- How is the land managed? Is there expertise in the donor country to help?

Humanitarian aid (emergency aid) also comes into this category

UK government pays money to institutions such as the UN, the EU and the World Bank each of which has its own aid programme. These agencies work with donor and recipient governments and non-governmental organisations (NGOs).

Multilateral aid has the advantage of having no political ties and not being linked to specific projects. However, the amount of aid available is too limited, much time is lost in organising projects and the interest rates put the recipient deeper into debt.

Economic factors

The following may be taken into account:

- The state of the donor economy, levels of poverty at home, the rate of inflation, level of trade recession and unemployment levels in the donor country
- Domestic social services and economic recovery may take priority over aid
- The ability of a recipient country to pay back a loan
- Possibilities of trade or other financial benefits which might develop to the donor's interest if aid is given (tied aid/boomerang aid)
- Would bilateral aid assist the donor economically?
- Would multilateral aid cause the donor country to lose prestige, power or glory?
- What opportunities for business or trade exist?
- Does the recipient country have raw materials that the donor needs?

Non-Governmental Organisation aid

Voluntary organisations such as Oxfam and Christian Aid raise money in the developed world to support projects in poorer countries. No political ties are made and the projects are on a small and realistic scale.

Emergency aid

All aid agencies from governments to NGOs hold special funds to pay for emergencies such as famine or war.

Political factors

The following may be taken into account:

- What benefits would come to the donor eg. power, world standing?
- Would giving aid improve the image of the party in power in the donor country?
- Is the potential recipient country at war? If so, which side, if any, should the donor country support?
- Is the leader of a recipient country politically sympathetic to the donor? Is a common political ideology shared?
- Is the recipient country democratic?
- Would supporting a particular country upset or offend others? If so, it may not be advisable to give aid

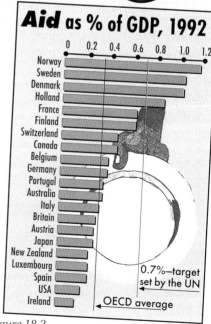

Figure 18.2

Britain sends food aid to Ethiopia

QUANTITY OF AID

While there is food insecurity and hunger, can aid ever be enough? It is impossible to walk through an emergency feeding centre in Sudan and believe that governments of the world are doing enough. Nevertheless, aid is only one of the many claims on a government's limited power to spend.

The usual measurement for comparing the size of governments' aid programmes is the percentage of the country's Gross National Product(GNP) given as aid. There is a recognised target set by the United Nations of 0.7% GNP, yet this is reached by very few countries. (See Figure 18.2.)

QUALITY OF AID

The quality of aid is even more important than the quantity. The crucial question is how effectively does aid improve the standard of living of the very poor?

Food aid can be good or bad. Food aid is vitally needed in times of severe famine but, in other circumstances, it can be a handicap for the poor. The bulk of food aid is not used in emergencies and, as a former head of the Overseas Development Administration (ODA) said, "is frankly more a means of disposing of European agricultural surpluses than of helping the poor." Food aid is always the subject of lively debate which often revolves around four principal issues.

● Speed
Governments are warned of impending famines by sophisticated early warning systems, but normally it is only when TV brings the famine to everyone's homes that governments begin to take serious action. Even when it is decided to provide food aid, procedures are often very slow. An example of this is in Mali when food aid arrived up to four months late. By the time it arrived, it coincided with the best harvest for five years. As there was so much food available, market prices remained extremely low and the poor farmers were hit.

● Food aid use
Food aid can make life difficult for small farmers and can encourage developing countries' governments to place less emphasis on improving their countries' agriculture. There is no clear-cut answer to this problem. Some countries, especially in Africa, are dependent on food imports and if they can get them free through food aid this clearly saves precious foreign exchange.

● Country allocation
Often food aid distribution bears

THE ONE THAT WENT WRONG

World Bank urged to shell out over nuts blunder

Factories have closed and thousands have been laid off in the poorest country in the world—Mozambique—because of World Bank-ordered policies which have been shown to be wrong.

Cashew nut processors in Mozambique are demanding $15 million in compensation from the World Bank. A policy imposed by the World Bank was said to be totally wrong and should be "abandoned." More than 7,000 workers were laid off and the cashew processing industry was almost bankrupt.

Cashew nuts are Mozambique's second largest export. Tens of thousands of peasants cultivate cashew trees and the country had a relatively sophisticated processing indus-

try employing 9,000 people, mostly women, to crack the nut's hard shell to expose the kernel.

At the World Bank's insistence these factories were privatised and were taken over by local business people. The Bank then disclosed a study which said the industry was so inefficient that the country lost money on every nut processed. The Bank insisted that the raw nuts be exported to India where the kernels are cracked by families working at home. Mozambique then

imposed an export tax on India to make up for the loss of revenue. However, the World Bank said that this was not allowed. It said that Mozambique would only get help from the World Bank and IMF if the export tax on cashew nuts was removed.

Mozambique is one of the world's most aid dependent countries and relies on aid from the World Bank. One Mozambique official said privately: "They told us we must say this is our policy and we cannot say it is imposed by the Bank. We know aid is conditional on

World Bank approval and now we must lie to get World Bank approval. And we will, but we will remain totally opposed to a policy that will destroy the cashew industry."

This case study illustrates the point that not all aid or advice from organisations like the World Bank is necessarily appropriate to the needs of the country.

(Adapted from Gemini News Service home page, November 1997)

---

little relation to need. For example, in the 1985 famine about 20% of the European Union's food aid went on famine relief, but Egypt received more EU food aid than Ethiopia.

● Quantities and kind

The amounts of food aid given are related to EU surpluses which are often inappropriate, for example milk powder and butter oil.

UK GOVERNMENT POLICY ON OVERSEAS FOOD AID

The Overseas Development Administration (ODA) was the aid wing of the UK government. It managed Britain's development assistance to developing countries, working with more than 150 countries. In 1996–97 its budget was £2,154 million. The purpose of the ODA was to improve the quality of life of people in poorer countries by reducing poverty and suffering. It did this by providing:

☞ technical cooperation to help develop human skills

☞ support for projects to improve health, education etc.

☞ finance for projects such as building roads and schools

☞ emergency aid for refugees

☞ aid channelled through international organisations such as the EU, the UN and the World Bank

☞ support for British NGOs such as Oxfam and VSO.

Following the General Election in May 1997, a new Department for International Development (DFID) was created. In November 1997 the UK government published a White Paper on International Development—the first for 23 years. It was entitled *Eliminating World Poverty: A Challenge for the 21st Century*. A number of clear development targets have been adopted by the UK government. These include:

✶ progress towards equality between men and women and equality for girls and boys in primary and secondary education by 2005

✶ access to family planning services for all individuals of

appropriate ages as soon as possible and no later than 2015

✶ reduce by half the proportion of people living in extreme poverty by 2015

DFID uses the World Food Programme (WFP) as a means of delivering emergency food aid. The UK government can, however, decide which countries the food aid goes to. It appears under emergency aid in the DFID budget.

AID VIA THE WORLD BANK

The World Bank is the world's largest funding source for agricultural development. The World Bank is one of a trio of institutions [along with the International Monetary Fund (IMF) and the World Trade Organisation (formerly GATT)] established at the end of the Second World War by major capitalist countries. The aim was to bring stability and thus prosperity to the global economy.

Every member country contributes to the World Bank's capital according to their strength in the global economy. The biggest shareholders get the most votes on the Executive Board. The Bank's strategic agenda aims to reduce poverty and to improve the quality of people's lives. It does this by working in partnership with all parties "who have a stake in the outcomes and who can make a difference." (World Bank report 1996)

The Special Programme for Assistance to Africa (SPA), established in December 1987, is the most important forum for the coordination of aid to the continent. Its aims are to give adequate finance in support of African countries which are undertaking economic reforms and to improve the effectiveness of donor assistance. The second aim is addressed through the Sector Investment Programmes (SIPs). These programmes coordinate donor assistance instead of the fragmented approach which often exists.

The World Bank also collaborates with United Nations agencies. It participates in the UN's Special Initiative for Africa which was launched in 1996. It seeks to expand basic education and health care and to improve water and food security.

Close collaboration with the private sector has become an integral part of the World Bank's strategy. Through partnership among the World Bank, governments and the private sector, a number of units have been set up to oversee specific projects such as 'Agribusiness in southern Africa.' The World Bank is also committed to partnership with NGOs, community groups, cooperatives and women's groups.

Criticisms of the World Bank

The work of the World Bank has been criticised. It claims to make decisions on the basis of pure economics. However, it is said to sup-

port corrupt right-wing regimes while giving a wide berth to countries which challenge its free market philosophy.

"Zaire's notoriously corrupt President Mobutu has virtually destroyed his country's economy yet the dictator's embrace of free market rhetoric has resulted in unstinting support from the Bank." (*New Internationalist* December 1990)

Another criticism is that many of its projects appear to threaten the environment. "Millions of people have been forcibly displaced by Bank-supported hydro-electric dams and resettlement programmes." (*New Internationalist* December 1990)

FOOD AND AGRICULTURAL ORGANISATION (FAO)

Most estimates suggest that more than 20% of aid never reaches poor people directly. Two-thirds of the world's poor live in ten countries which together receive less than a third of official development assistance.

One of the United Nations Specialised Agencies is the Food and Agricultural Organisation (FAO). It was founded in October 1945 with a mandate to raise levels of nutrition and standards of living, to improve agricultural productivity and to improve the conditions of rural populations. The FAO's 1996–97 biennial budget was set at US $650 million and FAO-assisted projects attracted more than US $3,000 million per year from donor agencies and governments for investment in agricultural and rural development projects. Since its incep-

tion, the FAO has worked to alleviate hunger by, among other things, pursuing food security—that is the access of all people at all times to the food they need for an active, healthy life.

The FAO offers direct development assistance, collects, analyses and disseminates information, provides advice to governments and acts as an international forum for debate on food and agricultural issues. It plays a major role in dealing with food and agricultural emergencies. To carry out many of these tasks the FAO created the Sustainable Development Department (SD) in 1995.

Development Assistance

Sustainable agricultural and rural development provides an essential foundation for improving the nutrition, food security and standards of living of millions of people living in

developing countries. The FAO promotes development which provides long-term solutions to the fundamental problems of poverty and hunger.

In promoting sustainable agricultural development, the FAO gives practical help to developing countries through a wide range of technical assistance projects. By encouraging people's participation the FAO aims to draw on local expertise and ensure a cooperative approach to development. On average, the FAO has some 1,800 field projects operating at one time.

DEVELOPMENT ASSISTANCE:
PROMOTING AQUACULTURE FOR FISH AND PROFIT

The Aquaculture for Local Community Development Programme (ALCOM) helps rural populations in nine southern African countries to improve their living standards and nutrition by fish farming. Activities are broad-based and involve studies, investigations and pilot projects for the integration of aquaculture with farming systems. They also promote a wider role for women in fish farming.

Small farmers see aquaculture as a way of making their food supply more secure by spreading their risks. If pests or diseases decimate the maize or rice, they still have fish to eat or trade for other foods. Aquaculture has the advantage of being sustainable since fishing does not diminish water resources or conflict with most other uses.

FAO SMALL GROUP APPROACH

The rural poor must be given the opportunity to participate in development. However, there is a problem in that most of the decision making is done in the towns and not in the rural areas. Low income rural people are not connected to the political system. They are often isolated and thus have limited access to newspapers and other forms of communication. They have poor access to markets and seldom see an agricultural extension agent. Likewise, governments find it too costly to provide services and resources to large numbers of scattered, isolated households.

How can rural people ever gain access to the services they need in order to increase their production and in-

comes? The FAO set up the People's Participation Programme (PPP) and has implemented small-scale projects in rural communities around the world eg. Kenya, Tanzania, Zimbabwe and Zambia.

The 'small group' approach brings together 10 to 15 people. Groups are cost-effective receiving systems for development assistance. It is easier to deliver training and other services to a group than to each and every rural household. Farmers can share skills and talents.

Groups are encouraged to start their own savings fund. Often this is done in kind. For example, members bring to their weekly meetings a small bag of, say, rice which is collected and later sold. Once there is enough money a bank

account will be opened.

Using their savings and new farming knowledge, the groups can undertake a variety of income generating activities.

A Zambian women's group began cultivating groundnuts and hiring out their labour to other farmers. Soon they earned enough to buy seed and fertiliser and start a two hectare maize plot. Now they are harvesting nearly four tonnes of maize each season. Some groups have gone into vegetable farming which provides extra income and helps to improve family nutrition. After carrying out their own feasibility study, one group planted an orange grove which now provides five tonnes of fruit per season.

Once the PPP ends its

support, most groups continue to function—unlike those projects where the participants have little or no control. As one FAO spokesperson maintained, "I think the small group approach has great potential because at present, although there are rural development programmes that incorporate participatory activities, it is a haphazard experience. Usually there is a top-down exercise where the problems are identified by people higher up and solutions are provided by them. It is now very important that we promote this participatory approach in all our rural development efforts, because only then will we be tackling their problems, their real needs."

FOOD SECURITY AND GOVERNMENTS

The importance of the state and government in bringing about food security cannot be underestimated. The state can act by:

- giving direct support and assistance
- creating appropriate environments
- defining long-term goals and objectives

One of the biggest challenges facing the state is to determine the extent and nature of the intervention in the food security process. Several guidelines must be considered in deciding the most effective form of involvement. Some of these are:

- to be effective, food security initiatives must be sustainable
- information is one of the most vital ingredients for effective decision making
- science and technology must be utilised in the struggle for food security
- development must be gender-equal

Two basic conclusions can be proposed:

- governments bear the greatest responsibility for ensuring food security at the global, national and local levels
- the precise form, extent and function of government involvement is determined by a combination of factors and conditions—both local and global.

Governments are not alone in their struggle for food security. They must form partnerships and alliances, where appropriate, in order to ensure the successful accomplishment of these objectives. Partnerships lead to many benefits. They can lead to increased scales of economy: they can provide a wider resource base and can augment the amount of information available to decision makers.

Information and Support Services

Knowledge is a vital tool for development. The FAO undertakes a variety of information and support services. Computer databases are maintained on topics ranging from fish marketing information to trade and production statistics and records of current agricultural research. The Organisation's Geographic Information System provides data on soils, vegetation cover and other aspects of land use. Satellite imagery is among the many tools used by the Global Information and Early Warning System (GIEWS) to monitor conditions affecting food production and to alert governments and donors to any potential threats. The FAO's information activities also include grass roots communication programmes which reach rural people directly, encouraging community awareness and action on agricultural and environmental issues.

Early warning – a step ahead of famine

The most important information is that which saves lives. The FAO's Global Information and Early Warning System (GIEWS) monitors the crop and food outlook at global and national levels to detect emerging food shortages and assess possible food requirements. Between its inception in 1975 and 1996, the system had issued 338 special alerts to the international community on the deteriorating food supply prospects in various parts of the world.

The system issued warnings of developing drought in southern Africa in 1991/2 and again in 1994/5, some 3 to 4 months in advance of the harvest. This enabled the countries to make critical decisions on imports and food stocks.

GIEWS works in the following way. Every day analysts study dozens of indicators which affect food supply. Satellite images and weather station data show how the growing season is progressing in broad areas of the world. Socioeconomic indicators are monitored. In an emergency, major aid donors and humanitarian organisations are alerted by fax. FAO missions are dispatched to the affected area to confer with the local authorities and to study the situation at first hand. National and international efforts are mobilised to provide food for the hungry and to restore production and distribution.

Potential partners can come from all areas. They range from intergovernmental organisations and non-governmental organisations to village groups. The FAO is dedicated exclusively to assisting governments in their struggle for food security.

World Food Programme

The World Food Programme (WFP) is the frontline UN agency mandated to combat hunger and to encourage long-term food security in the poorest regions of the world. It is the world's largest international food aid organisation having become operational in 1963. The aims of the WFP are:

- to save the lives of people caught up in humanitarian crises

- to support the most vulnerable people, especially women and children, when food needs are critical so that they are better able to attain their human potential

- to help the hungry poor become self-reliant and build assets such as roads, schools and irrigation systems in their communities.

WFP has projects in 84 countries worldwide. All contributions to WFP are voluntary. They come from donor nations, inter-governmental bodies such as the European Union and individuals. Contributions are in either commodities, cash or services.

WFP provides about a third of global food aid—more than 2.2 million metric tons a year. WFP aid is provided primarily to the least developed and low-income, food deficit countries. WFP is not now so concerned with development but is an action-oriented crisis agency geared to save lives in emergency situations. For example, in mid-1992 severe drought threatened 20 million people in ten southern African countries. WFP quickly responded to the alarm raised by national warning systems. It coordinated the flow of relief food into the region for nearly a year with over 6 million tons of food commodities transported to the ten countries for distribution to poor, very hungry people.

In Somalia, WFP was first in and last out. It provided vital assistance to starving people before the arrival of the UNOSOM (United Nations Organisation in Somalia) troops. When insecurity led to the departure of most NGO and UN staff, WFP's continued presence allowed the supply of basic food to continue to meet urgent needs at a crucial time in the peace negotiations.

WFP's effective responses to crises are due to a number of factors.

☛ **Dedication of staff** —WFP staff risk their lives to provide humanitarian aid to those who need it.

☛ **Expertise in logistics**—Food is bought locally or borrowed from WFP or other donor programmes which may have a strategic grain reserve. WFP acts efficiently to overcome obstacles to delivering the food to the regions.

☛ **A rapid response infrastructure**—In 1994, Rapid Response Teams were established to help WFP at the outbreak of emergencies.

☛ **Participatory approach**—In order to reach the grass roots level, WFP works with local organisations, including government, churches and women's groups.

☛ **Linking relief and development**—WFP gives priority to disaster prevention, being prepared for emergencies and post-disaster rehabilitation. It plays a major role in laying the foundations for peace and stability after an emergency.

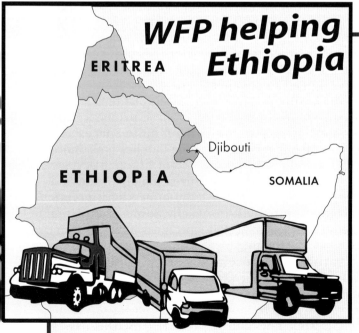

WFP helping Ethiopia

ERITREA

Djibouti

ETHIOPIA

SOMALIA

In June 1998, as the Ethiopian government called upon its nationals to prepare for war against Eritrea, the World Food Programme (WFP) revealed that some 4.3 million people in the country were in need of emergency food aid. WFP said that it had decided to establish and expand alternative transport arrangements to ensure the delivery of urgently needed humanitarian food aid to the vulnerable people of Ethiopia. On behalf of other UN partners, WFP has negotiated with the Ethiopian government that the much needed food will be regularly processed through the port of Djibouti and safely delivered by rail and truck. WFP is in the process of hiring some 200 commercial trucks to ensure that once food aid is released from the port it can be distributed quickly to the needy. "By expanding our operations with a dedicated trucking fleet, we'll create a new lifeline for millions of Ethiopians and refugees in that country who depend on food aid to help them and their families make it through to the next harvest," said Ramiro Lopes Da Silva, WFP's Director of Transport and Logistics and Head of the Mission.

The 240,000 tonnes of food were contributed to Ethiopia by WFP, the EU, the USA and Canada. A small proportion of the aid will go to NGOs working in Ethiopia.

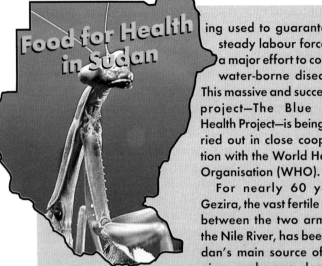

Food for Health in Sudan

Food is being used to improve health. In one important food-for-health project in Sudan, WFP food is being used to guarantee a steady labour force for a major effort to control water-borne diseases. This massive and successful project—The Blue Nile Health Project—is being carried out in close cooperation with the World Health Organisation (WHO).

For nearly 60 years Gezira, the vast fertile area between the two arms of the Nile River, has been Sudan's main source of foreign exchange derived from agricultural exports, particularly of fine, long-staple cotton, the principal cash crop. Several years ago a major outbreak of malaria reduced the labour force so much that the government had to enlist the army and school children to help with the harvest. Losses still ran into millions of dollars.

To prevent another such epidemic, Sudan's government embarked on an ambitious plan for the prevention and control of water-borne diseases—malaria, bilharzia and diarrhoea—in the irrigation schemes of Sudan.

The health project required expensive imported equipment and chemicals plus thousands of workers to spray irrigation canals with insecticides and carry out water supply construction and health education activities. Yet it was hard to retain a sufficient labour force until WFP supplied food aid which was used as part of wages.

Since then malaria has been reduced in the Gezira region to an incidence of less than 1% of the population. To complement public health efforts, a preventive educational campaign is being waged to improve hygiene and keep water clear of human waste.

Food aid to promote food production

Basic Grains Production projects in several countries show farmers how to increase crop yields dramatically. WFP provides food both as an incentive and as a guarantee. The production of staple foods like maize, sorghum, rice and beans has not kept up with need. These foods are largely produced by marginal farmers who till plots of two hectares or less. Their yields are low and after feeding their families they do not have much left over for marketing.

Basic Grains projects make it possible and attractive for these farmers to improve their techniques. Those who participate agree to try out new methods and use new inputs, working with and learning from government agricultural extension workers. Banks have agreed to advance credit for the new, more expensive seeds, fertilisers and other inputs necessary. Their guarantee is that, with the supervised instruction and the project's support the farmers' crops will increase and the loans will be repaid promptly.

Participants receive WFP food during two growing seasons. Farmers may also receive rations for the work they contribute to land improvements. One farmer received aid while he terraced his land and convinced not only himself but the entire community when his yield increased ten times! One other agent noticed that a farmer received higher yields than his neighbours simply because his small son made the holes for the seeds—since the boy took shorter steps the crops were more densely planted.

These projects have been quite successful. The families have more to eat, the banks have been rapidly repaid and the farmers have more to sell. Some of the big projects have also encouraged participation in local cooperatives which brings the farmers many benefits, including better access to credit. Food aid used in this way has proved to be a marked incentive for production.

NON-GOVERNMENTAL ORGANISATIONS (NGOs)

There are over 100 NGOs in Britain actively involved in overseas development. Some like Oxfam and Save the Children Fund (SCF), are household names but there are others, some smaller and more specialised, which are active in helping the developing world. Many of these smaller organisations concentrate on particular aspects of aid work such as health or technology.

These organisations raise money for much of their work from voluntary and private sources. This means that they are able to determine their policies and priorities independently of the government's official aid programme. Special appeals are used to raise money for specific emergency relief operations, but long-term development projects need regular funding and steady sources of income.

Most NGOs work with partners overseas such as community groups, churches and local NGOs whose projects are run mainly by the local people with assistance when needed. Many NGOs also work with international organisations like the European Union.

The traditional role of NGOs was primarily that of providing emergency relief overseas—responding to famine, disaster, natural and man-made emergencies. However, for many years now there has been mounting emphasis on long-term development aid. NGOs cover the full range of overseas aid which makes it difficult to generalise about their work, but there are common threads. The key element is their ability to work in direct partnership with poor communities in developing countries at a highly personal level. They are most effective at getting help directly to the poorest people.

Save the Children

Famine is closely linked to economic decline, lack of investment in agriculture and ecological degradation. These conditions have resulted in food insecurity across many parts of Africa. Food insecurity becomes famine when resources are exhausted and destitute families have no choice but to abandon their villages and migrate in search of food and work.

Famine relief and prevention

Save the Children Fund began life as an emergency relief agency and many of its long-term programmes have grown out of emergency work. It is now increasingly concerned with famine prevention. Emergency food aid does not solve the underlying problems. Famine prevention must begin before food insecurity becomes food crisis. Here are some of the ways in which SCF tries to prevent famine.

- *Crop assessments* – These give early warnings of harvest failures.
- *Providing seeds and tools to poor farmers* – This gives the farmers the chance to start again after a famine year when seed grain has been eaten.

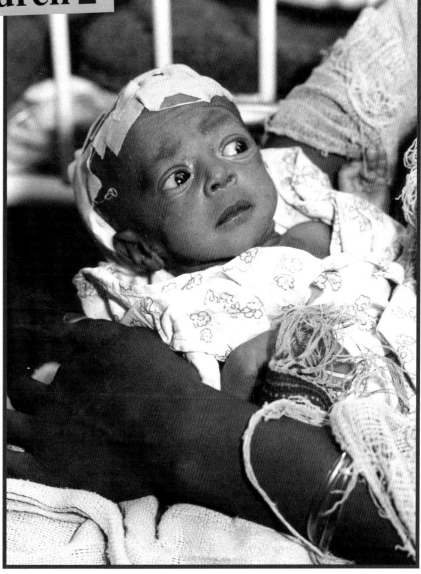

- ☀ *Providing bridges* – In areas cut off by war, famine prevention can mean keeping roads open so that food delivery is not disrupted. In Mozambique, SCF donated 27 emergency 'Bailey bridges' which can be reassembled by local construction workers to provide a lifeline to villages needing relief supplies.

- ☀ *Cash for work and food for work schemes* – These community projects give vital income to poor families as well as creating much-needed village amenities such as schools and wells.

- ☀ *Credit for village cereal banks* – After a poor harvest, household stocks are soon exhausted and families are forced to buy high priced grain on the open market. In Mali, SCF provided loans to a number of villages enabling them to establish their own cereal banks. This means that people can buy grain at a reasonable price when their own crops have failed.

Post-war reconstruction

Food is no problem in the town of Mopeia, Mozambique. The problem was that, for a while, there was no one to eat what was available. After an attack by a group of rebels, many fled the town or were killed, wounded or kidnapped. Mopeia had been a thriving community. Every family had its own smallholding, the soil was fertile, the nearby river was rich in fish and there was lots of small game around. The people who took refuge in nearby towns were given emergency food aid by SCF. When they returned to Mopeia the town had to be rebuilt, but there was still fish in the rivers and the game had multiplied. Where SCF supported the community was by helping to rebuild schools, clinics and the maternity hospital. As the basic services were re-established, the people began to return to Mopeia knowing that there was food waiting for them as well as a rebuilt community.

Food on the hoof

The Ogaden, one of the most insecure areas of Ethiopia, was hit by a crisis in 1992 when 250,000 destitute returnees from Somalia came home, swelling the population by 25%. The returnees were fleeing the civil war in Somalia. The miracle was that they were absorbed into the host population through a hidden relief operation. Rural farmers and herders shared what food they had, but at great cost to themselves.

The fragile food situation of the Ogaden came under further pressure when the livestock trade with Somalia, on which the Ogaden farmers depended for grain, broke down as a result of Somalia's civil war. Two years of severe drought then hit harvest, pasture and water resources, leading to lower milk production and depleted herds.

The impact of these changes on the people of Ogaden was unknown, so SCF decided to make the first needs assessment survey for 20 years. The survey was unusual for two reasons. Firstly, the region is vast—about the size of Wales —and mostly inaccessible, so helicopters were used to cover the maximum area in the minimum possible time. Furthermore, the survey was designed to look at ways in which food aid could be used to boost trade and the local economy, as well as to assess current emergency needs.

Although the community had been able to survive one year of stress, the survey revealed an economy at breaking point. Grain prices were high and livestock were in poor condition and were being sold off at a fraction of their normal value. SCF recommended that emergency food aid should be sold at subsidised prices in order to stabilise the terms of trade between livestock and cereals and help people to survive the dry season with their herds intact. The World Food Programme acted on this recommendation and began releasing food onto local markets. Emergency food aid was also given to the most vulnerable groups such as young children.

How to cope with drought

Poverty and irregular rainfall keep causing chronic food insecurity for the 1.3 million people in the Darfur region of Sudan. To help them to cope with this, the people use strategies which are centuries old.

- ● As a safety measure, farmers planted a variety of crops over large areas to take advantage of variations in rainfall. This increases the chances of at least harvesting something.

- ● Surplus crops from good harvests are stored underground for use in times of drought. Some communities insist on eating in public to see that food is shared out!

- ● Families often choose to split up for the duration of the food shortage. Men migrate in search of work and boys drive the animals south for pasture.

Other SCF Projects

SCF has tried to improve food security and lessen dependence on food aid through long-term development, village projects and cash or food for work schemes. These include the following:

- de-silting of natural water reservoirs
- advice on water spreading methods to improve crop yields
- vegetable gardening
- goat loan projects—families keep the goat milk and kid and the goats are returned after two years

SCF works to achieve food security for children and the communities in which they live. SCF suggests that the following are issues which have to be tackled if lasting progress is to be made:

- governments should reaffirm the right to food as a basic human right
- multilateral food aid funds should be built up to guarantee urgent humanitarian relief without political bias
- famine prevention and relief must be prioritised by food aid donors and NGOs working at community level
- the response of donor governments and multilateral agencies should be swifter and more flexible
- coordination between donors, UN agencies and NGOs should be improved
- subsidised food aid sales should be used more widely as an emergency intervention
- long-term investment should be made to improve roads and distribution in famine prone regions.

About 2 billion people rely on agriculture which is largely untouched by modern technology. In general these farmers are working with poor quality soils which are easily eroded. They cannot afford expensive tools and machinery. Concern Worldwide works with these farmers in order to improve their livelihoods and food security. The organisation operates in countries such as Mozambique, Ethiopia and Tanzania to help the farmers increase their yields without damaging the environment which sustains them. Concern Worldwide is very conscious that, while these farmers need to increase their yields substantially, they cannot afford to take risks or spend large amounts of money. The approach to agriculture therefore must be based on low external inputs. (External inputs include such things as machinery, tools and inorganic fertilisers.) It must also be sustainable in the longer term.

Simple methods of soil and water conservation are a major component of Concern Worldwide's agricultural programmes. Planting trees helps to prevent soil erosion

A tree nursery in Ethiopia. Planting trees helps to prevent soil erosion and can also provide a valuable source of income for the farmers.

and can also provide a valuable source of income for the farmers. The approach of LEISA (Low External Input Sustainable Agriculture) substitutes affordable and locally available knowledge, labour and management skills for expensive and often unaffordable inputs.

In Ludewa, in Tanzania, for example, farmers have been sowing a traditional crop—cassava—for many years. This crop is attacked on a periodic basis by the mealy bug which can destroy the crop. Concern Worldwide works with farmers to help them find ways of improving this situation. Methods employed would include crop diversification and proven organic methods of pest control. The community works together to improve crop production in the area and to find affordable ways to do this without damaging the environment.

In all Concern Worldwide project areas, the people who participate are being asked to identify their own priority needs and Concern Worldwide responds, where appropriate, with advice, materials and financial support. Adequate time is given for discussion and consultation with the people so that their needs are successfully met. To ensure that development projects are successful over the long term, organisation by the community is actively encouraged. Tackling the issues of food security comprehensively in a community takes time and effort. Many of the measures that Concern Worldwide use are simple and are designed to last in the community for many years after their introduction.

WaterAid in Tanzania

The WAMMA programme is an example of an international NGO successfully supporting a government partner in a participatory, integrated approach to water projects.

During the five years up to March 1996, a collaborative partnership between the Tanzanian government and WaterAid helped a total of 86 communities in the Dodoma region in Tanzania to provide themselves with improved water supplies and sanitation systems. The WAMMA programme is still going from strength to strength. It has come to be held up as a model of an integrated participatory approach to community water supplies and it has shown that governments and NGOs can be effective partners in development programmes. Crucially, it has also demonstrated the strong motivating effect which comes from empowerment.

In the WAMMA programme, village priorities dictate the type and pace of water and sanitation development. Government, donor and NGO support fill technical and financial gaps and ensure that the project meets national standards. The end result is team work. Government staff, WaterAid and the villagers share common goals, recognise the benefits of collaboration and build on their successes.

A typical village water project begins when a group of villagers approaches the Water Department with a request for assistance. The WAMMA team will meet with the villagers to explain what kind of help they can give. There are no set

procedures as the needs of each project are different. Once the project is decided, a formal contract between the villagers and the government is drawn up and signed. The villagers are responsible for setting up a water fund and gathering most of the materials needed. Once the project is completed the WAMMA team makes regular follow-up visits.

This example shows that there are powerful reasons for governments to work with NGOs to help communities obtain basic services. In this case, once a community has a good water supply other essentials such as food supply will also improve. Governments have national remits to provide services for their people. Governments are also best placed to provide sustained long-term support to community-based projects.

Many NGOs are committed to a grass roots approach and can bring experience and expertise to participatory projects. They can help governments to work successfully in communities and they have the flexibility to adjust their approaches and the form of support provided in a responsive way as programmes mature. NGOs are free to try out new ideas, change them if they do not work and adopt them if they do.

The Tanzanian government has many under-utilised resources such as equipment and trained staff. Through this empowering process of the Dodoma programme, these resources are being used effectively to bring much appreciated sustainable services to needy communities. At the same time, once WaterAid support is withdrawn the governments will continue to have the expertise to allow the projects to expand.

ARE ALL THE NGOs EFFECTIVE?

Some relief organisations take the Saturday flight into famine-threatened Somalia and spend three days seeing what it is like. Then they take the Tuesday flight back to London and declare, 'We are set up in Somalia now.' They are now in a position to appeal for money to carry out humanitarian work. This is the description put forward by Geoffrey Dennis, International Director of the British Red Cross. There is widespread cynicism about the mushrooming of poorly-run, unaccountable NGOs.

In 1984, a handful of NGOs went to help in the early stages of the Ethiopian famine in which 2.5 million people were threatened with starvation. Ten years later, following the massacre in Rwanda and the flight of the refugees into Zaire (now Democratic Republic of the Congo) more than 170 NGOs went to help. No-one knows how many of these groups there are in the world today. In 1995, the Commission on Global Governance found 28,900 international NGOs.

NGOs provide more aid in Africa than the World Bank. They deliver more than 75% of humanitarian relief. They no longer just fill the gaps left by national governments and international organisations such as the United Nations—they spearhead the humanitarian relief business.

However, as NGOs multiply they are increasingly fighting each other for funds, media coverage and market share. In the process, they are undermining each other. A common criticism is the uncoordinated response in the wake of a disaster. "Too often," says Gary O'Shea of the International Rescue Corps, "people think they can help by jumping on a plane and going to the disaster site even though they have no training or experience. All this does is put greater stress on the host country."

Margie Buchanan-Smith, head of the emergencies unit at the British charity Action Aid says, "We all co-ordinate already. If we need to send someone to Burundi we get on the phone to SCF or Oxfam and ask if they have someone available." She says that NGOs need to learn from mistakes, such as giving poorly qualified and inexperienced people responsibility for medical programmes in refugee camps in Zaire in 1994. "There was a case where a medical team was putting drips into people and then leaving them completely unsupervised," she recalled. "Even if you are a qualified nurse, the first time you go to Africa you don't want to end up in the middle of some disorganised and complex political emergency." Margie wants to see the establishment of an accreditation process for individual aid workers as well as agreement on which courses relief workers would be required to take before working overseas.

NGOs are finding it harder and harder to raise funds. Anxious aid workers catch themselves fighting back the surreptitious desire for the next big disaster to come quickly and fill up their collecting tins once more. The total cash they raise is, in any event, less than a tenth of official aid.

AID MUST ERADICATE POVERTY

Much of the poverty in African countries is absolute poverty. This means the absence of 'basic needs' like food, drinking water, shelter, education or health care. Poverty has been increasing everywhere for the last 20 years.

Between 1965 and 1980, 200 million people saw their incomes fall. In the years between 1980 and 1993 the figure rose to more than a billion. The people in Rwanda, Sudan, Zaire and Zambia are poorer now than they were in 1960.

In sub-Saharan Africa, enrolments in primary education have fallen by as much as a half.

Meantime, aid from rich to poor governments (official development assistance—ODA) keeps falling and in 1995 reached its lowest level ever.

It might be supposed that the increase in poverty is a direct result of the drop in aid—so increase aid and poverty will decrease. Unfortunately it does not work this way. Less than a quarter of the $59 billion ODA total—equivalent of about $8 a head each year—ever reaches poor people. ODA is siphoned off to promote 'development' objectives and mega-projects 'tied' to

purchases from donor countries or paid in 'debt relief' straight to Northern banks. Most poor people never see a penny of it.

Furthermore, the changes that are being made to aid are making the problem worse rather than better.

The final and possibly fatal folly is that the remains of ODA have now been tied in their entirety to 'structural adjustment programmes' (SAPs). SAPs require privatisation, cuts in public expenditure, increases in exports and adherence to the principles of 'free trade'

and 'free market'.

These principles are, by definition, indifferent to the eradication of poverty; they are largely responsible for its creation. Now not only do poor people get less money, they have to spend more time and effort explaining why they need it in the first place.

So, what is to be done? If aid is to survive it must be made to adhere to humanitarian principles—with the eradication of poverty as its principal objective. This has to be the responsibility of the people of the North.

IS ALL AID EFFECTIVE?

There are eight points which should be considered to determine if aid is effective.

1. Aid should go to the people in the rural areas who need the help. It should be directed towards agriculture rather than industry.
2. The poor people who are receiving the aid should be consulted and involved in the running of the project.
3. The aid projects should be small-scale and sustainable in terms of the resources available.
4. The role of women should be recognised particularly when dealing with food production.
5. Aid should help to sustain the natural environment.
6. Aid should involve the recipient country in decisions about where to buy equipment and technology.
7. Aid should be given to countries which need it rather than being given for political reasons.
8. Aid should be distributed through partnerships with NGOs, since most of them have workers who are in close touch with the local communities

Many of the first development projects in Africa were over-ambitious. The following are some examples of aid projects through official overseas aid which did not quite meet the needs of the people concerned.

The great groundnut scheme

This scheme was thought up in London but was carried out in Tanzania. Vast areas of grazing land were destroyed to grow groundnuts. Eventually it was realised that intensively grown groundnuts could not survive in Tanzania.

Milk in Sudan

There is lots of milk in Sudan so it was decided to bottle it. The only problem was that the Sudanese people only like milk fresh from the cow—they do not like bottled milk. The bottling plant which was built never produced a bottle of milk.

Grain storage in Senegal

The Americans spent $2 million on grain storage silos in Senegal. However, they have remained empty because they were built in places where peasant farmers never go.

Village woodlots in Uganda

Development projects are supposed to be small-scale, with appropriate user-friendly technology. Where charcoal burning has destroyed the forests, women still need timber to cook with. So in Karamoja village, Uganda, woodlots were started. The locals were all in favour and planted the trees themselves. The only input from aid agencies was that planting eucalyptus trees would be a good idea. However, nobody told the villagers that eucalyptus does not burn well and is not good for cooking purposes. There were also other problems with the trees which made them unsuitable for that area.

The Village Fishponds Programme

This project seemed to do everything correctly—it was sustainable, low tech and community oriented. Small ponds were created for fish so that the locals could get more protein in their diets. The fish they put in were Nile perch which are carnivorous and grew into monsters of six feet in two years. These perch escaped into Lake Victoria and ate all the native lake species. The people used to dry their catch in the sun but nobody told them that Nile perch are too oily and have to be smoked. So the fisherfolk cut down the trees for charcoal with soil erosion and desertification following.

The outcome of this project was a desert, eroded soil and deforestation, 180 species of fish extinct and the largest fresh water lake in the world dead because of the algae covering it.

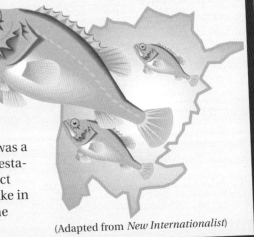

(Adapted from *New Internationalist*)

The European Union and Aid

Aid from the European Union is multilateral aid. It is mostly directed to developing countries in Africa through the Lomé Convention. Below is a series of frequently asked questions and answers about aid from the European Union.

What is the Lomé Convention?

The Lomé Conventions are the framework for cooperation between the EU and the African, Caribbean and Pacific countries (ACP). There have been four Lomé Conventions. The Conventions cover both trade and aid. Aid given under the Lomé Convention is organised through the European Development Fund (EDF).

In 1975, the nine Member States of the European Community (the Federal Republic of Germany, Belgium, Denmark, France, Ireland, Italy, Luxembourg, the Netherlands and the United Kingdom) and the 46 countries of the Africa, Caribbean and Pacific area signed the first Lomé Convention in Lomé, the capital of Togo.

Several revisions of the initial text followed in 1980, 1985, 1990 and 1995. The Convention now links 15 Member States of the European Union and 70 ACP countries representing a total of some 500 million people. Of the total aid received by developing countries, half is provided by European citizens, of which 15% is administered by the European Commission. Fifty per cent of this EU aid is distributed to the countries of the African, Caribbean and Pacific area.

Why continue providing development aid when the results are disappointing?

There is currently a crisis of faith concerning development and its results. Nonetheless, the economic balance sheet indicates more variation than is commonly believed. Many ACP countries have successfully completed what we might call 'initial development', breaking the vicious circle of under-development. All of the indicators—increased life expectancy, access to safe water, spending on health and adult literacy, and falling infant mortality rates—place them squarely on the path to a brighter future.

The signs of recovery abound and priorities have been revised to take these factors into account. Economic reforms are under way everywhere, while political change is finally becoming possible with the abolition of the ideologies which pitted one 'block' against another. Forecasts of per capita real-income growth between 1990 and 2000 are positive for the first time in many years (0.3% compared to -2% for Africa in 1990) and justify a certain degree of optimism.

Why finance development cooperation when unemployment is on the rise in Europe?

To appreciate fully the importance of development, we must keep in mind that the EU is not exclusively a lender of funds but is also a trading partner of the countries receiving aid. While Europe provides a vital market for developing countries, a greater share of EU exports are destined for these nations than for the United States or Japan. Experience has shown that over the medium term, development in countries receiving aid leads to increased consumption, which in turn produces growth in their imports of goods and services from donor countries. In other words, development aid to the least advanced countries can only benefit our own economies. Reducing or cutting off this aid would deprive us of promising markets.

For every 100 ECU spent on aid, the EU recovers 48 ECU in the form of projects, supplies and technical assistance purchased from European companies.

What are the advantages of EU development aid as opposed to bilateral aid by the Member States?

EU development aid has grown considerably over the years, with an increase in financial resources and a broadening of geographical coverage to the entire developing world. EU development cooperation (multilateral aid) continues to offer indisputable advantages over bilateral aid.

✦ Aid, which consists mostly of donations and is distributed through the Lomé Convention, does not increase the debt burden of the recipient countries.

+ The ACP countries are not denied the opportunity to express their opinions or to assert their demands.

+ The Lomé Convention is the non-political link between the EU's development policies and those of its member states.

+ The EU has never financed armaments and carefully avoids any involvement with aid of a political nature.

+ The Lomé system allocates substantial aid for regional cooperation. This allows the EU to make decisions about Structural Adjustment Programmes (SAPs). SAPs help poor countries to repay their debts by introducing economic reforms such as cutting governement expenditure, privatising industries or promoting exports. For example, in Tanzania SAP cuts in health service spending have led to a serious decline in the facilities at local clinics and hospitals.

Nevertheless, EU aid clearly does not and never will prevent the Member States from playing a role in bilateral arrangements. The two systems work in complement, not in competition.

Is aid to the EU 's partner countries unconditional?

The European Development Fund operates according to the priorities negotiated with the recipient countries and only at their request. These countries' development policies therefore determine what type of aid the EDF provides. In practice, however, a number of considerations may influence how this principle is applied.

The recipient countries' priorities are negotiated with the European Commission on a country-by-country basis. These negotiations culminate in the signing of a five-year 'national indicative programme'. Without this programme, cooperation cannot begin and no financing can be provided. In short, the partner countries may not receive any aid without first establishing an overall programme to which the Commission has agreed.

The European Union has stated very clearly its intention to deal exclusively with those countries demonstrating respect for human rights and working resolutely towards democracy and the rule of law. Europe considers this principle so important that failure to respect it may lead to the suspension of all but humanitarian aid.

What is the cost to European citizens of development aid to the ACP countries?

In 1994, European development aid cost the 370 million citizens of the 15 Member States of the European Union almost 64 ECU each. The countries differed in how much they spent on aid. For example, each Dane spent 222 ECU to support development, while Britons paid only 43 ECU each and the Portuguese 25 ECU per person.

The 63.9 ECU that the average European contributed to development is more or less equivalent to the cost of a good concert ticket, and represents some 10% of what a one-pack-a-day smoker spends on cigarettes in a year.

What are the primary areas of cooperation within the framework of the Lomé Conventions?

When the first European Development Fund was created in the 1960s, decolonisation dictated that the bulk of investment should go to supplying infrastructures which the colonial powers had not provided and to reconstructing those which had been destroyed. This overall policy was pursued under Lomé I and Lomé II.

During negotiations on Lomé III in 1985, it was noted that the least developed countries were being provided with infrastructures while their people were dying of hunger. It was therefore decided to emphasise rural development and food security, without completely abandoning the infrastructure component. Lomé IV, signed in 1990, introduced the idea of support for structural adjustment. The distinguishing feature of this new type of aid was that it would be earmarked for social welfare such as health and education. Intensive aid for rural development also remained one of the primary objectives of Lomé IV.

The Maastricht Treaty also lists a number of themes which were defined as being of primary concern. These themes, incorporated into the revised Lomé IV Convention in November 1995, include the promotion of democracy and a market economy, the fight against poverty, commercial competitiveness and the improved effectiveness of aid.